SOCIETY AND LITERATURE IN ENGLAND 1700-60

Also by W. A. Speck:

Tory and Whig: The Struggle in the Constituencies (1970)

Stability and Strife: England 1714-1760 (1977)

The Butcher: The Duke of Cumberland and the Suppression of the Forty-five (1981)

W. A. SPECK

SOCIETY AND LITERATURE IN ENGLAND 1700-60

GILL AND MACMILLAN
HUMANITIES PRESS

First published 1983 by
Gill and Macmillan Ltd
Goldenbridge
Dublin 8
with associated companies in
London, New York, Delhi, Hong Kong,
Johannesburg, Lagos, Melbourne,
Singapore, Tokyo

7171 0977 1

Published in 1983 in USA and Canada by Humanities Press Inc.
Atlantic Highlands, New Jersey 07716
ISBN 0-391-02945-2

Origination by Print Prep Ltd, Dublin
Printed and bound in Great Britain by Biddles Ltd,
Guildford and King's Lynn

Contents

Preface

This book has grown out of a long-standing interest in the problems of using literature as a historical source. Although I had earlier toyed with the relationship between history and literature, I began to take it seriously in 1965 when Kenneth Grose, then senior English master at Bradford Grammar School, kindly asked if I would contribute a study of Swift to the *Literature in Perspective* series which he was editing. While engaged on this task I received invaluable help from colleagues in the Department of English Literature at the University of Newcastle-upon-Tyne. Two were especially helpful. Philip Roberts collaborated with me in the writing of the book, contributing a chapter on Swift's verse. The late James Maxwell arranged for me to attend the Swift tercentenary conference in Dublin in April 1967, a gathering of scholars from both sides of the Atlantic who held a symposium in every sense. There I met Frank Ellis, who later invited me to help him edit the seventh volume of *Poems on Affairs of State*. Thanks to the support of George deForest Lord, the general editor of the series, and of the University of Newcastle-upon-Tyne, which granted me leave of absence, I spent the academic year 1969-70 at Yale University. During that sabbatical I incurred many debts of scholarship to Frank, and of hospitality to him and his wife Connie. I also benefited from discussions with Jim Leheny, who was then working on his definitive edition of Addison's *Freeholder*. By the end I felt I had learned something from the application of two disciplines to a particular kind of literary evidence.

This encouraged me to put on a course dealing with society and literature in Augustan England when I taught at Portland State University in the autumn term of 1973. Subsequently

I have taught similar courses at Newcastle, Cambridge, and latterly Hull. The stimulus of teaching made this new departure for me much more rewarding than it would otherwise have been. All those who attended the courses have helped me to develop and defend my views. Jeffrey Hopes went on to do graduate work, studying for his doctoral thesis on the English stage controversy of 1690-1740 under my supervision. Our discussions have influenced my approach considerably. Alan Downie is another former student at Newcastle who made the transition from history to literature with me, and from whose friendly collaboration I have benefited greatly. The most rewarding interdisciplinary co-operation confirmed John Cleveland's paradox

> England's a perfect World, has Indies too;
> Correct your Maps, Newcastle is Peru.

Paul Stigant, one of the editors of *Literature and History*, got me involved with that provocative journal from the outset and recommended me to Messrs Gill and Macmillan as the potential author of an interdisciplinary study. They have been extremely accommodating about my requests for extra time to deliver the typescript. The delay was not due to lack of material. Quite the reverse, I was almost overwhelmed by literary sources, especially after spending the academic year 1979-80, on study leave from the University of Newcastle-upon-Tyne, in Cambridge, where the University Library afforded excellent facilities for exploring Augustan literature, and particularly drama. Rather the problem was what to make of it all. At one time I was tempted to conclude with some other historians that literature was best avoided by those seeking to reconstruct the realities of a past society. This was a depressingly negative conclusion, as I must admit to finding essays, novels, poems and plays somewhat more interesting than parish registers, port books, and other quantifiable sources which are held to be more reliable records. While wrestling with the problem I thought I detected a more positive connection between literature and historical evidence, which involved a completely fresh start. The first draft of my revision was efficiently typed by Janice Cumming. John Cannon and Pat Rogers kindly undertook the chore of reading this revised version and tried to prevent my enthusiasm running away with me. If it has nevertheless done so, then I hold myself to be entirely responsible. For coping with even more revisions than usual I am more indebted than ever to my wife Sheila for her secretarial and other assistance.

Beverley, September 1982

Introduction

> How easy it would be to collect from our own comedians the follies, clownishness, barbarities and sottishness of country gentlemen: hence to draw a monstrous character of an illiterate, brutal drunkard, and then to say you are a country gentleman.
>
> *The Letter to Sir J—— B—— Examined* (1710)

Literary works have traditionally been used as prime sources for the history of English society. The chapters on the eighteenth century in G. M. Trevelyan's popular *English Social History*, which significantly he entitled 'Defoe's England' and 'Dr Johnson's England', are sprinkled with quotations from those authors and a host of other writers. So much was the illustrative value of literature taken for granted by an older generation of historians that, in his Oxford history *The Whig Supremacy*, Basil Williams discussed Fielding's Squire Western and Smollett's Matthew Bramble as though they were real people. Thus when dealing with the 'great middle class', as he called them, he wrote:

> Their lives were generally spent in their own small towns or countryside, within which their outlook was mainly confined. Travel was too irksome or expensive for most to pay more than one or two visits to the great world of London, and such visits rarely repaid them. Squire Western was frankly bored with his journey thither in pursuit of his errant daughter, and though Squire Bramble, more serious-minded and better educated, found much of interest in his long journey through a large part of the island, he was glad enough to find himself back at Brambleton Hall, and declared 'it must be something very extraordinary that will induce me to revisit either Bath or London'.[1]

The rise of what might be termed the new social or sociological history, however, has called into question the validity of literary evidence. W. A. Armstrong summed up the aims of the new approach when he observed:

> Ashton has written that economic historians (we might now add social historians) are concerned primarily with groups. Their subject is not Adam, a gardener, but the cultivators of the soil as a class; not Tubalcain, a skilled artificer in brass and iron, but metal workers or industrialists in general. They deal less with the individual than with the type. The now widely-agreed need to concentrate on the typical and the general rather than the unique or particular reflects perhaps the most fundamental influence of the social sciences on historical methods in this century. There will always remain those who dabble among the sources of history for the quaint and the unusual, and antiquarianism cannot be wholly condemned. But those who hope to see their researches make some contribution to the mainstream development of the subject must necessarily mark Ashton's words well.[2]

In their search for the statistically demonstrable modern historians are suspicious of sources which are inherently intuitive rather than quantitative, subjective rather than objective. They seek to establish what was typical about past societies with the assistance of masses of information from such quantifiable sources as parish registers, tax schedules and judicial records. Novels, plays, ballads, essays and other forms of literature do not lend themselves to exercises in Cliometrics, as the new methodology has been rather inelegantly dubbed. On the contrary, its high priests anathematise the use of literature as heretical. Thus Peter Laslett warns that 'It is indeed hazardous to infer an institution or a habit characteristic of a whole society or a whole era from the central character of a literary work and its story, from *Pamela*, for example, or from Elizabeth Bennet in *Pride and Prejudice*. . . . The outcome may be to make people believe that what was the entirely exceptional, was in fact the perfectly normal.'[3] He himself showed that notions of teenage marriages being commonplace in Tudor England, which could be derived from *Romeo and Juliet*, were at odds with the mean ages of marriages recorded in parish registers. By the same token it could be said that the Brambles and Westerns of the eighteen century, so far from being typical, were the unique creations of their authors. Certainly it is hazardous to generalise about geographic mobility among the 'middle class' from their fictional experiences.

The prime example of the pitfalls into which historians can tumble if they regard such fictions as fact is Macaulay's study of the country gentry of the late seventeenth century. A typical country gentleman appears in the pages of the celebrated third chapter of his *History of England* with the following characteristics:

> His chief serious employment was the care of his property. He examined samples of grain, handled pigs, and, on market days, made bargains over a tankard with drovers and hop merchants. His chief pleasures were commonly derived from field sports and from an unrefined sensuality. . . . His table was loaded with coarse plenty; and guests were cordially welcomed to it. . . . The coarse jollity of the afternoon was often prolonged till the revellers were laid under the table. . . . His opinions respecting religion, government, foreign countries and former times . . . were the opinions of a child. . . . His animosities were numerous and bitter. He hated Frenchmen and Italians, Scotchmen and Irishmen, Papists and Presbyterians, Independents and Baptists, Quakers and Jews. Towards London and Londoners he felt an aversion which more than once produced important political effects.

Perhaps worst of all, 'the gross, uneducated, untravelled country gentleman was commonly a Tory'.[4]

Macaulay concluded this remarkable account of the gentry with an even more breathtaking footnote. 'My notion of the country gentleman of the seventeenth century', he wrote, 'has been derived from sources too numerous to be recapitulated. I must leave my description to the judgement of those who have studied the history and the lighter literature of that age.' It is this claim which makes Macaulay's version of the landed gentry peculiarly appropriate to a discussion of the relationship between history and literature. It seems to me to present a prime example of the dangers, no less than the rewards, to be encountered by historians when they use literary materials to illuminate the past. For Macaulay has been heavily criticised for his use of 'the lighter literature of that age' to paint his picture of the country gentleman. As one critic said, 'His contempt for the gentry was not of the kind that familiarity breeds.' While the criticisms are, as we shall see, to a large extent valid, it would be wrong to conclude from them that literary productions are useless for social history.

According to Sir Charles Firth, 'Anyone who reads his description can see how much that notion of the gentry was influenced by their representation on the stage.'[5] Certainly Restoration comedy has as a stock character the stage squire, a rough rustic bumpkin, often from the West Country, which was regarded as the most 'hick' part of England at that time, though as Addison pointed out in the prologue he wrote for Steele's *The Tender Husband* in 1705:

> But now our British Theatre can boast
> Droles of all kinds, a vast Unthinking Hoast . . .
> Rough-country Knights are found of ev'ry Shire . . .

Notwithstanding this, Sir Harry Gubbin, the rustic squire of *The Tender Husband*, hails from the west of England! Another backwoods retreat for stage squires was Shropshire, home of Sir Willful Witwoud in Congreve's *The Way of the World* (1700), who is vilified as a 'Salopian' when marched off stage in a drunken condition. The very names of squires in Restoration and sentimental comedy reveal something of the contempt with which they could be held by dramatists – Sir Jolly Jumble, Sir Nicholas Culley, Sir Ralph Brute (a Yorkshire example) and the incomparable Sir Tunbelly Clumsy, to name but four. As Sir Charles Firth concluded:

> Take these dramatic personages and generalise from them about the class, if you like; but you are not basing your conclusions on facts and it is no good asserting that you are. You are only copying certain fictions which were accepted as facts by the pit and gallery; you are building on humourous exaggerations of the facts. Macaulay does this far too much in his description of the country gentlemen.[6]

It would be wrong, however, to imply, as Firth does here, that Macaulay relied exclusively upon plays for his depiction of the gentry. They were, it is true, the main materials extant from the actual period Macaulay was describing – England in the 1680s. But in his search for evidence for his third chapter he had no compunction in wandering right outside that decade – as far back as Chaucer for his account of English inns; as far forward as Sir Walter Scott's journal for the rude state of the border with Scotland. Indeed, it is one of the more telling criticisms of Macaulay that his sources were not restricted to the era between the Restoration and the Revolution. Croker compared the third chapter to an old curiosity shop into which 'the knick-knacks of a couple of centuries are promiscuously jumbled'. This was a little unfair, for Macaulay kept as close as he could to 1685. But the sheer paucity of relevant evidence available to him inevitably forced him to look further afield; and as far as the country gentlemen were concerned he drew on the literature of the whole Augustan period, from Pepys's diary for the 1660s to the novels of the 1740s. Not only are booby squires of Restoration comedy discernible below the surface of it; so are the grosser aspects of such fictional country gentlemen as Sir Roger de Coverley and even Squire Western. His account of the gentry's beer-drinking bouts could well have come from John Gay's vision in *The Birth of the Squire*:

> Methinks I see him in his hall appear,
> Where the long table floats in clammy beer.
> Midst mugs and glasses shatter'd o'er the floor,
> Dead drunk his servile crew supinely snore.
> Triumphant o'er the prostrate brutes he stands,
> The mighty bumper trembles in his hands.
> Boldly he drinks, and like his glorious Sires,
> In copious gulps of potent ale expires.

There is one source from the early eighteenth century which so perfectly fits Macaulay's description of backwoods gentry that it is hard to imagine that it was not part of the lighter literature of the age which he had in his mind when he wrote it. This was Joseph Addison's *Freeholder*. Macaulay had written a review of a life of Addison for the *Edinburgh*

Review in 1843, when he was hard at work on the first volume of his *History*. In it he observed that

> Towards the close of the year 1715, while the Rebellion was still raging in Scotland, Addison published the first number of a paper called the Freeholder. Among his political works the Freeholder is entitled to first place. Even in the Spectator . . . [there is] no satirical paper superior to those in which the Tory Foxhunter is introduced. This character is the original of Squire Western, and is drawn with all Fielding's force, and with a delicacy of which Fielding was altogether destitute.[7]

Addison introduced Foxhunter in the *Freeholder* for 5 March 1716, claiming to have encountered him in a remote part of England:

> Our Conversation opened, as usual, upon the Weather, in which we were very unanimous, having both agreed that it was too dry for the Season of the Year. My Fellow-Traveller upon this observed to me, that there had been no good Weather since the Revolution. I was a little startled at so extraordinary a Remark, but would not interrupt him till he proceeded to tell me of the fine Weather they used to have in King *Charles* the Second's Reign. . . . He affirmed roundly, that there had not been one good Law passed since King *William*'s Accession to the Throne, except the Act for preserving the Game. . . . I ask'd him if he had ever Travelled; He told me, he did not know what Travelling was good for, but to teach a Man to ride the Great Horse, to jabber *French*, and to talk against Passive-Obedience. . . . As we rode Side by Side through the Town, I was let into the Characters of all the principal Inhabitants whom we met in our Way. One was a Dog, another a Whelp, another a Cur, and another the Son of a Bitch, under which several Denominations were comprehended all that Voted on the Whig Side in the last Election of Burgesses. . . . He expatiated on the Inconveniencies of Trade, that carried from us the Commodities of our Country, and made a Parcel of Upstarts as rich as Men of the most ancient Families of *England*. He then declared frankly, that he

> had always been against all Treaties and Alliances with Foreigners; *Our Wooden Walls*, says he, *are our Security, and we may bid Defiance to the whole World, especially if they should attack us when the Militia is out*. . . . He would undertake to prove, Trade would be the Ruine of the English Nation. I would fain have put him upon it; but he contented himself with affirming it more eagerly, to which he added two or three Curses upon the *London* Merchants, not forgetting the Directors of the Bank.[8]

It is obvious that Foxhunter is an archetype of Macaulay's country gentleman. If Macaulay was misled by his reliance upon literary sources into caricaturing the gentry, then Addison was more to blame for misleading him than Restoration playwrights or eighteenth-century novelists. The outstanding question is: was he misled?

Even since Croker's hostile review of Macaulay's *History* there has been a steady chorus of complaint that his picture of the gentry was distorted, partly by his partisanship but mainly by his use of the lighter literature of the age. The main attack has been aimed at his methodology, namely that he asked the wrong questions of the wrong sources. The problem 'What were the gentry really like?' cannot be solved by literary evidence. After Macaulay's death two developments revolutionised the historiography of the late seventeenth century. One was the development of so-called scientific history, which trained historians to be far more critical and objective about their sources than Macaulay ever was. This tended to dismiss as worthless the partial evidence of literature. The second major change was the discovery of fresh evidence, totally unknown to Macaulay, which throws a great deal of light on the state of the landed classes in early modern England. The foundation of the Historical Manuscripts Commission in the late nineteenth century unearthed an abundance of private archives in England, stuffed for the most part with the private letters and papers of the aristocracy and gentry of the seventeenth and eighteenth centuries. The establishment of local record offices in the twentieth century has made available far more of the same kind of evidence. These sources document the lives of the gentry as they really lived. As Sir Charles Firth observed, 'Any one familiar with the domestic correspondence of the period will form a more favourable impression of the manners and intelligence of the country gentry. Collections of correspondence . . . prove that there were many families with habits and ideals as high as those of the corresponding class in Macaulay's own time.'[9]

This is undoubtedly true. Almost any volume calendered by the Historical Manuscripts Commission, or bundle of letters deposited in a county record office, testifies to the literacy and indeed the sophistication of at least a section of the gentry of the late Stuart period. Such qualitative evidence also gives the lie to another claim by Macaulay, that 'Few knights of the shire had libraries so good as may now perpetually be found in a servants' hall, or in the back parlour of a small shopkeeper. An esquire passed among his neighbours for a great scholar, if *Hudibras* and Baker's *Chronicle*, Tarlton's Jests and the Seven Champions of Christendom lay in his hall window among the fishing rods and fowling pieces.'[10] On the contrary, as Firth again commented, 'The seventeenth-century libraries which occasionally come into the market, bills for books, references in letters and other indications show that there was more reading done in the country houses than Macaulay admitted.'[11]

However, these conclusions, though based on more reliable evidence than Macaulay's, are still as impressionistic. Moreover, these impressions are not necessarily at odds with each other. It seems possible that the letters and papers which have survived document the lives of the upper ranks of the gentry, and that the lesser gentry might still have exhibited the characteristics which Macaulay attributes to the whole class. After all, there were some 16,000 gentry families in England at the time of the Revolution, and the gradations of wealth between the richest and the poorest were enormous. By distinguishing between the component elements of the class Firth resolves the conflict of evidence:

> The level of culture varied as greatly as the average amount of wealth. The smaller gentry were naturally less cultivated than those who could afford to spend liberally on the education of their children, and to travel. In the remoter parts of the country the gentry were less educated and less civilised than those who lived nearer to the capital. In the

> picture which Macaulay draws of the class as a whole these shades of difference are suppressed; he generalises too much from the lower half of the class and makes no adequate allowance for the large number of educated and intelligent men it contained.[12]

This resolution of the matter seems to have found general acceptance. Thus Professor Charles Wilson in *England's Apprenticeship* has agreed that it is in the lower ranks of the squirearchy that historians encounter the coarse bucolic country gentlemen characterised by Macaulay.[13]

Unfortunately this happy compromise cannot be sustained, because the literature on which Macaulay based his character of the gentry made no such distinction. Although Addison's Foxhunter was almost certainly one of the lesser gentry, other literary portrayals of country gentlemen placed them in the upper reaches of the squirearchy. It was one of Jeremy Collier's many objections to *The Relapse; or Virtue in Danger* that Vanbrugh made Sir Tunbelly Clumsy 'a Justice of Peace and a Deputy Lieutenant and seats him fifty miles from London: But by his character you would take him for one of Hercules's monsters or some Gyant in Guy of Warwick'.[14] He even objected to Sir Tunbelly's offering young Fashion a cup of sack-wine, since 'sack-wine is too low for a petty constable'. Playwrights are supposed to have responded seriously to Collier's strictures, but Vanbrugh took little notice of this particular criticism judging by the characters of Polidorus Hogstye of Beast Hall in Swine County, who appears in *Aesop*, and of Sir Francis Wronghead, a country gentleman in *The Provok'd Husband; or A Journey to London*. Polidorus makes his appearance with the stage direction 'Enter a country gentleman, drunk, in a hunting dress'. Yet he is a justice of the peace and captain of the militia, worth £3000 a year, with woods valued at £2000.[15] Although Sir Francis is MP for Guzzledown, an imaginary Yorkshire borough, he arrives in London 'gaping and stumping about the streets in his dirty boots'. His family is even more clownish than himself, especially his booby son Richard, who, upon being invited to play at ombre provides Vanbrugh with an opportunity of making a grotesque pun by responding: 'What! th' Humber! Hoy day! Why, does our River run to this Tawn, Feather?'[16]

Fictitious country gentlemen therefore seem to bear very little resemblance to the real gentry whose lives are documented in non-literary sources. Social historians, seeking to reconstruct social realities from quantitative data, would have their suspicions confirmed by Macaulay's example that literature is not only worthless as evidence but positively misleading.

It is, of course, possible to argue that there is no necessary link between literary stereotypes and contemporary realities. They could be regarded as stock characters who inhabit a world created purely by writers, existing in a tradition outside historical developments. The booby squire, after all, had a pedigree going back at least to Elizabethan and Jacobean drama. Falstaff, for instance, displays many of his characteristics. The country gentleman was so much a standard type that he appeared in *The English Theophrastus; or The Manners of the Age, being the Modern Characters of the Court, the Town and the City*. Although this was published in 1702, it was largely a digest of types from a variety of sources, including La Bruyère, Francis Bacon and Sir Walter Raleigh, as well as more recent authors. The Theophrastan squire conforms closely to the archetype:

> His conversation is wholly taken up by his horses, dogs, and hawks, and the more senceless animals that tend 'em. His groom, his huntsman and his falconer are his tutors, and his walk is from the stable to the dog kennel. . . . He wearies you in the morning with his sport, in the afternoon with the noise, repetition and drink, and the whole day with fatigue and confusion. His entertainment is stale beer and the history of his dogs and horses, in which he gives you the pedigree of every one, with all the exactness of a Welch-Herald. . . . He is very constant at all Clubs and meetings of the country-gentlemen, where he will suffer nothing to be talked or heard of, but his Jades, Curs and Kites, and is least impertinent when most drunk.

It could be, therefore, that such stereotypes exist in a literary limbo unaffected by the mere passage of time.

And yet one Augustan who did see a definite connection between stage squires and his own age was Jeremy Collier. In his influential *Short View of the Prophaneness and Immorality of the English Stage* (1698) he roundly condemned playwrights who exhibited country gentlemen as ignorant clowns on the grounds that they were undermining respect for authority. Paradoxically, he himself had so little respect for the authorities that he refused to take the oaths of allegiance to them. Collier was a Non-juror, i.e. one of those who did not recognise the legitimacy of the government established after the Revolution of 1688. To the Non-jurors the Revolution, so far from being 'Glorious', was a disaster which had overthrown not only the principle of divine, indefeasible hereditary right but also the old ruling hierarchy, replacing it with a regime of social upstarts. Collier himself claimed that erosion of respect for the traditional ruling elite had been in a large measure responsible for the Revolution, and that these subversive trends still continued, as witness the disrespect with which figures of authority such as country gentlemen were treated on the stage.[17]

Although one could question his analysis of the social trends of the late seventeenth century, Collier was right in his assumption that dramatists after 1688 overwhelmingly supported the Revolution settlement. Those who created stage squires, such as Mrs Centlivre, Congreve, Farquhar, Steele and Vanbrugh, were Whigs. So was Addison, the originator of Foxhunter. They did not represent what country gentlemen were really like, so much as how they were perceived by the Whigs. Since Whigs held most of the gentry to be their enemies, they were not regarded in a flattering light. Indeed, the stereotype was not confined to Whig writers of fiction. The Whig historian Gilbert Burnet, Bishop of Salisbury, made some very unflattering observations on them. 'They are for the most part', he wrote in his *History of My Own Time*,

> the worst instructed and the least knowing of any of their rank I ever went amongst. The Scotch, though less able to bear the expense of a learned education, are much more knowing. . . . A gentleman here is often both ill-taught and ill-bred; this makes him haughty and insolent. . . . Can there be any thing more barbarous, or rather treacherous, than for gentlemen to think it is one of the honours of their houses, that none must go out of them sober; it is but a

> little more infamous to poison them; and yet this passes as a character of a noble house keeper, who entertains his friends kindly.[18]

What these works do, therefore, is to recapture, not what the gentry were really like, but how they appeared to Whigs. Now one thing that Macaulay did get right was that the majority of country gentlemen were Tories. The county electorates were on the whole overwhelmingly Tory, and the gentry formed a significant element among the freeholders who voted in the counties. Not only were they more inclined to vote Tory, they were particularly prone to do so in the West Country. The counties of Cornwall, Devon and Somerset were almost solidly Tory throughout the late seventeenth and early eighteenth centuries. This confirms up to the hilt the contemporary assertion that 'The majority of the gentry upon a poll will be found Tories.'[19]

Macaulay's description, therefore, is not of a sociological reality but of a political stereotype. We are looking at the backbone of the Tory party through his own Whig eyes and the Whiggish glasses of his literary sources. This process distorts the picture, so that the gentry's principles appear as prejudices; their attachment to the Church of England is refracted into bigotry; their dislike of continental contacts is conveyed as xenophobia; their suspicion of the city is represented as narrow provincialism; and so on, until by a process of political refraction they cease to be real and become stereotypes. These tell us little or nothing about real country gentlemen, but a great deal about contemporary Whig ideology.

The following study seeks to show that much Augustan literature was charged with similar ideological preconceptions. If, like Macaulay, we use it to try to document social realities, we shall be seriously misled. If, however, we read it with an appreciation of the partisanship of its writers, then it can become a prime source for the ideologies of the period 1700-60.

This work is not intended to be a literary history in the sense of providing the 'background' to Augustan literature, although it might serve that purpose. Rather it is an attempt to reclaim creative writing as a legitimate source for the historian. The literary student's 'background' is therefore very much the foreground of this study: hence its title 'Society and Literature' and not 'Literature and Society'. Its focus is largely on problems which have concerned political and social historians in recent years, in order to show what light, if any, literary texts throw on these. The first chapter discusses Augustan ideologies to demonstrate the political commitments of many authors in the period. There follow chapters which pick up themes which have recently attracted the attention of social historians. Fielding and Smollett have been selected for individual case studies because their novels seem so vividly realistic that they are often used to illustrate aspects of Augustan society. The relationship between authors and their readers is explored to indicate that literature helped to form as well as to reflect attitudes. The conclusion reaffirms the central thesis that Augustan literature does not document 'reality' so much as contemporary ideologies.

1
Politics and Literature

> He [the King of Brobdingnag] could not forbear taking me up in his right hand, and stroaking me gently with the other, after an hearty fit of laughing, asked me whether I were a Whig or a Tory.
>
> Jonathan Swift, *Gulliver's Travels* (1726)

G. M. Trevelyan defined social history as 'the history of a people with the politics left out'.[1] However acceptable his definition might once have been, it would not command general support nowadays. Historians who study past politics no longer see them primarily as the interplay of a handful of politicians operating in a void, but place political activity in a social context. At the same time social historians are becoming increasingly aware that concepts such as class and the family have political implications.

Even if politics could safely be ignored when dealing with the use of literature as evidence for social history in other periods, they would still be essential for studying links between literary works and society in the years 1700-60. In that period every major writer and many minor writers contributed to contemporary political debates. Addison, Defoe, Fielding, Steele and Swift, to name five in the front rank, wrote pamphlets and contributed to periodicals defending or attacking prominent politicians. Poets from Matthew Prior to Alexander Pope wrote poems on affairs of state. The drama of the day was politically committed. Even novels handled themes which were ultimately political in nature.

The political historian, however, needs to be no less careful than his colleagues in social history about the use he makes of this kind of evidence, for literature can be just as misleading about politics as it is about society. The case study of the country gentlemen in the Introduction showed that there was an almost complete discrepancy between the booby squire of fiction and the way the gentry behaved in fact. This was due to the manipulation by Whig writers of a stereotype squire for partisan purposes. Similarly, Tory propagandists depicted the Whig party as being composed of undesirable elements in society. Thus *The Old Pack*, a Tory poem of 1710, described Whigs who sat in the House of Commons in the early months of that year as having various more or less unsavoury origins:

> Some were bred in the Camp, and some dropt in the Fleet,
> Under Bulks some were litter'd, and some in the Street;
> Some are good harmless Curs, without Tooth or Claw,
> Some were whelp'd in a Shop, and some Runners at Law;
> Some were poor wretched Curs, Mungrels, Starters and
> Setters,
> 'Till dividing the Spoil they put in with their Betters.[2]

The association of Whigs with professional and business men linked their politics with social types which had a very unfavourable image in contemporary literature. This was taken to extremes in *The Character of a Whig under Several Denominations* (1700), whose very list of contents indicates the guilt-by-association technique. Among the characters which it contains are: 'the factious seditious illiterate whig lawyer, a bold treacherous whig attorney, the jugling whig physician, the mechanick or scoundrel whig physician, an amphibious latitudinarian aldermanlike whig, and a politick tricking overreaching trading whig'. One of the traits common to most of these 'characters' is their low birth. 'The factious seditious illiterate whig lawyer' is depicted arriving in rags from Scotland, to be clothed by an uncle's charity and a collection; 'a bold treacherous whig attorney' is described as 'an animal descended from the plough tail, swept out o' th' shop or kick'd from a justice of the peace's or lawyer's clark into a gentleman'; and a 'mechanick or scoundrel whig physician' is 'a mixture of broken tradesman, decayed serving man and discarded hostler'. They contrive to rise in the world by totally unscrupulous means. Of the Whig lawyer we learn that 'That which prevents many honest men from being lawyers, viz a scrupulous conscience and an inflexible honesty, never hinders him, for he carries no such things about him.' He is in league with a Nonconformist parson who introduces him to rich clients, for whom he draws up wills, ensuring that he and his partner both benefit therefrom. 'Thus the whigs engrossing all the arts of money catching among themselves, our lawyer is soon grown rich and opulent.'[3]

After the Revolution of 1688 the Whigs set up institutions of public credit, including the Bank of England, which brought into existence stock-jobbers and others associated with the financial machinery. These were transformed into new stereotypes who were depicted as parasites by Tory propagandists. Thus another Whig 'character' was created, most brilliantly that of Tom Double in Charles Davenant's *The True Picture of a Modern Whig* (1701) and its sequels. Double damns himself out of his own mouth in a dialogue with a Mr Whiglove. Thus he tells Whiglove that he 'was first bound to a shoemaker in London', but left shoemaking to buy a place in the customs administration after his grandmother 'who sold barley broth and firmity by Fleet ditch' died, leaving him three hundred pounds. In James II's reign, however, he was convicted of fraud and was turned out of the customs service. Where he had previously been a loyal Tory, he now 'became a furious Whig'. When his grandmother's legacy ran out he was 'forced to be a corrector of a private press in a garret, for three shillings a week'. Then the Revolution improved his condition, for he was able by an outrageous confidence trick to pass himself off as an agent from the Prince of Orange, and by even more brazen cheating at dice to win money from the man he had conned. He then set out to make a fortune from the new regime, starting with shares in the discovery of concealed Crown lands, and moving into the big time with enormous frauds in the disposal of confiscated Irish estates. Double claimed to have devised the whole machinery of public credit, the million lottery, the leather tax, malt duty, window tax, Bank of England, New East India Company and Exchequer Bills. Whiglove observes: 'I always understood we Whigs had been the devisers of the new taxes and remote funds, but did not know till now the share you have had in it.' To this Double replies:

> I have done my part, and think I have reason to pretend to a great deal of merit. For what would have become of

> our Party if it had not been for these projects? 'Tis true we have run the nation head over ears in debt by our funds and new devices, but mark what a dependance upon our noble friends this way of raising money has occasioned. Who is it sticks to 'em but those who are concern'd in tallies and the new stocks?

The 'master piece' of his 'dexterity' was to act as receiver of the taxes, when £50,000 stuck to his fingers; and although it cost him £20,000 to buy off a parliamentary inquiry by bribing MPs, he still had enough left to live at ease, with his country seat, a town house and a coach and six. 'You have given me a very succinct accompt of your self', Whiglove acknowledges, 'from the time you crept out of your garret, to the prosperity in which you flourish at present.' 'You have the History of my life,' concludes Double, 'but it may serve as a looking glass in which most of the Modern Whigs may see their own faces.'[4]

Despite this assertion, Davenant's allegedly 'true picture' is a manifest fiction. The ways in which the penniless adventurer Double rises to riches by a career of corruption are patently absurd, for even someone with his 'familiar confidence' could not have hoodwinked so many people. Although he asserts that most modern Whigs had similar careers, no historian would dream of generalising about the Whigs from such a source in the way that Macaulay did about the Tory gentry from similarly hostile evidence. And yet Davenant's fictitious character Tom Double seems to have appealed to enough people at the time for two sequels to *The True Picture* to appear, one in 1702 and the other as late as 1710. The first was a tract with the title *Tom Double Returned out of the Country*, referring to his efforts in a general election, in which he sent to Gloucestershire 'five portmanteaus stuft full of libels, every freeholder in the country had one of each sort sent to his house'. The revealing title of the second was *Sir Thomas Double at Court and in Great Preferments*.

Double's mirror, indeed, reflects more the kind of person Davenant was addressing, or at least whom he thought he was addressing, than it does the modern Whig himself. A superficial reading might lead one to conclude that the pamphlets were designed for consumption by Tories. Davenant was a

Tory writer, and he portrays a Whig who admits that he and his kind are utterly unscrupulous. Yet Double is described not merely as a Whig but as a *modern* Whig, with the emphasis very much on the adjective. Davenant was anxious to appeal not only to Tories, but also to a significant section of post-Revolution Whigs who had become disillusioned with the party leadership. Before 1688 the Whigs had been essentially an opposition party, but the Revolution brought them to power. The new generation of leaders, especially those lords who were known collectively as the Junto, rose to high office during the 1690s. Many of their erstwhile followers, however, retained their opposition stance, and became disillusioned when they saw the Junto adopting the essential compromises that the responsibility of office entailed. They were particularly incensed when the Whig ministers tried to retain a large standing army after the Treaty of Ryswick in 1697, and they joined with the Tories to reduce the armed forces to 10,000 that year and 7000 in 1698. It was this opposition or, as it was called at the time, 'Country party' of Tories and the so-called Old Whigs that Davenant was anxious to keep alive in his Double tracts. They extol the virtues of the Old Whigs and depict the modern Whigs as apostates who had shed all ideological tinctures of true Whiggery in pursuit of their own aggrandisement and in defence of their ill-gotten gains.

The Junto's opponents went beyond the creation of a modern Whig *persona* to personal abuse in their polemical attacks. Those who wrote poems on affairs of state, for instance, did not hesitate to vilify them by name or innuendo in poem after poem.[5] Charles Montagu, Earl of Halifax, as Chancellor of the Exchequer in William's reign had presided over the creation of the machinery of public credit which Tories and Country Whigs claimed to be the greatest single source of corruption. He was consequently lambasted by the Junto's enemies as the architect of the nation's ruin. *Advice to a Painter*, an anonymous poem of 1697, for example, puts 'imperious Montague' at the front of 'the Mercenary Herd':

> Slavish Excises are his darling Sin,
> And 'Chequer-Bills the Product of his Brain;
> No publick Profit but conduces most
> To raise his Fortune at the Publick Cost.

Edward Russell, Earl of Orford, was also held to be corrupt. *A Conference between King William and the Earl of Sunderland* (1700) put into the king's mouth the words

> Ranalagh, Blaithwaite and Boyle I'le Skip ore
> Lest they smuggle the little that's yet left in Store,
> Or like my Lord Orford make up their Accounts,
> Though his Cowardly baseness their Cheating Surmounts.

On My Lord Somers (1700) described him as an 'Audacious Upstart' who was 'Blown up by Faction, and by Guilt Spurr'd on'. William Shippen accused Charles Spencer, third Earl of Sunderland, of showing 'a true Fanatick Zeal and Heat'.

But the most libelled of all the Junto was Thomas, first Marquis of Wharton. *An Acrostick on Wharton* (1710) summed up the main points of the Tories' charge against him:

> Whig's the first Letter of his odious Name;
> Hypocrisy's the second of the same;
> Anarchy's his Darling; and his Aim
> Rebellion, Discord, Mutiny and Faction;
> *Tom*, Captain of the Mob in Soul and Action;
> O'ergrown in Sin, cornuted, old, in Debt,
> *Noll*'s Soul and *Ireton*'s live within him yet.

Although Wharton is not named in *The Character of a Certain Whigg* (1711), he is undoubtedly its target. In it he is said to be a 'Sworn Enemy to God, his Church, and Laws'. The spleen of its author overflows in the closing lines:

> His *Mind* still working, *Mad*, of Peace bereft,
> And *Malice* eating what the Pox has left.
> A Monster, whom no Vice can bigger swell,
> Abhorr'd by Heav'n and long since due to Hell.

Swift was merely joining in a popular Tory sport when he baited the most reviled member of the Whig Junto in *A Short Character of His Excellency Thomas Earl of Wharton*.

This identification of real politicians in Augustan satirical verse complicates the relationship between literature and reality. Some literary critics have assumed that there must be some truth in such polemical poems, on the basis that there is no smoke without fire. Impartial historians, however, would require much more concrete, first-hand evidence than this biased testimony before accepting its verdict. Sympathetic biographers would object that it is nothing but a tissue of half-truths, deliberate distortions and downright lies. They could claim that the Junto were maliciously libelled by their opponents, and that in fact all five lords can be defended from the charges brought against them. Halifax was exonerated from the accusations of corruption, Orford's accounts were passed, Somers was not an upstart but the son of a country gentleman, Sunderland was not a 'fanatic', nor Wharton an anarchist.

The satires in which they were libelled, however, were not rooted in objective reality. Rather they were related to the fears and prejudices of their opponents, which found expression in the archetype of the modern Whig. Those who created this archetype in order to exploit those fears and prejudices made little or no attempt to be objective. Indeed, the author of *The Character of a Certain Whigg* explicitly admitted that he was not discussing a man but a monster. Such monsters tell us far more about the ideology of the Junto's opponents than they do about the five Whig lords themselves.

One of their leading opponents was Robert Harley. Harley's Puritan background made him a Revolution Whig in 1688, but also led him to espouse the Country opposition against what he saw as the corruption of the Court, even when it included Whig ministers. This attitude continued to inform the propaganda he wrote or inspired even in Anne's reign, when he himself rose to high office and became essentially a Court politician. Indeed, he was the first minister systematically to organise a government press, for which purpose he employed both Daniel Defoe and Jonathan Swift besides a host of lesser writers.[6] He even wrote or inspired political tracts himself, the most celebrated being *Faults on Both Sides*, in which Simon Clements incorporated Harley's own views, in 1710. A much more obscure treatise he penned himself in 1708, with the title *Plain English: to all who are honest or would be if they knew how.*[7] In it he argued that party politicians were essentially corrupt, while their leaders, High Church Tories on the one side, Junto Whigs on the other, kept up divisions in order to pursue their own selfish ends. In

Plain English he even accused Lord Treasurer Godolphin and the Duke of Marlborough of fomenting party strife in order to maintain themselves in power and thereby to amass wealth. Harley therefore genuinely appears to have believed that parties were perpetuated by corrupt politicians, and that moderate men would no longer follow them if their self-interest was exposed.

The theme of corruption consequently informs the Court propaganda campaign which Harley organised. Defoe lambasted High Church Tories like the Earl of Rochester and Sir Edward Seymour remorselessly in the *Review*, devoting issue after issue to an exposé of High Church fanaticism between 1704 and 1706. Some of his most telling strokes against them, however, appeared in his poem *The Dyet of Poland*, which he wrote in 1704 and circulated in manuscript before publishing it in 1705. In it Rochester was accused of 'crimes too black for Satyr to reveal', while Seymour was said to be 'hard'ned with bribes, with frauds and broken vows'.[8] By 1710, when Harley wished to discredit the leaders of the Whig ministry he had just supplanted, Swift turned his talents against them. He needed no prompting to vilify Wharton, having already written the damning *Short Character of His Excellency* before he teamed up with the new prime minister, though he was not averse to penning another exercise in character assassination by depicting the former Lord Lieutenant of Ireland as Verres, the corrupt governor of Roman Sicily, in the *Examiner*. Although his cold reception from the fallen Lord Treasurer left Swift with no love for Godolphin, Harley probably furnished him with some hints for his attack on the disgraced minister in *The Virtues of Sid Hamet the Magician's Rod*, in which he develops analogies between the white staff of office and a conjuring stick. Harley had drawn parallels between Godolphin and Marlborough and magicians in his unpublished *Plain English* which it is hard to believe he did not show to Swift. Certainly by the time he came to denounce the Duke of Marlborough as Crassus in the *Examiner*, and above all in *The Conduct of the Allies*, he used arguments strikingly similar to those employed in Harley's tract. In both a major theme is that a particular family, the Churchills, has been deliberately prolonging the War of the Spanish Succession in pursuit of its own advancement. Thus in *Plain English* Harley asserted: 'It is plain that everything they do is calculated to support either the power or profit of one family,' while in *The Conduct of the Allies* Swift claimed that 'We have been fighting to raise the wealth and grandeur of a particular family.'[9]

In the *Examiner* and *The Conduct of the Allies* Swift also developed the notions adumbrated by Davenant in his Double tracts, that the post-Revolution Whig leaders were engaged in systematic as well as individual corruption. 'Let any man observe the equipages in this town,' he observed in his very first contribution to the *Examiner*;

> he shall find the greater number of those who make a figure to be a species of men quite different from any that were ever known before the Revolution; consisting either of generals or colonels, or of such whose whole Fortunes lie in funds and stocks; so that *Power*, which, according to the old maxim, was used to follow land, is now gone over to money . . . so that, if the war continues some years longer, a landed man will be little better than a farmer at a rack rent, to the army, and to the publick funds.[10]

Like Davenant, he blamed this on the Whig leaders of William's reign, who

> argued that the war could not last above two or three campaigns; and that it was easier for the subject to raise a fund for paying interest, than to tax them annually the full expence of the war. Several persons who had small or encumbered estates, sold them, and turned their money into those funds to great advantage; merchants as well as other monied men, finding trade was dangerous, pursued the same method: But the war continuing, and growing more expensive, taxes were increased, and funds multiplied every year, till they have arrived at the monstrous height we now behold them. And that which was at first corruption is at last grown necessary, and what every good subject must now fall in with. . . . By this means the wealth of the nation, that used to be reckoned by the value of land, is now computed by the rise and fall of stocks.

Swift elaborated the notion that there was a conspiracy on the part of the Whigs to enrich themselves at the expense of the public in *The Conduct of the Allies and* (as the title continues) *of the Late Ministry in Beginning and Carrying On the Present War*. 'A set of upstarts,' he claimed, again referring to the Junto in William's reign, 'finding that the gentlemen of estates were not willing to come into their measures, fell upon these new schemes of raising money, in order to create a money'd interest that might in time vie with the landed.' By the accession of Queen Anne they had created 'a sort of artificial wealth of funds and stocks in the hands of those who for ten years before had been plundering the publick'. This interest, 'whose perpetual harvest is war', had forced England into the War of the Spanish Succession as a principal power fighting on land, when she ought only to have been an auxiliary deploying her main war effort to the sea. 'Thus', Swift maintained, 'there was a conspiracy on all sides to go on with those measures which must perpetuate the war.' This had laid an intolerable financial burden on the kingdom, one which through the National Debt would bear heavily on future generations. 'It will, no doubt, be a mighty comfort to our grandchildren', he predicted, 'when they see a few rags hang up in Westminster-Hall, which cost an hundred millions, whereof they are paying the arrears, and boasting, as beggars do, that their grandfathers were rich and great.' His conspiracy thesis was pushed to its ultimate conclusion when he asked:

> What have we been fighting for all this while? The answer is ready; we have been fighting for the ruin of the publick interest and the advancement of a private . . . to enrich usurers and stock-jobbers; and to cultivate the pernicious designs of a faction; by destroying the landed interest. The nation begins now to think these blessings are not worth fighting for any longer, and therefore desires a peace.[11]

During Anne's reign the main attacks upon the alleged corruption of the Whig leaders came from Tories or from writers associated with Robert Harley. Hardly any of the Country Whigs who had fulminated against the Junto in print at the time of the standing army controversy in the 1690s kept up the quarrel with them after William's death. As in so many other spheres of political life, the press was dominated between 1702 and 1714 by the conflict between the Whig and Tory parties. Writers fought paper battles over every issue which divided Whigs and Tories. Partisan views on the nature of monarchy, on religion and on foreign policy were vented in countless newspapers, pamphlets, plays and poems which poured like a torrent from the press. Most of this literature is no longer widely read, although the party warfare did produce some enduring works. The religious controversy between High Church Anglicans and Nonconformists inspired Defoe's *The Shortest Way with the Dissenters*. The Whig championship of liberty against tyranny imbues Addison's *Cato*. The Tory longing for an end to the War of the Spanish Succession and relief at the Treaty of Utrecht found expression in Pope's *Windsor Forest*. No one can read these works without becoming aware that under Anne the literary world was polarised into Tory and Whig camps along with the rest of a deeply divided society.

After the succession of George I, however, a situation somewhat similar to that which had followed the Revolution was again experienced. The Whigs once more came to power, this time for the best part of fifty years. The Tory party as it had existed before 1714 was never in a position to act as an effective rival in the struggle for power. The victorious Whigs then fell out among themselves, to some extent along lines which had divided them under William. Thus opposition or Country Whigs emerged who accused the Whig ministers of perpetuating their rule by corruption. Indeed, a leading champion of the Country Whigs at the time of the standing army dispute, John Trenchard, became perhaps the foremost critic of the new regime. He had written the most influential tract against the upkeep of armed forces in peace-time in 1698, *An Argument Showing that a Standing Army is Inconsistent with a Free Government*. In 1720, at the height of the South Sea Bubble scandal, he collaborated with Thomas Gordon to contribute *Cato's Letters* to the *London Journal*.

The theme of shady financiers and corrupt politicians driving the nation to destruction was explored more fully in *Cato's Letters* than in any previous publication. Its essence is encapsulated in the eighteenth letter. Indeed, the very title sums up a central theme in the letters: 'The terrible tendency of publick corruption to ruin a state, exemplified in that of Rome, and applied to our own'. It described how the consuls of ancient Rome, who obtained their posts by intrigue or bribery, indulged in an orgy of conspicuous consumption, until having 'spent their private patrimonies they endeavoured to make reprisals upon the Publick; and, having before sold every thing else, at last sold their Country. The public Treasure was squandered away and divided amongst private men; and new demands made, and new taxes and burdens laid upon the people, to continue and support this extravagance.'[12] Although 'Cato' expressed the hope that 'we ourselves have none of these corruptions', and even ended by flattering George I, it is clear that the application to contemporary England was meant to be direct. The only way to avoid the fate of the Romans was to practise republican virtue and constantly be on guard against the machinations of men in high places, who as incessantly sought to deprive Englishmen of their liberties by corrupting them.

Cato's Letters called for a coalition of Tories and opposition Whigs in a Country party to fight the Court. This appeal was taken up by the *Craftsman*, which was launched by the Tory Bolingbroke and the opposition Whig William Pulteney in 1726, with the significant subtitle *The Country Journal*. In it they concentrated on exposing the workings of 'state-craft', claiming that 'From this grand fountain of corruption flow all those little streams and rivulets, which have spread themselves through every part of this kingdom, and debauched all ranks and orders of men.'[13]

The *Craftsman* was by no means the only voice of the opposition to the ministry of Sir Robert Walpole. On the contrary, the 'Great Man' was assailed by a whole host of writers who raised a deafening chorus of complaint against his government. Despite their differing motives for opposition, by and large they shouted the same slogans: that the old party distinctions were now dead, and that all honest men should combine on a Country platform against the Court. Amongst a galaxy of talent arrayed against the prime minister were Jonathan Swift, John Gay, Alexander Pope and James Thomson.

Swift's *Gulliver's Travels*, which appeared in 1726, a few months before the first *Craftsman*, contains political puzzles which still perplex readers. As far as its party line is concerned, however, it is usually described as a Tory satire. Certainly Swift became converted to Toryism in Anne's reign, though it is significant that he described himself as an Old Whig;[14] moreover, in assessing the political attitudes which he expressed in his most famous work it is as important to distinguish between Swift and Gulliver as it is when appraising its literary stance. During his second voyage Gulliver was asked by the king of Brobdingnag whether he were a Whig or a Tory, and although he does not indicate his answer it is clear that all his attitudes are Whiggish and that at the outset of his travels he supported the Court. The description of England which he gave to the Brobdingnagian ruler is a panegyric which a government hack might well have penned. Peers are described as 'persons of the noblest blood, and of the most ancient and ample patrimonies', bishops as clergymen who 'were most deservedly distinguished by the sanctity of their lives, and the depth of their erudition', and the Commons as comprising 'principal gentlemen freely picked and culled out by the people themselves, for their great abilities, and love of their country, to represent the wisdom of the whole nation', while parliament was 'the most august assembly in Europe'.

The king, however, not content with this description, probes below its surface to ask how peers are created, and whether 'a design of strengthening a party opposite to the publick interest ever happened to be motives in those advancements'. He then wonders whether the bishops 'had never been compliers with the times, when they were common priests'. Above all, he inquires into parliamentary elections, and 'whether such zealous gentlemen could have any views of refunding themselves for the charges and trouble they were at, by sacrificing the publick good to the designs of a weak and vicious prince, in conjunction with a corrupted ministry'. In the light of his inquiries the king is forced to the conclusions 'that ignorance and vice are the proper ingredients for qualifying a legislator', and while he observed 'some lines of an institution which in its original might have been tolerable', these had become 'half erased, and the rest wholly blurred and blotted by corruptions'.

Although Gulliver himself says that 'great allowances should be given to a king who lives wholly secluded from the rest of the world', his complacent acceptance of English institutions has plainly been shaken. If a significant theme in the *Travels* is his education, changing him from being gullible, as his name implies, into a disillusioned cynic, his political education can be said to be a process whereby he changes from a Court Whig, not into a Tory so much as into a Country Whig. It is furthered in the third voyage, and especially in Glubdubdrib, 'the island of sorcerers or magicians', whose Governor can summon up the dead. Gulliver asks to see the Senate of Rome and a modern representative side by side: 'The first seemed to be an assembly of heroes and demigods; the other, a knot of pedlars, pickpockets, highwaymen and Bullies.' The more he compared the present with the past, the more he became 'disgusted with modern history': 'Three kings shewed with great strength of reason, that the royal throne could not be supported without corruption, because that positive confident, restive temper, which virtue infused into men, was a perpetual clog to publick business.' This contrasts not only with the virtue of ancient Rome but also with the polity of Brobdingnag, which appears as a very model of the Country ideal. Government is not the intricate statecraft deplored by Country writers, but a simple, straightforward art. There is no standing army, but a militia, another embodiment of Country aspirations. Indeed, the whole political philosophy of *Gulliver's Travels* reflects Country more than Tory attitudes.[15]

The same applies to an even greater degree to *The Beggar's Opera*, for, unlike Swift, Gay was never a Tory. Although he knew Bolingbroke and Pope before Anne's death, he attached himself to William Pulteney early in the reign of George I, and it was probably this connection which procured for him the post of Commissioner of State Lotteries in 1723. Even after Pulteney went into opposition Gay tried to obtain further preferment at court, cultivating his friendship with Mrs Howard, wife of the groom of George I's bedchamber, and dedicating his *Fables* to the infant prince William Augustus, the future Duke of Cumberland. However, none of Gay's political associates were to Walpole's liking, and the most that the prime minister was prepared to offer in the way of further advancement was the place of gentleman usher to Princess Louisa, which the poet regarded as an insult and turned down. Shortly afterwards, in January 1728, *The Beggar's Opera* was first performed. Parallels between criminals and ministers are made throughout the opera, Peachum, master criminal and thief-taker, comparing his trade with that of a statesman in the very first air, while a direct hit at the court is aimed in the air

> When you censure the age,
> Be cautious and sage,
> Lest the Courtiers offended should be:
> If you mention vice or bribe
> 'Tis so pat to all the tribe,
> Each cries – That was levelled at me.[16]

The *Craftsman* took up the parallels in mock outrage at 'the most venomous allegorical libel against the government that hath appeared for many years past'. 'There are some persons', it maintained, 'who esteem Lockit, the keeper or prime minister of Newgate to be the hero of the piece; to justify which opinion they take notice that he is set forth on the stage . . . as a very corpulent bulky man,' i.e. resembling the gross Walpole. He and Peachum 'have a numerous gang of thieves and pickpockets under their direction, with whom they divide the plunder, and whom they either screen or tuck up, as their own interest and the present occasion requires'. The use of the word 'screen' would strike contemporaries as an obvious allusion to the prime minister, who had been called by that name ever since his alleged cover-up of those involved in the South Sea scandal. 'But', continued the *Craftsman*,

> I am obliged to reject this interpretation . . . and to embrace another, which is more generally received; viz that Captain Macheath, who hath also a godly presence and hath a tolerable bronze upon his face, is designed for the principal character and drawn to asperse somebody in authority. He is represented at the head of a gang of robbers, who promise

to stand by him against all the enquiries and coercive force of the law. He is often called a great man.[17]

Where Gay depicted ministers 'under the prime characters of a Thief-catcher, a Jaylor, and a Highwayman', Pope's *Dunciad* painted them and their literary supporters as dunces. Pope affected political impartiality in the lines

> Diff'rent our parties, but with equal grace
> The Goddess smiles on Whig and Tory race,
> 'Tis the same rope at sev'ral ends they twist,
> To Dulness, Ridpath is as dear as Mist.[18]

Yet, as Bertrand Goldgar has pointed out, this is very misleading, since the poem names at least twenty-four government hacks and only three opposition writers.[19] Moreover, the contrast between George Ridpath and Nathaniel Mist is an instructive one. Ridpath was indeed a Whig writer, but Mist was a Jacobite, who had been forced to flee the country in 1728 after printing a treasonable article in his *Weekly Journal*. Pope was therefore distancing the opposition from the Jacobites by referring to him and not mentioning any of the writers associated with the *Craftsman*.

Although it teems with the names of hack writers and scribblers in the government's cause, the *Dunciad*'s prime target is not the dunces themselves but those 'great Patricians' who 'inspire these wond'rous works'. Among the 'Patricians' are the kings themselves ('Still Dunce the second reigns like Dunce the first') and the Whig oligarchs who had ruled England since 1714 and were now presided over by Walpole. By ignoring men of genuine taste and wit, and by employing Grub Street hacks, they had lowered the Court to the gutter, and were bringing 'The Smithfield Muses to the Ear of Kings'. Instead of upholding polite values, therefore, they were threatening them with extinction, and along with them all art and science, learning and culture until, in the words of the *Dunciad Variorum* of 1729,

> Lo! the great Anarch's ancient reign restor'd.

Pope also attacked the Court Whigs who upheld the 'Patricians'. When the Goddess Dulness proclaims the games

She summons all her sons: An endless band
Pours forth, and leaves unpeopled half the land;
A motley mixture! in long wigs, in bags,
In silks, in crapes, in garters, and in rags;
From drawing rooms, from colleges, from garrets,
On horse, on foot, in hacks, and gilded chariots,
All who true dunces in her cause appear'd,
And all who knew those dunces to reward.[20]

By implication, the other half of the land, who did not attend the games, were the Tories and opposition Whigs who upheld traditional, Country values.

When Pope came to rewrite the poem the political content became more explicit, with Walpole appearing as an old wizard and a tyrant supreme, while the closing vision became even grimmer, until at last

Lo! thy dread Empire, CHAOS! is restor'd;
Light dies before thy uncreating word:
Thy hand, great Anarch! lets the curtain fall;
And Universal Darkness buries all.[21]

Between the *Dunciad Variorum* and the *Dunciad in four books* of 1743 Pope wrote the *Epistles* which are generally called *Moral Essays*. Those to Lords Bathurst and Burlington on 'the use of riches' crystallise the notion that a corrupt monied interest had risen by devious ways not available in traditional times. Thus bribery could be more clandestine with the use of bills of exchange than was possible in more primitive economies, where either goods or coins were exchanged. Pope has great fun imagining bribery on a massive scale in an exchange economy:

A statesman's slumbers how this speech would spoil!
'Sir, Spain has sent a thousand jars of oil;
Huge bales of British cloth blockade the door;
A hundred oxen at your levee roar.'

Even coins, though less visible and more discreet, were still capable of detection:

Once, we confess, beneath the Patriot's cloak,
From the crack'd bag the dropping Guinea spoke,

And gingling down the back-stairs, told the crew,
'Old Cato is as great a Rogue as you.'

Bills of exchange, however, drawable on the London money market that had come into existence since the Revolution of 1688, facilitated the secret exchange of enormous and undetectable sums:

Blest paper-credit! last and best supply!
That lends Corruption lighter wings to fly!
Gold imp'd by thee, can compass hardest things,
Can pocket Senates, can fetch or carry Kings;
A single leaf shall waft an Army o'er,
Or ship off Senates to a distant Shore;
A leaf, like Sibyl's, scatter to and fro
Our fates and fortunes, as the winds shall blow:
Pregnant with thousands flits the Scrap unseen,
And silent sells a King, or buys a Queen.

Pope quotes a prophecy which the *Epistles* reveal to have come true:

At length Corruption, like a gen'ral flood,
(So long by watchful Ministers withstood)
Shall deluge all; and Av'rice creeping on,
Spread like a low-born mist, and blot the Sun.[22]

The metaphor of the mist's low birth emphasises the Country conceit that the Court politicians were upstarts, *nouveaux riches* of humble origins, like Tom Double. To the opposition Walpole's ministry was crammed with Sir Thomas Doubles.

One of the few good writers whom the prime minister had rewarded was James Thomson, who received £50 in 1727 for dedicating to him his *Poem Sacred to the Memory of Sir Isaac Newton*. Two years later, for reasons which remain obscure, he attacked the ministry in *Britannia*, which warned of luxury eating out the heart of liberty, and narrow selfishness, 'sapping the very frame of government' until 'the whole state in broad corruption sinks'. Like Gulliver, Thomson became a Country Whig rather than a Tory. His poem *Liberty* (1736) encapsulated the Country ideology in verse. It even includes a potted history of Britain, which records how Norman tyranny was thrown off with the granting of Magna Carta, whereafter

Through this, and through succeeding reigns affirmed
These long-contested rights, and wholesome winds
Of opposition hence began to blow
And often since have lent the country life.
Before their breath corruption's insect-blights.
The darkening clouds of evil counsel, fly;
Or should they sounding swell, a putrid court,
A pestilential ministry, they purge,
And ventilated states renew their bloom.[23]

During the 1730s the opposition Whigs were joined by the Earl of Chesterfield, himself a literary man, and George Lyttelton, who not only wrote against Walpole but was regarded as the patron of a group of Country Whig poets, of whom the most celebrated was Richard Glover. Lyttelton's major contribution was his *Letters from a Persian in England to his Friend at Ispahan*, which appeared in 1735. These were by no means all directly political, since the epistolary device was used to satirise many aspects of English life. Frontal attacks on the regime, however, occur in a few of the letters, which repeat the clichés that liberty, precariously preserved throughout English history, is now threatened by a wicked minister and by a standing army at the disposal of the Crown. These particular letters also develop a distinctly Country Whig view, by stressing the parliamentary rather than the hereditary title to the Crown, and by observing that opposition Whigs, 'like other dissenters', were 'punished for their separation by being excluded from all places of trust and profit'.[24]

Early in 1737 Frederick, Prince of Wales, to whom Lyttelton was equerry, went into opposition, so that the elements opposed to Walpole now had a fresh focus for their campaign. Among those who pinned their hopes on Frederick was the London merchant Richard Glover, whose long epic poem *Leonidas* (1737) was puffed by Lyttelton in *Common Sense*, a new Country newspaper, subtitled *The Englishman's Journal*, which soon eclipsed the *Craftsman*. Glover's Leonidas is a prince in whose eyes blazed

The inextinguishable spark, which fires
The souls of patriots

and who died defending virtue and liberty at Thermopylae.[25] It is now universally cause for astonishment that the nine books of blank verse in which Glover developed this theme proved to be a best-seller, since modern critics seem to be agreed that the poem is unreadable.

A more enduring treatment of the same notion is Bolingbroke's *The Idea of a Patriot King*, which was written in 1738. Having despaired of the opposition's chances of toppling Walpole, Bolingbroke's hopes revived when the Prince of Wales joined its ranks. He argued that

> A Patriot King is the most powerful of all reformers, for he is himself a sort of standing miracle, so rarely seen and so little understood, that the sure effects of his appearance will be admiration, and love in every honest breast, confusion and terror to every guilty conscience, but submission and resignation in all. A new people will seem to arise with a new king.

Frederick was the somewhat unlikely candidate for this miraculous role. What the Country coalition could not obtain under George II would be realised under Frederick I: 'His first care will be, no doubt, to purge his court, and to call into the administration such men as he can assure himself will serve on the same principles on which he intends to govern.' Some of those discarded 'will be abandoned by him; not to party fury, but to national justice . . . to make satisfaction for wrongs done to their country, and to stand as examples of terror to future administrations'. Thus Bolingbroke envisaged the future for Walpole when his day of reckoning finally came. Ideally, party divisions would disappear during such a reign, but at the outset the nation would still be divided, and the Patriot King 'may and he ought to show his dislike or his favour, as he judges the constitution may be hurt or improved by one side or the other'.[26] In other words, the Court Whigs would be proscribed and the Country party promoted on Frederick's accession. Thereafter their programme would be implemented, trade would be encouraged, taxes would be lightened, and the navy advanced at the expense of the army. Ideologically there were few differences by now amongst the leading opposition writers. Lyttelton was a great admirer of Bolingbroke, and many of the political ideas in his *Persian Letters* were derived from the Tory peer's contributions to the *Craftsman*, particularly his *Dissertation upon Parties*. Bolingbroke's own *Idea of a Patriot King* was a major contribution to the cause of the Prince of Wales, who made Lyttelton his secretary in 1737.

By the late 1730s Bolingbroke and the 'patriots' were sponsoring or inspiring a whole range of writings. These included plays by James Thomson, David Mallet and Henry Brooke, two of which, Thomson's *Agamemnon* and Mallet's *Mustapha*, somehow got past the Lord Chamberlain and onto the boards, though Brooke's *Gustavus Vasa* and Thomson's *Edward and Eleonara* were banned. Drama was so steeped in opposition rhetoric that George Lillo could not resist a dig at the government even in an otherwise completely non-political play, *Fatal Curiosity* (1737). Set in Penryn at the time of the trial of Sir Walter Raleigh, it contains but one allusion to the event, when Old Wilmot, on hearing that Raleigh 'must lose his head to satisfy the Spaniards', laments: 'There's now no insolence that Spain can offer but to the shame of this pacifick reign poor England must submit to.'[27]

How far opposition writings were concerted into a Country programme is disputable. There are those who see Country writers as a tightly knit group, and who talk of 'Bolingbroke and his Circle'.[28] This probably exaggerates the degree to which even the Scriblerians acted together, and certainly could not be applied to all who wrote against Walpole. Bertrand Goldgar, on the other hand, regards them as disparate individuals who for their own particular reasons found themselves writing against him.[29] One thing which they had in common, he claims, was their frustration at the prime minister's alleged indifference to literary talent. Pushed to extremes this could become a worm's eye view of the situation. It does not explain why Thomson wrote opposition poems despite his payment for *Newton*. Nor can one imagine Pope writing panegyrics if Walpole had paid him more than the £200 he received from the king as 'encouragement to the work of translating the Odyssey of Homer into English verse'. So far from writing polemics against the Great Man because they were not preferred, they were refused his patronage because they criticised his politics.

What they shared was an opposition or Country ideology. They argued that Walpole's administration was undermining fundamental English liberties by systematic corruption. Places and pensions had been liberally bestowed on MPs, and government funds made available in the constituencies, to buy the votes of a majority of the House of Commons and of the electorates in most boroughs. So far from asserting its traditional role of acting as a check on the executive, the legislature had become a mere rubber stamp to the government. It kept in power an unscrupulous Court Whig oligarchy of upstarts who had profited from the 'financial revolution', acquiring estates in the countryside and fortunes on the Exchange. These had supplanted the traditional rulers of the country and the city, the independent squires and merchants. Although Tories had previously been identified with the country gentry, and Whigs with city merchants, during Walpole's ministry they came together to articulate a Country opposition to him.

Whether or not Walpole and his political associates did form a narrow and corrupt oligarchy, and whether or not the 'financial revolution' did result in a transference of wealth from one section of society to another, are questions of current interest to historians. Some defend him from the charges of his opponents by pointing out that, although he undoubtedly exploited the Crown's patronage for political advantage, he could not depend upon a parliamentary majority purely by the judicious bestowal of places and money to MPs and voters. To acquire a majority necessitated the support of a significant number of members and even of electors impervious to his influence.[30] Others insist that Walpole's administration alienated the majority of his fellow-countrymen, and that only ruthless and cynical manipulation of the system kept him in power.[31]

Again, some historians are sceptical about claims made for long-term social and economic changes in the period after the Revolution of 1688. Although the wars against Louis XIV and the accompanying financial measures might have produced a short-term transfer of income from taxpayers to state creditors, after their conclusion the traditional relationships of land, trade and money reasserted themselves.

Walpole, it is claimed, deliberately cultivated landed men by keeping direct taxes low, and merchants by shifting the incidence of indirect taxes from customs to excises. Nevertheless, others insist that the success of the opposition in the counties and the larger boroughs indicates the failure of these approaches. The big constituencies were almost all opposed to him. His relations with the city of London strikingly demonstrate his vulnerability to opposition criticisms, for throughout his ministry he kept close contacts with the major financial corporations, the Bank of England and the East India and South Sea companies, while those outside their charmed circle resolutely resisted him. Thus the four members of parliament for London, elected by the freemen of the city, consistently sided with the opposition.

These divergent interpretations cannot be resolved by citing literary sources. The exact nature of Walpole's dealings with MPs and voters can be documented only by a systematic analysis of the careers of politicians and of individual constituencies such as has been provided by the History of Parliament Trust. Shifts of wealth from one social group to another can be established only by a similarly exhaustive study of estate records, business ledgers and the books of the big corporations. Historians who try to document the political realities of the period from propaganda fall into the same trap as Macaulay did with the country gentlemen. Flimnap, the acrobatic prime minister of Lilliput, who performed the high-wire act so dexterously, may well have been intended by Swift to represent Walpole. So may Gay's Macheath and Pope's old wizard. Indeed, he has been identified with over forty fictitious characters in the polemical literature of the period. Yet these characters also link up with stereotypes of corrupt, self-seeking and upstart politicians which go all the way back to Charles II's reign and even beyond.

Such stereotypes illuminate the ideology of Walpole's opponents rather than the realities of his regime. The notion that there was a deliberate conspiracy to perpetuate the rule of an oligarchy which had usurped power by means of corruption appealed to all those whom he had alienated. Tory gentry and clergy, stripped of all hopes of preferment in state or church, found the conspiracy thesis attractive. They were joined by disillusioned Whigs driven into opposition by Walpole's measures. Their resentment fused into a Country ideology which diagnosed corruption as the prevalent disease and prescribed patriotism as the cure.

The Court did not sit still and leave these taunts unanswered. Its more sophisticated supporters evolved a Court Whig ideology to offset the opposition's, while cruder propagandists attacked their political attitudes and threw mud at their proponents in the public prints.

Although the ministries of Walpole and the Pelhams could not deploy such an impressive array of authors as the opposition could muster against them, they were not as bereft of literary talent as is often alleged. Daniel Defoe defended the government throughout the 1720s, and Henry Fielding during the 1740s, though their contributions fell somewhere between the more erudite expositions of Court Whig philosophy and the hatchet jobs of ministerial hacks. Their novels and pamphlets never rose as high as the former, while their journalism never descended quite so low as the worst of the latter. Among those who developed a Court Whig ideology were Lord Hervey, Benjamin Hoadly and Samuel Squire. Reed Browning has demonstrated how such writers countered Country criticisms by claiming that no government could be perfect and that excessive liberty became licence, while the existing regime was the best possible and preserved essential liberties. Where some opposition authors asserted the sovereignty of the people, the Court Whigs stressed that of the king in parliament. They also held a more optimistic view of human nature than their opponents, which led them to conclude that ministers should be trusted, or at least given the benefit of the doubt, since they were not inevitably prone to corruption and an overweening ambition for power. At its most elevated, Court Whig ideology proposed Cicero as an alternative model of the virtuous citizen to the Country idealisation of Cato.[32]

When attacking the opposition rather than defending the regime, Court writers could plunge from such lofty heights to the level of the gutter press. Walpole hired a whole team of writers to rebut the arguments of his opponents in such newspapers as the *Daily Courant*, the *Free Briton*, the *London*

Journal and the *Corncutter's Journal*. William Arnall, Matthew Concanen, Benjamin Gould and James Pitt, the journalists who wrote these papers and a number of government tracts, are now chiefly remembered as dunces in Pope's *Dunciad*, Arnall and Pitt especially with their pseudonyms of Walsingham and Mother Osborne. They, of course, denied that the government was corrupt, and even asserted that the monied interest was not a sinister corrupting element in the body politic but a beneficial and healthy development for the country's economy as well as its finances. The standing army, so far from being a danger to the liberties of Englishmen, was absolutely essential to defend them from the threat of a Stuart restoration backed by a French invasion, which the opposition's disloyalty made more likely. They bespattered their opponents individually with personal abuse and collectively denigrated them as an unholy alliance of Tories who were really Jacobites and opportunist Whigs. They insisted that the party distinctions of Anne's reign were still the most significant dichotomy in politics, with a Whig party in power being opposed by a Tory party, while the dissident Whigs were merely a minor complication of this fundamental division.

Some historians also argue that practical politics still revolved around the old party rivalries, and that the Country coalition was little more than a pipe-dream conjured up by the *Craftsman*.[33] While the detailed documentation of this case largely lies outside literary sources, there are some Court effusions which are cited in its support. One in particular is quoted approvingly as demonstrating that the real division was still that of Tories against Whigs as late as 1740. This is Sir Charles Hanbury Williams's *Political Eclogue . . . occasioned by the Great Contest between Mr Lechmere and Mr Pytts, Tories, who afterwards carried the election; and Lord Derehurst and Mr Lyttelton, Whigs (all four being violent opposers of the Court) who should represent the county of Worcester in the ensuing parliament.*[34] An attempt by the four opposition candidates to come to an agreement before the general election of 1741, and to share the representation of the two Worcestershire seats, broke down. Williams wrote a dialogue in which the Whig George Lyttelton tries unsuccessfully to persuade the Tory Edmund Lechmere to stand down for the good of the common cause. When asked why he insists on opposing Lyttelton he replies:

> Because, Sir, you're a Whig, and I'm a Tory
> Howe'er with us you the same schemes pursue
> You follow those who ne'er will follow you;
> My principles to you I'll freely State,
> I love the Church and Whiggism I hate;
> And tho', with you, Sir Robert I abhor
> His Whiggish heart is what I hate him for.
> And if a Whig the minister must be
> Pult'ney and Walpole are alike to me.

The quotation of these lines in refutation of the argument for an alignment of Court against Country is a signal instance of the care which historians need to exercise in the use of literature as evidence. The dialogue is, of course, fictitious. Williams, the Paymaster of Marines, was a Court Whig anxious to discredit the opposition. He imagined this exchange in order to embarrass the Country interest in the general election of 1741 by emphasising and exaggerating the breakdown of an attempt at a joint candidature of a Tory and an opposition Whig in one constituency. Had such failures to combine been commonplace, the poem would have lost much of its point. In fact the circumstances appear to have been unique.

Moreover, if words exchanged in a fictitious dialogue can legitimately be cited as evidence for political realities, then those allegedly uttered by Lyttelton deserve equal weight with those of Lechmere:

> What can be hoped when friends from friends divide
> And weaken fatally the weaker side?
> Our party by itself is overcome,
> By Roman arms thus perished fated Rome. . . .
> Don't we in all things act and vote the same
> And both on one foundation build our fame
> Equally hating Walpole's noxious name? . . .
> Whoe'er of all us four obtain their ends
> The party still must lose two zealous friends.

It could be concluded from these lines that Lyttelton and

Lechmere both belonged to the same 'party' which acted and voted the same way 'in all things'. Even those historians who argue that Tories and opposition Whigs shared a common ideology have not asserted that they united into a Country party as disciplined as Sir Charles Hanbury Williams here implies.

The political propaganda of the period, whatever other evidence suggests about the actual disposition of political groups in parliament or the constituencies, has persuaded most historians who have worked on it that, by the reign of George II, it makes far more sense to classify it into Court and Country rather than into Whig and Tory rhetoric.[35] Although there were many shifts of political alignments between 1740 and 1760, this rhetorical context remained largely fixed in the pattern formed during Walpole's ministry. David Hume, for example, writing *Of the Parties in Great Britain* observed: 'There are parties of PRINCIPLE involved in the very nature of our Constitution, which may properly enough be denominated COURT and COUNTRY parties.'[36] The Jacobite rebellion of 1745 temporarily reasserted the distinction between Tories and Whigs, but its effects were shortlived. In the general election of 1747 the propaganda campaign was largely conducted along Court and Country lines. Thus Henry Fielding contributed to it *A Dialogue between a Gentleman of London, Agent for Two Court Candidates, and an Honest Alderman of the Country Party.*[37] It was not until the upheavals associated with Pitt's rise to power, the accession of George III, and the radical issues raised by Wilkes that the political dialogue began to take a new form.

2

Social Structure and Literature

> Those Graves, with bending Osier bound,
> That nameless heave the crumbled Ground,
> Quick to the glancing Thought disclose,
> Where *Toil* and *Poverty* repose.
>
> The flat smooth Stones that bear a Name,
> The Chissels slender help to Fame,
> (Which e'er our Sett of Friends decay
> Their frequent Steps may wear away)
> A *middle* Race of Mortals own,
> Men, half ambitious, all unknown.
>
> The Marble Tombs that rise on high,
> Whose Dead in vaulted Arches lye,
> Whose Pillars swell with sculptur'd Stones,
> Arms, Angels, Epitaphs and Bones,
> These (all the poor Remains of State)
> Adorn the *Rich*, or praise the *Great*.
>
> Thomas Parnell, *A Night Piece on Death* (1722)

Unlike political history, which has arguably been overworked of late and could profitably be left to lie fallow for a while, the field of social history in the first half of the eighteenth century has not yet been fully cultivated.[1] This, however, has not prevented historians from generalising about major trends in society. Indeed, the bolder generalisations tend to be made about those areas which have been least investigated. This has produced some confusion about the very nature of eighteenth-century society. Ignoring minor discrepancies, and setting aside for the moment the objections of those who consider the concept of 'class' to be anachronistic in this period, there are three contradictory views, for example, about the class divisions which existed in the years 1700-60. Some say that there was only one class, others that there were two, while there are those who perceive three.

The principal advocate of a 'one-class society' throughout this period is Peter Laslett. In *The World We Have Lost* he argues that, although there were numerous status groups in pre-industrial England, there was only one class, the gentry. This was because status rests on a vertical scale, while class requires a horizontal dimension. There were many rungs on the status ladder. Gregory King in a somewhat overused table described no fewer than twenty-six, ranging from the peerage at the top to vagrants at the bottom. At least some of these rungs would be evident in every community in the country, while some large towns, and especially London, could run the whole gamut. But few people in those communities would consciously identify themselves with the wider society outside and feel solidarity with those on the same rungs in neighbouring towns, let alone throughout England. The only group with such a national sense of identity were the gentlemen. It was this, according to Dr Laslett, which made the gentry the one true class before the onset of industrialisation.[2]

E. P. Thompson has challenged this notion with the two-class model. One was indeed that identified by Laslett as the only class, for Mr Thompson sees the landowners of Hanoverian England as a ruling class. The other was the great mass of the people – tradesmen, craftsmen, labourers and paupers. These, he insists, were conscious of themselves as being collectively different from, and at odds with, the ruling class, a conflict which he characterises as one between the patrician upper class and the plebeian lower class. There was no middle class between them, for the professional and business community was in a client relationship with the landowners, and as such dependants of the ruling class. Thus he sums up his model of social structure:

> Of course no one in the eighteenth century would have thought of describing their own as a 'one-class society'. There were the rulers and the ruled, the high and the low people, persons of substance and of independent estate and the loose and disorderly sort. In between, where the professional and middle classes, and the substantial yeomanry, should have been, relations of clientage and dependency were so strong that, at least until the 1760s, these groups appear to offer little deflection of the essential polarities.[3]

Various historians have preferred a threefold division of society. Nicholas Rogers, for instance, concludes from his study of London that there was a bourgeoisie in the capital.[4] Although E. P. Thompson apparently concedes that London was exceptional, he still maintains that provincial England did not witness the development of a middle class in the first half of the eighteenth century. Yet Peter Borsay, in a survey of the development of provincial urban culture in the late seventeenth and early eighteenth centuries, observes that 'there appears to have been a rapid expansion in the "middling" groups in society'.[5]

It might be thought that here was a controversy which literature was eminently well qualified as a historical source to resolve. After all, writers surely described social divisions as they were perceived by contemporaries? It should therefore follow that a careful analysis of literary descriptions of cleavages in society would indicate which model was more appropriate.

Unfortunately the answer is not so simple. Writers in the period 1700-60 used such diverse terms when dealing with social distinctions that the proponents of all three views could find supporting evidence for their case in contemporary literature. Although Dr Laslett eschews literary sources, he could have cited the works of several dramatists to support his view that social gradation was very subtle, and that only those at the top had any collective or class consciousness. For playwrights displayed remarkable discrimination in their handling of distinctions in their own society. The *dramatis personae* of plays in this period were usually listed not in their order of appearance but according to their position in the hierarchy. For example, Bonniface, the landlord of a Lichfield inn, appears first on stage in George Farquhar's *The Beaux' Stratagem* but is next to the last in the list of male characters. (Female characters, of course, are listed separately after the men, for this was a sexist as well as an elitist age.) Before him are listed, in order, Aimwell and Archer, two gentlemen of broken fortunes; Count Bellair, a French officer; Sullen, 'a Country blockhead' (i.e. gentleman!); Freeman, a gentleman from London; Foigard, a French priest; Gibbet, a highwayman, and Hounslow and Bagshot, his companions;

while after Bonniface comes Scrub, Sullen's servant. The four ill-assorted guardians to Mrs Lovely in Susannah Centlivre's *A Bold Stroke for a Wife* are socially graded in the *dramatis personae*: Sir Philip Modelove, the old beau, heads the cast, followed by Periwinkle, a silly virtuoso, Tradelove, a changebroker, and Obadiah Prim, the Quaker hosier. Sir Richard Steele's *The Conscious Lovers* opens with Sir John Bevil and his servant Humphrey on stage. In the cast, however, they are separated by four other characters, though as Sir Philip's servant Humphrey is named before those of Bevil junior's and Indiana's. Even among servants, therefore, Steele is aware of subtle distinctions. Vanbrugh showed a similar awareness of the gradations among tradesmen when he observed in *Aesop* how many were being ruined by the social aspirations of their wives. Aesop declaims:

> This is an age where most people get falls by clambering too high to reach at what they should not do. The shoemaker's wife reduces her husband to a cobbler by endeavouring to be as spruce as the taylor's; the taylor's lowers hers to a foreman, by perking up to the merchant's; the merchant's wears hers to a broker, by strutting up to quality.[6]

The introduction of the concept of the 'quality' is the first 'class' distinction Vanbrugh uses, in line with Laslett's distinction between the gentlemen and the rest.

Both E. P. Thompson and Peter Borsay actually do cite contemporary literature in support of their two- and three-class models. Thus Thompson writes that 'For Fielding the evident division between the high and the low people, the people of fashion and no fashion, lay like a cultural fissure across the land:

> Whilst the people of fashion seized several places to their own use, such as courts, assemblies, operas, balls, etc., the people of no fashion, besides one royal palace, called His Majesty's Bear-Garden, have been in constant possession of all hops, fairs, revels, etc. . . . So far from looking on each other as brethren in the Christian language, they seem scarce to regard each other as of the same species.

This is a world of patricians and of plebs.'[7] For Peter Borsay, on the other hand, 'Addison's "Foxhunting Gentleman", Fielding's Squire Weston [*sic*] , or Smollett's Matthew Bramble, all perplexed and upset by their contact with metropolitan culture, inhabit a world in which urbanisation was creating real tensions in society.'[8]

One reason why literature can be used to document variant views of eighteenth-century social structure is that contemporary writers were as involved in a debate about the nature of their society as historians are today. Their writings therefore should be read with awareness of this ideological dispute. If we look at different levels of society in the years 1700-60 through the eyes of creative writers of the time, their divergent attitudes soon emerge, as we shall see in the following discussion, which examines literary evidence for the landed elite, 'the middle station of life' and 'the lower orders'.

* * *

There are two distinct views of the characteristics of most landowners in eighteenth-century England. One view sees them as benevolent, employing their authority beneficially for those beneath them, so that their servants were well treated, their tenants fairly dealt with, and transgressors brought before those of them who were magistrates obtaining justice tempered with mercy. The other regards them as self-seeking, exploiting their position in society to safeguard their own interests at the expense of others, browbeating their servants, rack-renting their tenants, and visiting the full force of the law on those upon whom they sat in judgement, especially those accused of breaking the game laws. These are modern stereotypes, reflecting the ideologies of present-day social historians.[9] The first could be described as the 'patriarch', and the second as the 'patrician'.

Similar stereotypes are discernible in the works of eighteenth-century writers who dealt with the landowners on their country estates. These are for the most part country gentlemen, for though there are plenty of aristocrats in Augustan literature, very few are depicted in their rural habitations.

Almost all the peers in the drama of the period are shown living in their town houses in St James's and district, many as ridiculous fops and beaux. Lord Modeley was a familiar name for a fashionable London-based lord, appearing in three plays published in the 1730s: *The Connoisseur; or Every Man in his Folly*, *The Modish Couple* and *A Tutor for the Beaus*. Like Lord Foppington, their great original, they are characterised by affected speech, French fashions and a totally frivolous attitude towards life. Conscious of themselves as 'the quality', they live a life of ease distinguished by conspicuous consumption. The play with most peers in it, *The Humours of Whist* (1743), which names no fewer than four in its *dramatis personae*, while 'several lords' are included among the extras, takes place mainly in White's chocolate-house, London's leading gambling casino. These are not patriarchs or patricians so much as parasites.

Fielding objected that stage aristocrats bore no resemblance to the reality, but were

> those strange monsters in lace and embroidery, in silks and brocades, with vast wigs and hoops; which, under the name of lords and ladies, strut the stage, to the great delight of attornies and their clerks in the pit, and of citizens and their apprentices in the galleries; and which are no more to be found in real life, than the centaur, the chimera, or any other creature of mere fiction.[10]

Even peers who appear in novels tend to be encountered in London rather than in the country, like Lord Fellamar and Lady Bellaston in *Tom Jones*. An exception is Swift's Lord Munodi, whom Gulliver met in Balnibari. Munodi is presented as an archetypal patriarch. 'Everything about him', Gulliver recorded, 'was magnificent, regular and polite.' He treated the traveller with much kindness and in a most hospitable manner in his town house, and then took him to his country seat, where Gulliver did not 'remember to have seen a more delightful prospect'. The estate was divided into neat and prosperous farms, while the house was 'indeed a noble structure, built according to the best rules of ancient architecture. The fountains, gardens, walks, avenues and groves were all disposed with exact judgment and taste.'[11] One of the characteristics of a patriarch in literature was to display architectural taste.

Pope's Timon, by contrast, reveals from the outset that he is a patrician by his tasteless villa:

Two Cupids squirt before; a Lake behind
Improves the keenness of the Northern wind.
His Gardens next your admiration call,
On ev'ry side you look, behold the Wall!
No pleasing Intricacies intervene,
No artful wildness to perplex the scene;
Grove nods at grove, each Alley has a brother,
And half the platform just reflects the other.
The suff'ring eye inverted Nature sees,
Trees cut to statues, Statues thick as trees,
With here a Fountain, never to be play'd,
And there a Summer-house that knows no shade.

Timon has no sense of serving the community. He uses his wealth only to indulge his own vanity. His dining-room is described as a temple, the object of his worship being himself. Although he appears at first sight to be hospitable, like Lord Munodi, in fact his visitor leaves 'Sick of his civil Pride from Morn to Eve'.[12]

While the Lord Munodis and Timons are rather thin on the ground, there are plenty of country gentlemen in Augustan literature. At the outset of the eighteenth century, however, they tend to be neither patriarchs nor patricians but, as we have seen, boobies. The Foxhunters and Sir Tunbelly Clumsys did not altogether disappear as the period progressed. On the contrary, the stock character was still very much to the fore in Henry Carey's *A Wonder; or An Honest Yorkshireman*, published in 1736. Squire Sapskull, the principal character, makes a typical entry, his opening words being 'Wuns-lent! What a mortal big place this same London is? Ye mun ne'er see End on't for sure; – Housen upon Housen, Folk upon Folk – one would admire where they did grow all of 'em.'[13]

With the appearance of Sir Roger de Coverley in the pages of the *Spectator*, however, Addison and Steele presented a more subtle and more sympathetic portrait of a country squire. Sir Roger, 'the best master in the world', is an archetypal patriarch, with 'a mixture of the father and the master of the family'. 'Family' is here used to denote Sir Roger's household as well as his immediate kin. His servants have a particular fondness for him, greeting him with joy when he makes his way from London to his Worcestershire seat in the company of Mr Spectator: 'Some of them could not refrain from tears at the sight of their old master, every one of them pressed forward to do something for him, and seemed discouraged if they were not employed.' The baronet's kindness to his servants extends to their children, so that he pays the premium for his coachman's grandson to become apprenticed.[14]

The treatment of servants is a significant indication of whether a landowner is a patriarch or a patrician. Mr B in Richardson's *Pamela* exploits his power over the heroine in a sustained campaign to seduce her. Had he succeeded, then in the eyes of contemporaries she would have been ruined, the fate awaiting servants who had lost their 'virtue', according to the literature of low life, being utter degradation. The path from a gentleman's bedroom to a cell in Newgate prison via a brothel was a well-worn one in many tracts for the time.[15] Mr B's tyranny is emphasised by being contrasted with the gentle treatment of Pamela by his mother. As Pamela told her parents when informing them of her death, 'She was a dear good lady, and kind to all us her servants.'[16] Where her first employer displayed patriarchal, or rather matriarchal, traits, Mr B is by comparison a patrician. Fielding reversed the sexes of Mr B and Pamela in his satire on Richardson's novel by presenting Lady Booby as the mistress and Joseph Andrews, Pamela's alleged brother, as the servant. While this turns the sexual melodrama into farce, the social exploitation is still significant. Lady Booby is just as tyrannical as Mr B over her servants, dismissing Joseph on the spot without notice, having him stripped of her livery, and cast out of her door in borrowed clothes. By contrast, it is a hallmark of Sir Charles Grandison's worthiness that his servants 'are honest worthy men' who 'love their master'.

Sir Charles was also a patriarch to his tenants. Mr Dawson, a Nottingham attorney, gave him 'such a character, respecting his goodness to his tenants and dependants only, as will render credible all that even the fondest love, and warmest gratitude, can say in his praise'.[17] Sir Roger de Coverley, too, is kind to his tenants as well as to his servants, so that 'the greatest part of Sir Roger's estate is tenanted by persons who have served himself or his ancestors'. Being a good churchman, he has given all his fellow-parishioners a hassock and a copy of the Book of Common Prayer. In short, as Sir Roger confides to Mr Spectator, he 'resolved to follow the steps of the most worthy of my ancestors . . . in all the methods of hospitality and good neighbourhood'. In return he is 'beloved and esteemed by all about him. He receives a suitable tribute for his universal benevolence to mankind in the returns of affection and good-will which are paid him by every one that lives within his neighbourhood.'[18]

Another patriarch who earned the devotion of his neighbours was Pope's Man of Ross.[19] Again, we are introduced to him by a description of his estate, which is one where Art and Nature are in happy combination. Thus water is not uselessly tossed in columns, as in the Emperor fountain at Chatsworth,

> But clear and artless, pouring thro' the plain
> Health to the sick, and solace to the swain.

The Man of Ross is so much the father of his community that his neighbours turn to him for medical and legal advice. His charity is especially conspicuous.

It is obvious from these examples that, if a historian wished to ascertain whether the typical country gentleman in the eighteenth century was a patriarch or a patrician, literary evidence would not be very helpful. A selective use of literature could be used to support either interpretation. The historical problem which this poses is that of why these two stereotypes existed side by side, even in the work of a single author.

As with the booby squire, one answer is that the stereotypes reflect the political attitudes of their creators. Opposition writers especially regarded the patriarch as an ideal, and one which seemed to them to be vanishing as a rising breed of country gentlemen and aristocrats who supported the Court replaced it with a patrician norm. Swift makes this transition quite clear in *Gulliver's Travels*, where Lord Munodi admits that his methods of estate management are old-fashioned, and that 'he doubted he must throw down his houses in town and country, to rebuild them after the present mode; destroy all his plantations, and cast others into such a form, as modern usage required; and give the same directions to all his tenants'.[20]

Although the Man of Ross was modelled on an actual contemporary of Pope's, John Kyrle, he stands for outmoded values. Kyrle was, after all, born in 1637, and his Herefordshire acquaintances appear to have been mostly Tory gentlemen.[21] Timon, on the other hand, is a Whig grandee, possibly Sir Robert Walpole himself, though more likely an amalgam of several, including the Dukes of Devonshire and Marlborough. The political implications of Timon's villa were brought out in one of Lyttelton's *Persian Letters* in which the Persian visits a similar mansion of a *nouveau riche* landowner, catches a cold from a north-east wind blowing into the garden, and mistakes a saloon for a mausoleum.[22]

Admittedly Sir Roger de Coverley poses problems for an interpretation of fictional country gentlemen which sees them as ideological stereotypes. Here is a Tory knight of the shire being sympathetically portrayed by Whig writers. Of course, in the *Spectator* Addison and Steele were very anxious to play down their partisanship and leaned over backwards to depict an archetypal adversary in a favourable light. When Addison next described a Tory gentleman it was for an avowedly political purpose, to denigrate Jacobites and their fellow-travellers at the height of the rebellion of 1715. As we have seen, he then represented Foxhunter in very crude terms. Even in the *Spectator*, however, Whiggish prejudices are discernible below the surface presentation of Sir Roger. Mr Spectator preferred the anonymity and bustle of London to the inquisitiveness and monotony of the country and was glad when his visit to Sir Roger's seat came to an end. That the writers of the *Spectator* shared his rather than the knight's values is at least implied in this passage, which concludes with him, 'having found by experience that the country is not a place for a person of my temper', expressing a preference for the town where he can 'enjoy all the advantages of company with all the privileges of solitude'. There is an explicit rejection of Sir Roger's values in favour of others in a passage wherein he and Sir Andrew Freeport discuss charity. Sir Andrew objects to the knight's indiscriminate benefaction:

> If to drink so many hogsheads is to be hospitable, we do not contend for the fame of that virtue; but it would be worthwhile to consider whether so many artificers at work

> ten days together by my appointment, or so many peasants made merry on Sir Roger's charge are the more obliged? . . . Sir Roger gives to his men; but I place mine above the necessity or obligation of my bounty.

His practical rather than sentimental approach to such matters is extolled when he buys an estate himself and plans to run it on lines very different from the traditional methods employed by Sir Roger:

> This will give me great opportunity of being charitable in my way, that is, in setting my poor neighbours to work, and giving them a comfortable subsistence out of their own industry. My gardens, my fish ponds, my arable and pasture grounds shall be my several hospitals or rather workhouses, in which I propose to maintain a great many indigent persons, who are now starving in my neighbourhood. . . . As in my mercantile employment I so disposed my affairs, that from whatever corner of the compass the wind blew it was bringing home one or other of my ships; I hope, as a husbandman, to contrive it so, that not a shower of rain, or a glimpse of sunshine shall fall upon my estate without bettering some part of it, and contributing to the products of the season.[23]

Sir Roger de Coverley is indeed old-fashioned, and to those who admired these attributes he was a sympathetic character. In Joseph Dorman's play *Sir Roger de Coverley; or The Merry Christmas*, published in 1740, the idea that he belonged to a vanished breed was driven home. Indeed, the Worcestershire knight's patriarchal traits are almost sickeningly sentimentalised, with his generous Christmas boxes to his servants and his open-house hospitality for his neighbours. 'Would to heaven there were more Sir Roger de Coverleys in the nation,' his butler is made to say.

> Complaints then wouldn't be so common, that they never see their landlord's face. That they never warm their fingers by his fire, nor can get a sup of his beer, tho' they were perishing with thirst – England, Sir, isn't what it was – Its hospitality decays – Its Quality folks are all show.[24]

The Sir Roger de Coverleys have been replaced by the Sir Andrew Freeports, a trend to which the Court Whig *Spectator* gave its blessing. To Swift, ideologically opposed to the Court, Sir Roger might well have seemed to be like Lord Munodi, while Sir Andrew, who was going to make the very sun work for him, would doubtless have encouraged the academician of Lagdo who had

> been eight years upon a project for extracting sun-beams out of cucumbers, which were to be put into vials hermetically sealed, and let out to warm the air, in raw inclement summers. . . . He did not doubt in eight years more, that he should be able to supply the governor's gardens with sun-shine at a reasonable rate.[25]

The contrast between 'a true English country gentleman' and 'the senceless upstart whig country gentleman' was starkly pointed in *The Character of a Whig under Several Denominations*, published at the start of our period in 1700. 'The true English gentleman', it asserted,

> keeps a constant table for his friends and family, and unexpected visitors can never surprise him. His kindness to his friends or civility to strangers does never interrupt his devotions, and those that sit with him at his table must kneel with him in his chapel. . . . His servants thrive, his tenants grow rich, and the poor in his parish are employed and well provided for. He administers justice with an equal hand.

He also, it goes without saying, was a Tory. The upstart Whig, on the other hand, is not of ancient gentility, for 'Heraldry knows nothing of his ancestors on either side, for like mushrooms they grew up in a night of rebellion by plundering the loyal party.' At one stage he was 'confined within the compass of a leather jacket, echoing about the streets "great hard dry faggots, five for six pence, faggots" ', until a series of deaths in his family brought him into an estate unexpectedly, so that 'he now perches up into squire', though he has no other qualification 'than a large stock of whiggism, hypocrisy and confidence'.[26]

By the time of Walpole's ministry the contrast is no longer

one between a traditional Tory gentry and upstart Whigs, but between country gentlemen and peers in the opposition on one side and those who support the Court on the other. It was such lords as Bathurst, Burlington and Cobham, all opposed to Walpole, who earned Pope's respect for upholding what has been called the 'country house ideal':

> His father's Acres who enjoys in peace,
> Or makes his Neighbours glad, if he encrease:
> Whose chearful Tenants bless their yearly toil,
> Yet to their Lord owe more than to the soil
> Whose ample Lawns are not asham'd to feed
> The milky heifer and deserving steed;
> Whose rising Forests, not for pride or show,
> But future Building, future Navies grow:
> Let his plantations stretch from down to down,
> First shade a Country, and then raise a Town.[27]

* * *

When writers in the early eighteenth century referred to 'the middle station of life' it was usually to extol it as a kind of golden mean, between the extremes of harsh poverty and the excess of affluence. As a character in *The Coquet's Surrender* put it, 'Fortune has placed me in a middle station of life, above the darts of Poverty and beneath the envy of Grandeur.'[28] David Hume preferred it to the status of 'the great' and 'the poor'.[29] Robinson Crusoe's father told his son

> that mine was the middle state, or what might be called the upper station of low life, which he had found by long experience was the best state in the world, the most suited to human happiness, not exposed to the miseries and hardships, the labour and sufferings of the mechanick part of mankind, and not embarrassed with the Pride, Luxury, Ambition and Envy of the upper part of mankind.[30]

The 'middle station' was quite a wide category. Crusoe's father, for instance, had 'a good estate'. At the other end of the spectrum were the characters in Mrs Weddell's *The City Farce* (1737). As the authoress explained in 'an Address to the Pitt', farce 'was designed to yield some benefit as well as diversion by exposing those follies which affect chiefly the middle station of life, and are therefore beneath the province of comedy, which is principally confined to the genteel part of mankind'. The characters in her play are mostly tradesmen, while there is even a scene set in a haberdasher's shop.

How far those in the middle station developed a distinct sense of being a separate 'class' is difficult to determine, for there was a tendency whereby some people in this category identified themselves more with the gentry above them than with their fellows. This can be seen in the appropriation of the title of gentleman by members of the business and professional communities during the course of the eighteenth century, the expressions 'gentleman farmer', 'gentleman lawyer' and 'gentleman merchant' being all widespread by 1760. Writers satirised this tendency. Defoe highlighted Moll Flanders's social pretensions by having her exclaim: 'I was not averse to a tradesman, but then I would have a tradesman, forsooth, that was something of a gentleman too; that when my husband had a mind to carry me to the Court, or to the play, he might become a sword and look as like a gentleman as another man.' What is more, she found 'this amphibious creature, this land-water thing, called a gentleman-tradesman' in the person of a draper.[31] By Fielding's time she could have gone lower, since Partridge, the barber in *Tom Jones*, boasted: 'I am no man's servant – for tho' I have had misfortunes in the world, I write gentleman after my name; and as poor and simple as I may appear now, I have taught grammar school in my time.' Even Mrs Seagrim proudly asserts: 'Poor as I am, I am a gentlewoman,' because she was the daughter of a clergyman.[32] Lady Booby drew the line at Joseph Andrews, for when Parson Adams called him 'Mr Joseph' she expostulated: 'Pray don't Mister such fellows to me.'[33] Even this is ironic, however, since Joseph is later revealed to be Mr Wilson's son, and therefore fully entitled to call himself a gentleman.

Such satire cannot, of course, be used to substantiate a case that barbers, drapers, gamekeepers' wives and menservants were in fact calling themselves gentlefolk, let alone that they were getting away with it. What it does at least suggest, however, is that the most significant division in society was that between the gentry and the rest. The aspirations of the middle station were not distinctly 'bourgeois' but to be accepted as gentlemen. How far these aspirations arose from their client status, as E. P. Thompson contends, can to some extent be gauged from a closer look at fictitious professional and business men.

The three traditional professions of religion, law and medicine were all given an unfavourable image in the drama of these years. All three were seen as middlemen who dealt not with goods of tangible value but with people's troubles, complaints and grievances. Lucy deplores their grasping avarice in Abraham Langford's *The Lover His Own Rival* when she says:

> If your estate is in danger, will the lawyer advise you? If your life is in danger, will the physician attend you? If your soul is in danger, will the priest pray for you; No, the Devil a bit will they do anything without you cram their fists full.

She then sings:

> The priests, like the lawyers, are all of a gang,
> All the Doctors, like bees, together do hang;
> The former won't pray nor the latter prescribe,
> Unless you induce 'em thereto by a Bribe.[34]

Playwrights were somewhat restrained from actually presenting individual clergymen on stage after the criticisms of Jeremy Collier, who had objected to their being represented as wordly hypocrites, though something of the old stereotype survived in the character of Dr Wolf in Colley Cibber's *The Non-Juror* (1717). As his very name implies, he is very far from being a good shepherd, but hopes to devour his flock, by depriving his master's eldest son of the estate and his wife of her virtue, while posing as a zealot for the Non-juring seceders from the Church of England. The ultimate hypocrisy appears when it is revealed that he is really a Roman Catholic in disguise.

There was no similar restraint in the treatment of doctors and lawyers. The medical profession was represented on stage by mercenary quacks who bilked their clients by pretending to be proficient in the science of physic, obscuring their ignorance in senseless jargon. The physician blinding the patient with science, like Fielding's *Mock Doctor*, was a stock character. A conversation between two in James Ralph's *The Cornish Squire* is a typical example. Squire Treelooby, though sane, has been committed to a private madhouse by a rival for the hand of the heroine, Julia. Two physicians attempt to diagnose the nature of Treelooby's alleged madness in the following exchange:

> *1st Physician*: I say . . . that our patient here present is unhappily attack'd, affected, possest and agitated with that sort of folly which we very well term melancholy Hypochondriac, a species of a very dreadful malady. . . . I call it melancholy Hypochondriac to distinguish it from the two others, for the celebrated Galen hath established very learnedly (according to his usual custom) three species of this distemper, which we call melancholy, so termed not only by the Latins, but likewise by the Greeks, which, by the way, is very material for us to observe in the present case.
>
> *2nd Physician*: You are in the right, brother, and, for an incontestible diagnostick thereof, you may only observe that great seriosity of countenance with which he views us; that sorrowfulness of face attended with fear and suspicion, signs pathognomic and individual of this distemper, so well mark'd by the divine old man Hippocrates; that physiognomy, those eyes red and haggard, that beard overgrown, that habitude of body, wasted, washy black and hairy, symptoms which denote him very much touched with this distemper arising from an error in the hypochondria. A malady which, by lapse of time being naturalis'd, antiquated, habituated, enrol'd and made free of his body, might well degenerate either into madness of phthisic, or apoplexy or in fine into phrenzy and distraction.[35]

The first physician then goes on to recommend liberal phlebotomy, purging, and bathing in water and whey 'to purify by the water the feculence of the dreggy humour and to clarify by the whey the nigridity of the black vapour'. On hearing these recommended cures for his imagined condition, Squire Treelooby, not surprisingly, escapes. Such treatment was more likely to kill than cure, a point driven home in many plays. Thus Seizecorpse, an undertaker in the macabre *Bickerstaff's Unburied Dead*, complains: 'The Doctors and we have been friends too long; they are as exorbitant in their fees with us, as with their patients; Besides they are so tedious of late in despatching, they take a fortnight . . . to kill a man.'[36]

Lawyers were likewise alleged to be pettifoggers who extracted extortionate fees by bamboozling their clients with legal gibberish. The avaricious pettifogger is represented by Latitat in *The Lawyer's Fortune; or Love in a Hollow Tree*. Latitat, 'a knavish attorney', cashes in after a fracas in an alehouse by urging those involved to sue the instigators. He draws up a bill for one ignorant countryman who had only been threatened with violence, and then demands a fee of ten shillings and twopence, which gives rise to the following dialogue:

> *Countryman*: How! Sir, that's more than I am worth.
>
> *Latitat*: Six shillings and eightpence the writ, two shillings and eight pence the warrant, twelve pence for postage and don't I deserve twelve pence for expedition? Come, give me ten shillings. I'll bate the two pence.
>
> *Countryman*: Your post is swift indeed, a pox take it.
>
> *Latitat*: Thou blockhead, if I had not one ready, I must have sent by post, then thou hadst staid a week longer and have paid so then. Do'st not know what is for thy advantage?[37]

The resort to meaningless jargon is well illustrated in a scene in Sir Richard Steele's *The Funeral* in which the aptly named lawyer Puzzle exhibits his skill in drawing up a deed by asking his clerk to 'read toward the Middle of the Instrument':

> *Clerk* (*reads*): I the said Earl of Brumpton, Do give, Bestow, Grant and Bequeath over and above the said Premises, all the site and Capital Messuage call'd by the name of Oatham, and all Outhouses, Barns, Stables, and other Edifices, and Buildings, Yards, Orchards, Gardens, Fields, Arbors, Trees, Lands, Earths, Meadows, Greens, Pastors, Feedings, Woods, Underwoods, Ways, Waters, Water-

courses, Fishings, Ponds, Pools, Commons, Common of Pasture, Paths, Heath-Thickets, Profits, Commodities, and Emoluments, with their, and every of the Appurtenances whatsoever (*Puzzle nods and snears as the synonimous words are repeating, whom Lord Brumpton scornfully mimicks*) to the said Capital Messuage, and site belonging or in any wise appertaining, or with the same heretofore used, occupied, or enjoy'd, accepted, executed, known, or taken as part, parcel, or member of the same containing in the whole, by Estimation four hundred Acres of the large Measure, or thereabouts, be the same more or less, all and singular, which the said site Capital Messuage and other Premisses with their, and every of their Appurtenances are situate, lying and being –

Puzzle: Hold hold good Tom; you do come on indeed in Business, but don't use your Nose long enough in Reading – Why you're quite out – you Read to be Understood – let me see it – I the said Earl (*reads in a Ridiculous Law-Tone, till out of breath*) – Now again suppose this were to be in Latin.[38]

Of professional men, only soldiers occasionally appear as reputable types, like Plume in Farquhar's *The Recruiting Officer*, Clerimont in Steele's *The Tender Husband* and Colonel Fainwell in Mrs Centlivre's *A Bold Stroke for a Wife*. An early farce by David Garrick, *Miss in her Teens; or The Medley of Lovers* (1747), drew on an established convention when it had Captain Loveit emerge as the only worthy claimant for Miss Biddy Bellair's hand against the foppish Fribble, the cowardly Flash and the superannuated Sir Simon. Loveit displayed such bravery in Flanders at the battle of Laffeldt that the Duke of Cumberland promoted him from ensign to captain. He demonstrates his professional pride when dealing with one of his rivals, Flash, who disgraced himself in the action. 'And now, Sir, have you dared to show your face again in open day,' Loveit asks him, 'or wear even the outside of a profession you have so much scandalised by your behaviour? I honour the name of soldier, and as a party concerned am bound not to see it disgraced; as you have forfeited your title to honour, deliver up your sword this instant.'

He then kicks him out of the house.[39] To be sure, there is something of a military stereotype about Loveit, the dashing, swashbuckling officer and gentleman; but it is at least a sympathetic stereotype, unlike the dramatic representations of the other professions.

Among the business men who appeared on stage there was a stock merchant character, who had profit as his only motive and treated people as commodities. Sir Humphrey Staple in Leonard Welsted's *The Dissembled Wanton; or My Son, Get Money*, deplores the representation of his kind in drama, complaining that

> The wits and poets make it their business in their plays and prologues to abuse their betters, and that they treat persons of good reputation very injuriously, giving them nicknames such as Nikin, Gripe, Scrape-all, Split-farthing and the like; Now Sir I must be plain to tell you that this licence is unreasonable, and that persons of substance and credit ought not to be libell'd by your poets and people of that character.[40]

Despite Sir Humphrey's complaints, there are signs that the image of business men in drama was slowly improving during these years. Sealand in Steele's *The Conscious Lovers* (1723) is often seen as a turning-point in the characterisation of the merchant, as he is eminently honest and upright. Not that Steele went very far down the social scale, for he made it quite clear that Sealand was a younger son in an ancient West Country family and had been an eminent citizen of Bristol before his downfall. It was not until the appearance of George Lillo's *The London Merchant* in 1731 that a major production extolled the virtues of trade in its principal characters.

Because of their tendency to stereotype, plays have to be used with considerable caution by the social historian.[41] Many of the stock characters were rooted not in eighteenth-century England but in earlier epochs and even in other countries. Two curiously similar plays of 1734, *The Cornish Squire* and *The Mother-in-Law; or The Doctor the Disease*, contain between them two booby squires, Squire Treelooby and Looby Headpiece, Esquire; four quack physicians; two conniving apothecaries; a pettifogging lawyer, Mr Cranny; and even a stage stepmother. Both claimed to be based on Molière, as was Fielding's *The Mock Doctor*. Steele went even further back in time for the original of his *The Conscious Lovers*, basing it on a play by Terence.

Yet if the stereotypes are timeless, the use made of them by contemporary authors does tell us something of changing perceptions in the first half of the eighteenth century. Most professional men are persistently represented as the mere clients of the aristocracy and gentry, to the point of being complete parasites; only the military types are shown to be honourable. The image of the merchant, on the other hand, slowly changes from being a despicable usurer, another social parasite, to appearing as honest and reputable in their own right, and with their own standards. So Barter, a city merchant in John Gay's *The Distressed Wife*, can declaim to Lord Courtlove, who frequents St James's and Westminster: 'We live on in the humdrum way of honesty and regularity; we think, we act differently from people at your end of the town.' And when Courtlove says to him: 'You merchants have your own way of thinking,' he replies: 'And of speaking and acting too. But you know, my Lord, we are a particular race of people.'[42] Sealand makes a similar point in *The Conscious Lovers* when he declares: 'We merchants are a species of gentry that have grown into the world this last century, and are as honourable, and almost as useful, as you landed folks.'[43] As far as the business community of London is concerned, dramatists appear to have perceived it more and more as a separate social entity, what might be termed a bourgeoisie.

Some literary historians have invoked the possibility that theatre audiences underwent a social change during this period in order to account for the changing image of the merchant on stage. The argument is that Restoration theatres attracted the Court aristocracy and gentry, who considered themselves to be superior to mere country gentlemen, despised professional men and looked down on merchants: hence the stereotype booby squires, professional hacks and usurious merchants. In the early eighteenth century, however, opera became fashionable for 'persons of quality', who forsook

Drury Lane and Lincoln's Inn Fields for the new Haymarket Theatre. The alleged vacuum created by this desertion was filled, so the theory goes, by the mercantile middle classes. While they too could jeer at the squirearchy, and even dislike lawyers and doctors, they took exception to seeing their own kind being presented as figures of fun. Playwrights consequently responded by improving the image of merchants in plays.[44]

This plausible explanation is not completely convincing, however, for two reasons. First, we know far too little about the actual nature of theatre audiences in the period to sustain such sweeping generalisation. Secondly, the improved image of the business community is not confined to drama.

Perhaps the best known of all fictitious merchants in these years was Sir Andrew Freeport of the Spectator Club. He is always treated with respect as a useful, sensible, honest and prudent man whenever he appears in the pages of the *Spectator.*[45] At his first appearance we are told that he is:

> a merchant of great eminence in the City of London; a person of indefatigable industry, strong reason and great experience. His notions of trade are noble and generous, and (as every rich man has usually some sly way of jesting, which would make no great figure were he not a rich man) he calls the sea the British common. . . . He abounds in several frugal maxims, amongst which the greatest favourite is 'A penny saved is a penny got'. A general trader of good sense is pleasanter company than a general scholar; and Sir Andrew having a natural unaffected eloquence, the perspicuity of his discourse gives the same pleasure that wit would in another man.

When he last appears he has left off paying his business bills to settle his account with God.

Joseph Addison created with Sir Andrew a Whig archetype just as ideological, albeit more subtle, as he did when he devised the Tory Foxhunter. In both the *Spectator* and the *Freeholder* he proclaimed the advantages of commerce to counter Tory arguments that it was detrimental to the economy. Thus he had Freeholder confounding Foxhunter by pointing out that they could not even enjoy a sneaker of punch without trade, since every ingredient except water was imported. Merchants, therefore, so far from being parasites, were essential middlemen. 'There are not more useful members in a commonwealth', Addison claimed in the *Spectator*, 'than merchants. They knit mankind together in a mutual intercourse of good offices, distribute the gifts of Nature, find work for the poor, add wealth to the Rich, and magnificence to the Great.'[46] The underlying ideology behind Addison's economic views was made most explicit in an essay on public credit which he contributed to the *Spectator* for 3 March 1711. This took the form of an allegorical dream in which Mr Spectator saw Public Credit as a beautiful virgin on a throne of gold. Upon the walls were such symbols of English liberty as Magna Carta, the Toleration Act and the Act of Settlement, which she cherished. Her health was quickly affected by news reports, which were hourly read to her. She was then menaced by six phantoms, Tyranny and Anarchy, Bigotry and Atheism, Republicanism and Jacobitism, the last in the person of the Pretender, who brandished a sword in his right hand and was rumoured to have a sponge in his left. The sword he pointed at the Act of Settlement, while the sponge was to wipe out the National Debt. At their approach Public Credit faints, while money-bags piled behind her throne shrink. Fortunately she is rescued by such friendly forces as Liberty and the future George I. This essay, appearing a few weeks before subscribers to the Bank of England had to choose between rival Tory and Whig candidates for directors, left his readers in no doubt as to which way he wanted them to vote.

Whig writers tended to share Addison's advocacy of trade, though not all were as enthusiastic about public credit. One who endorsed both was Daniel Defoe. He even introduced a real merchant, Sir Robert Clayton, into *Roxana*. Sir Robert lectures the heroine on the advantages of trade over land, telling her 'that an Estate is a pond, but that a Trade was a spring; that if the first is once mortgag'd it seldom gets clear, but embarrass'd the person for ever; but the merchant had his estate continually flowing'.[47] In *Robinson Crusoe* Defoe extolled both trade and Whiggism. Crusoe started out not as a merchant but as a mariner, leaving home at the age of eighteen when he was too old to be apprenticed either to a tradesman or as a clerk to an attorney. As a mariner, however, he made a profit on his first voyage to Guinea, exchanging toys worth £40 for gold dust worth nearly £300, which he says 'made me both a sailor and a merchant'. He therefore 'set up for a Guiney trader'.[48] Later he became a planter in Brazil, and after four years began to thrive and prosper, until he estimated that in another three or four years he would be worth £3000 or even £4000. Then he made the fateful decision to enter the slave trade, which led to his shipwreck and his long sojourn on the island. Defoe might seem from Crusoe's story alone to have found little to commend in the merchant's calling. Yet though Crusoe is inclined to blame Fate for his misfortune, Defoe makes him the author of his own misery, partly through his lack of piety, but mainly through his want of prudence. It is his impious refusal to obey his father's will which leads to his first shipwreck in the Yarmouth roads, but it is his imprudently overreaching himself in business ventures which indirectly causes his solitary confinement on the island. At a time when his plantation was beginning to flourish, as he himself admitted, 'for me to think of such a voyage, was the most preposterous thing that ever man in such circumstances could be guilty of'.[49] Crusoe triumphs over adversity by learning to be both pious and prudent. It is especially in his acquisition of skills for physical survival that Defoe indicates his admiration of the characteristics which enabled men to survive in trade. During his stay on the island Robinson Crusoe becomes a basketmaker, a boatbuilder, a carpenter, a miller, a potter, a tailor and an umbrella-maker.

Not only does Defoe eulogise trade in the novel; he also makes his hero a Whig. Crusoe himself indicates his approval of Whig principles when he finally acquires 'subjects' on his island. He notes that they were of three different religions: 'My man Friday was a Protestant, his father was a pagan, and a cannibal, and the Spaniard was a Papist; However, I allow'd Liberty of Conscience throughout my Dominions.'[50] When in his *Farther Adventures* he returns to the island he finds more people there and brings law and order to them. Those living together as man and wife are persuaded to marry. Yet he is not a tyrant. On the contrary, as he explains, he 'had no authority or power to act or command one way or other, farther than voluntary consent mov'd them to comply'.[51] His little colony was a Whig commonwealth. It was a miniature Great Britain, which Defoe described in his *Tour through the Whole Island* as 'the most flourishing and opulent country in the world'.[52]

Defoe, however, was critical of the corrupt manipulation of the money market. While he could extol the advantages which the nation gained from the 'financial revolution' in *An Essay upon Public Credit* and *An Essay upon Loans*, he could also castigate those who took advantage of it for their private ends. 'What will become of the honour of the English nation', he asked in *The Villainy of Stock-Jobbers Detected*, 'if the principal affairs relating to the credit both of the publick and private funds is dependent upon such vile people, who care not who they ruin, nor who they advance?'[53] He even called those traitors who brought down the price of stock in the Jacobite invasion scare of 1719.

Other Whig writers did not make Defoe's distinction between the advantages of public credit and the abuse of stock-jobbing. In *Cato's Letters* Trenchard and Gordon attacked not only the manipulation of stocks but also the great financial corporations which were an integral part of the machinery of public credit. 'The benefits arising by these companies', they asserted,

> generally and almost always fall to the share of the stock-jobbers, brokers, and those who cabal with them; or else are the rewards of clerks, thimble men, and men of nothing; who neglect their honest industry to embark in those cheats, and so either undo themselves and families, or acquire sudden and great riches; then turn awkward statesmen, corrupt boroughs, where they have not, nor can have, any natural Interests; bring themselves into the Legislature with their pedling and jobbing talents about them, and so become brokers in politicks as well as stock.[54]

What distinguished Trenchard and Gordon from Addison and Defoe were different brands of Whiggery. *Cato's Letters* were archetypal Country Whig writings. Although the polished and urbane style of Addison bears little resemblance to the rugged prose of Defoe, they did share a Court Whig attitude. Addison was, after all, a Secretary of State under George I, while Defoe wrote for the Whig government. Court Whigs favoured business activities of all sorts, including the London money market, whereas Country Whigs, while they countenanced merchants, disapproved of monied men. As Sir John Barnard, a leading opposition Whig, expressed it in a parliamentary speech in 1737:

> The publick funds divided the nation into two ranks of men, of which one are creditors and the other debtors. The creditors are the three great corporations . . . the debtors are the landholders, the merchants, the shopkeepers and all ranks and degrees of men throughout the kingdom.

This Country attitude was shared by Tory writers, even if some Tories, like Foxhunter, were suspicious of all commerce. John Arbuthnot's *John Bull* tracts, for example, criticised public credit but by implication endorsed trade. In them law is an allegory for war, and the famous statement 'Law is a bottomless pit' is a metaphor for the vast debt incurred by England in the War of the Spanish Succession. In order to finance his law suit 'John began to borrow money upon Bank stock, East India bonds, now and then a farm went to pot'. This put him in the hands of scriveners, i.e. state creditors: 'Such fellows are like your wiredrawing mills, if they get hold of a man's finger, they will pull his whole Body at last, till they squeeze the Heart, Blood and Guts out of him.' Yet John Bull is himself 'the richest tradesman in all the country'.[55] Pope, too, drew a distinction between city plutocrats associated with Walpole and the lesser London merchants opposed to him. Among the first is Sir Balaam, who appears in the *Epistle to Bathurst*. He displays many characteristics of the traditional merchant stereotype, his honesty being revealed as hypocrisy and his religion as self-interest. It is given a contemporary twist, however, when Sir Balaam becomes a Court Whig. He is almost the very reverse of Sir Andrew Freeport, who confided to Mr Spectator that 'Those lucky hits, which at another time he would have called pieces of good fortune . . . in the temper of mind he was then, he termed them mercies, favours in Providence and blessings upon honest industry,' whereas Sir Balaam

Ascribes his gettings to his parts and merit
What late he call'd a Blessing, now was Wit,
And God's good Providence, a lucky hit.

By contrast, Pope praised patriots like Sir John Barnard:

BARNARD in spirit, sense, and truth abounds.
'Pray then what wants he?' fourscore thousand pounds.[56]

Literary representations of merchants thus became involved in an ideological debate between the Court and its connections with high finance, and Country elements, including Whigs as well as Tories, who opposed these associations on the grounds that they were detrimental to the national economy.

Fictional professional men could also become the mouthpieces of rival ideologies. Although the stereotypes of the hypocritical clergymen, quack doctors and pettifogging lawyers remained largely unchanged, and did not improve as the merchant's image did, they were adapted by some writers for polemical purposes. At the outset of the eighteenth century the clergy were held to be almost entirely Tory, while the other professions were regarded as Whiggish. Hence a theatre dominated by Whig playwrights tended to represent clergymen unsympathetically and soldiers favourably, while Tory propagandists depicted quacks and pettifoggers as villainous Whig characters.

One of the few medical men not portrayed as an avaricious quack was Lemuel Gulliver, who confessed at the outset of his *Travels* that he was not a successful surgeon, 'for my conscience would not suffer me to imitate the bad practice of too many among my brethren'. Towards the end, in conversation with a Houyhnhnm, he spelled out what these were. They either prescribed a vomit or a purge, 'these artists ingeniously considering that in all diseases nature is forced out of her seat; therefore to replace her in it, the body must be treated in a manner directly contrary, by interchanging the use of each orifice; forcing solids and liquids in at the anus, and making evacuations at the mouth'. They also invented imaginary cures for imagined illnesses. Their skill in prognostication depended upon foretelling death as the consequence of any real disease, 'which is always in their power, if recovery is not', for if a patient unexpectedly recovers, 'rather than be accused as false prophets, they know how to approve their sagacity to the world by a seasonable dose'.

Clearly Swift did not make Gulliver a ship's surgeon in order to extol the medical profession. Why he cast him in this role is therefore curious. Given the genre of travel writing which he used for his major satire, his choice of hero was to some extent limited to somebody associated with sea voyages, but Gulliver could have been like Crusoe, who began as a mariner after running away to sea and subsequently became a trader. Instead, Gulliver's father, owner of a small Nottinghamshire estate, first sent him to Emmanuel College, Cambridge, and then apprenticed him to an eminent London surgeon, before contributing to his maintenance at Leyden University. Although Gulliver claims that he used some of his allowance in London to learn 'navigation and other parts of the mathematics useful to those who intend to travel', while his medical training in Leyden was undertaken in the knowledge that 'it would be useful in long voyages', this was scarcely a normal preparation for a maritime career. But however questionable his qualifications for seafaring might be, they were admirable Whig credentials. The choice of university, Whiggish Cambridge rather than Tory Oxford, is one clue, reinforced by Gulliver's attendance at Emmanuel, historically a Puritan foundation and perhaps the college most faithfully representing the Low Church tradition. His sojourn at Leyden associated him with Dissenting Englishmen, who were barred from Oxford and Cambridge, and therefore ultimately from the Royal College of Physicians, and perforce had to receive medical training elsewhere, many of them going to the Dutch university, which had an international reputation for medicine when Gulliver was there. His solid city addresses upon his return, Old Jury, Fetter Lane, a Dissenting neighbourhood, and his marriage to the daughter of a Newgate Street hosier, all identified Gulliver with Whiggish elements in society.

Swift used these associations to develop his own Country Tory ideology in two ways. First he employs Gulliver as a Whig foil, to satirise the values of the Court Whigs. As we have seen, the Captain begins his voyages imbued with naive faith in the excellency of his own country's laws and institutions. After his disillusionment, however, Gulliver himself reacts by vehemently rejecting the values of the Court Whigs, including their commitments to commercial expansion and the ascendancy of the Whig oligarchy.

Gulliver's attack upon the growth of commerce is made in one of his conversations with his Houyhnhnm host, in which he complained that in England he carried on his body 'the workmanship of a hundred tradesmen; the building and furniture of my house employ as many more; and five times the number to adorn my wife'. He was particularly scathing about the extravagance of women, asserting 'that this whole globe of earth must be at least three times gone round, before one of our better female Yahoos could get her breakfast, or a cup to put it in', while 'in order to feed the luxury and intemperance of the males, and the vanity of the females, we sent away the greatest part of our necessary things to other countries, from whence in return we brought the materials of diseases, folly and vice to spend among ourselves'.[57] This was a direct rebuttal of Whig writers like Defoe and Bernard Mandeville who extolled economic growth based on the exchange of goods between interdependent parts of the national and global economy. Defoe had boasted that 'This whole kingdom, as well as the people, as the land, and even the sea, in every part of it, are employed to furnish something . . . to supply the city of London with provisions.'[58] Mandeville had even argued that the exchange of English woollen cloth for foreign luxury goods directly stimulated economic growth. He also claimed that 'The variety of Work that is perform'd and the number of Hands employ'd to gratify the Fickleness and Luxury of Women is prodigious.'[59] The beneficial effects of vice to the economy lay behind his famous paradox 'Private vices, public benefits'. Gulliver came to see them as public calamities. Above all, where Mandeville had written approvingly of Pride for employing a million of the poor, this became the most deadly of all the seven sins as far as Gulliver was concerned. As he observed at the conclusion of the *Travels*, 'When I behold a lump of deformity, and diseases both in body and mind, smitten with *pride*, it immediately breaks all the measures of my patience; neither shall I be ever able to comprehend how such an animal and such a vice could tally together.'

The ultimate target of Gulliver's attack on commerce was not traders but the people whose luxury, pride and vanity they sought to gratify: the landed elite. One of the greatest indictments in the whole satire is that of the aristocracy. At the outset Gulliver eulogises the English peerage, informing the king of Brobdingnag, for instance,

> that they were persons of the noblest blood, and of the most ancient and ample patrimonies.... That these were the ornament and bulwark of the kingdom; worthy followers of their most renowned ancestors, whose honour had been the reward of their virtue; from which their posterity were never once known to degenerate.

Although the king queried this account, particularly inquiring whether those ennobled were always worthy men, the peerage survives his scepticism relatively well. In Glubdubdrib, however, Gulliver's expressed admiration for the aristocracy is considerably shaken when he is able to summon up the ancestors of several 'counts, marquesses, dukes, earls and the like':

> I could plainly discover from whence one family derives a long chin; why a second hath abounded with knaves for two generations and fools for two more; why a third happened to be crack-brained; and a fourth to be sharpers. ... How cruelty, falshood, and cowardice grew to be characteristics, by which certain families are distinguished as much as by their coats of arms. Who first brought the pox into a noble house, which hath lineally descended in scrophulous tumours to their posterity. Neither could I wonder at all this, when I saw such an interruption of lineages by pages, lacqueys, valets, coachmen, gamesters, fidlers, players, captains, and pickpockets.

Finally he gives a very different account of the aristocracy to his Houyhnhnm host from that which he had given to the king of Brobdingnag, telling him

> that our young noblemen are bred from their childhood in idleness and luxury; that, as soon as years will permit, they consume their vigour, and contract odious diseases among lewd females; and when their fortunes are almost ruined,

> they marry some woman of mean birth, disagreeable person, and unsound constitution, merely for the sake of money, whom they hate and despise. That the productions of such marriages are generally scrophulous, rickety or deformed children; by which means the family seldom continues above three generations, unless the wife take care to provide a healthy father among her neighbours, or domesticks, in order to improve and continue the breed.

This might be considered an indictment of the principle of an hereditary aristocracy as such. Yet Gulliver accepts and admires Houyhnhnm society, where there is an aristocracy based on race as well as upon birth. As his host informs him:

> Among the Houyhnhnms, the White, the Sorrel, and the Iron-Gray, were not so exactly shaped as the Bay, the Dapple Grey, and the Black; nor born with equal talents of mind, or a capacity to improve them; and therefore continued always in the condition of servants.

What Gulliver objects to is that the aristocratic ideal which he outlined to the king of Brobdingnag is not being observed by the contemporary English aristocrats, so that instead of being *hoi aristoi*, or the best, they were in fact the worst of mankind. Their physical degeneracy demonstrates this, for according to Gulliver,

> A weak diseased body, a meager countenance, and sallow complexion, are the true marks of noble blood; and a healthy, robust appearance is so disgraceful in a man of quality, that the world concludes his real father to have been a groom or a coachman.

He would have preferred a world in which physical characteristics complemented social status, so that the nobility were noble in body as well as in estate. This is in fact what distinguished him from the Yahoos, whom he 'far exceeded in shape, colour, and cleanliness'. It was presumably this which led the sorrel nag to bid farewell to him by saying: 'Take care of thyself, *gentle* Yahoo.'

The corruption of the aristocratic ideal by a degenerate breed of upstart peers was part and parcel of the Country complaint against the Whig oligarchy. In this connection it is significant that Gulliver rounds off his condemnation of the English aristocracy by making a political point:

> Without the consent of this illustrious body, no law can be enacted, repealed, or altered: and these nobles have likewise the decision of all our possessions without appeal.

With that conclusion Gulliver's conversion from being a gullible Court Whig to his creator's politics is complete. He is quick to correct the impression that he sprang from noble stock himself, stressing 'that my birth was of the lower sort, having been born of plain, honest parents, who were just able to give me a tolerable education'. It is perhaps interesting that when distinguishing himself from the aristocracy he identifies with the lower rather than with the middle sort, since in fact he came from what contemporaries called the middle station of life. Indeed, as the third of five sons born to the owner of a small estate in the Midlands he is almost archetypally from that category.[60]

While Swift used a ship's surgeon as a yardstick by which to judge the values of his political opponents, there was no similar employment of doctors or lawyers by Court Whigs in riposte to their denigration by opposition writers. On the contrary, Whig dramatists like Steele and Vanbrugh perpetuated the unflattering stereotypes of quacks and pettifoggers in their plays. The professions of medicine and the law never became as closely associated with a political party as the Church did with the Tories or the army did with their rivals.

Army officers and clergymen, indeed, were at the centre of the disputes between Tory and Whig in Anne's reign. Tories objected to English involvement in the War of the Spanish Succession as a principal and came to suspect the Duke of Marlborough and other military leaders of committing England to a land war for their own selfish ends. Swift played on these suspicions in his attacks upon Marlborough in *The Fable of Midas* and 'A Letter to Crassus', published in the *Examiner*. Whigs, on the other hand, were fully committed to the European conflict and glorified the means of waging it. None praised Marlborough or the military profession more than Joseph Addison in *The Campaign*, a poem celebrating the battle of Blenheim. The English troops who accompanied him to the Danube are described as

> Our British Youth, with in-born Freedom bold,

and

> Th' Illustrious Youth, that left their Native Shore
> To March where Britons never march'd before.

Marlborough himself is compared in a famous passage to an angel, who

> pleas'd th' Almighty's Orders to perform
> Rides in the Whirl-wind, and directs the Storm.[61]

Tories were concerned to defend the Church of England from what they considered to be the insidious challenge of Dissent, and regarded its clergy as front-line troops in a campaign equally as important as the war, if not more so. Swift devoted the whole of *Examiner* no. 21 to 'the Condition of the Church' and observed that 'For several years past there hath not, I think, in Europe, been any society of men upon so unhappy a foot as the clergy of England.'[62] Whigs, on the other hand, sought to protect the Dissenters from Tory proscription, and in their propaganda could be virulently anticlerical. Although they muted their attack on clergymen in plays, they did not spare them in print. A poem *On Dr Sacheverell's Sermon* in 1710, for instance, could write of the High Church clergy:

> They tell us they're Heaven's Plenipotentiaries,
> Alas! But we find 'em meer Incendiaries.[63]

John Tutchin could be particularly hostile. In the *Observator* for 19-23 May 1705 he wrote: 'When I see a priest at a man's house I presently conclude he's either come to pick the man's pocket or to make him a cuckold.' The Whig attitude to both the army and the clergy was beautifully brought out by George Farquhar in *Love and a Bottle*. A crippled beggar claims that officers were more charitable than clergymen: 'A captain will say Dam'me, and give me sixpence; and a parson shall whine out, God bless me, and give me not a farthing: Now I think the officer's blessing much the best.'[64]

Under the first two Georges, however, the roles of the army and the Church in the political disputes of the day shifted significantly. The army came to be associated with the Court in Country writings, which accused the kings and their ministers of employing it more for extending their domestic power than their European influence. These accusations were sustained by Country Whigs even more than by Tories. In 1720, for instance, Thomas Gordon and John Trenchard revived the Country Whig attack on the standing army which had featured so prominently in the late 1690s but which had been subdued in Anne's reign. Their *Cato's Letters* became an arsenal of ammunition for opposition writers to employ against the professional army throughout the reigns of George I and George II. The *Craftsman* often drew on its arguments and examples. Swift developed the Country case against the army in *Gulliver's Travels*, when the king of Brobdingnag objects to it, and shows his preference for a militia, by asking Gulliver 'whether a private man's house might not better be defended by himself, his children, and family; than by half a dozen rascals picked up at a venture in the streets, for small wages, who might get an hundred times more by cutting their throats'.[65] Court writers, by contrast, defended the military profession. Defoe's Colonel Jack emerges as a hero even though he sides with the Jacobites in the Pretender's abortive invasion of 1708 and the rebellion of 1715. To be sure, he subsequently recants when he learns of the passing of an Indemnity Act for those implicated in the '15 and fulsomely declares himself to be 'sincerely given in to the Interest of King George; and this from a principle of gratitude, and a sense of my obligation to his Majesty for my life'.[66]

It took longer for Country Whigs to change their attitude towards the Anglican clergy. Thomas Gordon's *Character of an Independent Whig* and his paper *The Independent Whig*, which appeared between January 1720 and January 1721, were as anticlerical as Tutchin's *Observator* had been, inveighing against 'high Church Jacobite priests'. The collected edition of *The Independent Whig* was significantly subtitled *A Defence of Primitive Christianity against the Exorbitant Claims and Encroachments of Fanatical Disaffected Clergymen*. In 1724 *The True Character of a Triumphant Whig* could depict Whigs as atheists who hated priests and priestcraft. There was no continuation of this vendetta by Whig contributors to the *Craftsman*, however. On the contrary, the main opposition paper in the first decade of George II's reign proclaimed that it was anxious to uphold the civil rights of the clergy. As the dedication to the collected edition of 1731 put it, 'We have no where endevour'd to deprive the clergy of any of their just rights and immunities.' Latent distrust of 'priestcraft' nonetheless survived in Whig circles, to surface in *The Old Whig*, a periodical published between 1735 and 1738. Henry Fielding played an important part in the opposition's task of educating its Whig supporters to accept the role of the Anglican clergy in English society. He contributed four articles under the heading of 'An Apology for the Clergy' to the *Champion* in 1740.[67] The first two stressed the biblical injunctions of humility and charity which the profession should uphold, and the third dwelt on the legal entitlement to its honours, immunities, revenues and restraints. The last dealt with such clergymen who fell from the high standards which they were supposed to maintain, saying of them:

> In what other light can such a wretch appear in the pulpit, than that of a quack Doctor on the stage, who trumpets over the virtues of his pills only to pick the pockets of the multitude, whilst he believes the direct contrary of what he says, and begs to be excused from taking any of them himself?

Yet he insisted that, while such disgraces to the profession undoubtedly existed, 'contempt or ridicule . . . can never fall with any weight on the order itself, or on any clergyman, who is not really a scandal to it'.

Whether or not professional and business men are portrayed in literature as being independent, rather than as parasites on the aristocracy and gentry, seems to be governed more by ideological considerations than by objective criteria. Writers of works examined here were not writing documentaries based on observation of social realities. They were all to a greater or lesser extent involved in a debate about the value of certain social types to society as a whole. Since doctors and lawyers did not represent interests crucial to the controversy, few of them were developed beyond the crudest stereotypes which depicted them as parasites. An important exception was Lemuel Gulliver; but one of the reasons why Swift chose to make his hero a ship's surgeon appears to have been precisely because he could use him to score political points off Court Whig aristocrats and merchants. Soldiers and clergymen, on the other hand, symbolised values which were central to the ideological dispute. In Anne's reign the argument tended to polarise Tory and Whig, while increasingly under her successors it divided Court and Country supporters. Thus in the opening decades of the century Whigs defended the military men and attacked the clergy, while Tories were opposed to the army and upheld the Church. Later Court apologists insisted on the need for a standing army even in peace-time, while Country critics were convinced that the military were a threat to English liberties and urged that all opposed to Walpole's ministry, Whigs as well as Tories, should unite to resist it. One of the obstacles to such unity was the residual anti-clericalism of many Country Whigs. Opposition leaders realised there was a problem here and tried to counter it. The *Craftsman* carried no attacks on the clergy, such as had been the stock-in-trade of Gordon's abusive *Independent Whig*. On the contrary, when it discussed them it was to advocate their value to society. Fielding continued this task of converting Country Whigs to accepting the role of clergymen in society in contributions to the *Champion*, and above all in his portrayal of Parson Adams, who epitomises the independent clergyman.

Most professional men, however, are depicted in fiction as clients rather than as independent practitioners of their professions. Judging by fictititous clergymen, lawyers and soldiers, the 'middle station of life' did not form a separate middle class in this period.

The business community, on the other hand, does emerge as one with its own characteristics. Again, this is due to its being involved in a heated discussion of its contribution to society. At the outset of the period Whigs extolled the value of the city, while Tories criticised its effects on the national economy. Later Country writers attacked what they considered to be the excessive influence of city plutocrats at court, while upholding the contribution of lesser business men to society. As the debate developed so it documented the emergence of a distinct 'bourgeoisie', at least as an ideological concept.

* * *

'One reason why many English authors have totally failed in describing the manners of upper life', observed Fielding, 'may possibly be that in reality they know nothing of it.'[68] He could have gone on to say, perhaps with more justice, that they knew next to nothing about the manners of low life either. It is interesting that when he portrayed his heroine Amelia at her most destitute she still contrived to keep a maid. Very few writers knew real poverty at first hand, an exception being Stephen Duck. There was a popular literary culture, dominated by almanacs and chapbooks, though even these were written not by but for the lower orders, and not necessarily in the eighteenth century. Indeed, their standard fiction consisted of traditional tales like the stories of Robin Hood, Jack the Giant Killer and Guy of Warwick.[69] For the most part, therefore, literature documents not the reality of life among the lower orders, but how it, and they, were perceived by those above them.

The difficulties which the historian encounters by drawing on literary works to illustrate the lives of people below the middle station of life can be demonstrated from the case of servants. These tended to be regarded very much from the employer's point of view, which was scarcely complimentary. On the contrary, much contemporary literature gives a most unflattering view of servants. Defoe, in *Everybody's Business Is Nobody's Business*, lamented the alleged insistence of modern maids on the maximum wages for the minimum work. *The Great Law of Subordination Considered*, another work by Defoe, also complained that 'The insufferable behaviour of servants in this nation is now (it may be hoped) come to its height; this measure of insolence, I think, may be said to be quite full.'[70] Swift wrote an ironic manual of *Directions to Servants* giving hints on how to get away with the most slovenly service while cheating and insulting their masters. For example, 'Never send up a leg of a fowl at supper, while there is a cat or dog in the house, that can be accused for running away with it: But, if there happen to be neither, you must lay it upon the rats, or a strange grey-hound.'[71] Steele in the *Spectator* claimed to 'know no Evil which touches all Mankind so much as this of the Misbehaviour of Servants'.[72]

On the basis of such writings it has been affirmed that servants in the eighteenth century really were insubordinate, unreliable and mercenary.[73] This is to accept the master's viewpoint at its face value. Literary sources which document how servants viewed their employers are, not surprisingly, scant. Robert Dodsley's poem *The Footman,* however, does provide a corrective to the employer's point of view, for it was based on experience. Dodsley had himself been employed as a footman by Charles Dartiquenave (Pope's 'Darty'), and by the Hon. Mrs Lowther. His poem describes the very busy day of the domestic servant, from cleaning glasses, knives and plates, a task he hated, as soon as he got up in the morning, even before he dressed, to attending his master or mistress at the play, assembly or opera in the evening, and then going home to a late supper. The 'only pleasant hour . . . in the twenty four' is spent when he waits at table and overhears polite conversation. From his description of it, however, it was apparently no more elevated than that recorded by Swift in *Polite Conversation*. Dodsley does not allow himself a direct criticism of his employers, but admits that the 'chief trade' of other servants was

> To rail against our lords and ladies:
> T' aggravate their smallest failings,
> T' expose their faults with saucy railings.

Although he expresses his hatred for a practice which lends confirmation to the view that servants were insolent, there is an undertone of resentment to being at the beck and call of superiors from morning until night. Certainly *The Footman* rather documents the drudgery than the idleness of servants.

Dodsley also wrote *The Footman's Friendly Advice to his Brethren of the Livery* (1731). While this advised servants to be honest, obedient, diligent, neat and discreet, it also admonished masters about their duties and took issue with Defoe on the subject of the insubordination of those in domestic service. Servitude, he suggested, was unnatural subjection, and not a state people would naturally choose. 'With what humanity then ought a master to treat that man whom fortune has subjected to be his servant?' he asked.

> How ought he to endeavour to mollify and alleviate the irksomeness of his servitude? and by the sweetness of his temper and mildness of his commands, make that be performed willingly which would otherwise be done with reluctance? always remembering that though he is advanc'd never so far above him by Fortune, he is yet nearly related to him by Nature; and that had it not been for some accidental circumstances, he might perhaps have been in his condition.

He objected very strongly to *Everybody's Business Is Nobody's Business*, which he found 'Stuft with nothing in the world but opprobious railings and spiteful invectives against the pride, laziness and dishonesty of gentlemen's servants'. Defoe's tract had been provoked by his mistaking a maid for her mistress because she wore fine clothes. 'What because a servant has one silk gown or so, to go abroad in now and then, does it follow that they have nothing but silks and satins to do the drudgery of the house in?' Dodsley expostulated. ''Tis very probable, Sir, if you had seen the chamber maid you was so complaisant to, an hour or two before, you had found her in another garb.' He turned the tables neatly on a typically Defoean economic argument, that if servants wore silk then the cloth industry would suffer, by pointing out that their fine clothes were cast-offs from their mistresses, and if they did not give them to their servants the clothes would go to second-hand shops and be 'worn amongst the common people's wives and daughters; and where then would be the difference, with respect to the woollen manufacture?' The effectiveness of this argument was rather offset, however, by his accusation that Defoe wanted a reduction in the wages of maids so that they would not be able to afford silk gowns.

'From our pride he proceeds to our pilfering,' continued Dodsley, 'and here too, with his usual justness and good nature, he accuses us in the lump, makes no supposition that some of us may be honest.' There were three allegations of pilfering which he contested: food and beverages for junkets;

purchasing meat at the master's expense; and obtaining commission from tradesmen. He admitted that some servants might help themselves to a little tea or sugar, but pointed out that this did not make them criminals on a level with Jonathan Wild, as Defoe seemed to think. He agreed that those who defrauded their masters when purchasing meat should be treated with the utmost severity, but thought that it was 'almost impossible to do it, since most butchers now send in a note with their meat every day'. As for the commission which some tradesmen gave servants, he argued that 'It is not so much we that expect it, as they that allow it to us.' The reason was that 'Gentlemen take larger quantities of provisions etc. than common people, their pay is generally better, and their custom more valuable; which, therefore, lest a trader should lose, he thinks a gratuity to the servant not ill bestow'd.'

Defoe objected to the giving of 'vails' to servants, since they regarded these tips as a normal part of their wages and not as a reward for good service. Dodsley replied that they should be an encouragement to the well-deserving rather than being bestowed as a matter of course. 'For my part,' he observed, 'I can't see how gentlemen can bestow a shilling better, than in thus encouraging each other's servants to do well; for I would have all my brother servants to look upon what they receive, as given with that design; and accordingly use their endeavours to deserve it.' His riposte concluded 'with an hearty and sincere wish, that those of my brethren, who do actually resemble the picture which squire Moreton [Defoe] has drawn of them, may never meet with a better master than he to encourage them'.[74]

Of course, Dodsley's protestations were special pleading. Vails, for instance, were regarded as an automatic tip rather than as a reward for good service. But his observations offer a valuable corrective to the overwhelmingly one-sided view of the master/servant relationship.

The medium which most frequently explored the relationship between master and servant in this period was the theatre. Almost any Augustan play, whether tragedy, comedy or farce, presented servants on stage attendant upon their masters or mistresses. It is interesting that they are hardly ever shown as having separate and conflicting interests.

Even titles which apparently indicate the portrayal of disloyal servants, such as Fielding's *The Intriguing Chambermaid* or Garrick's *The Lying Valet*, in fact assert the identity of interests between them and their employers. Lettice is impertinent to Mrs Highman in defence of her master Valentine, while Timothy Sharp employs his ingenuity to conceal his master's poverty from Melissa until he can marry her.

The plots of some plays even depend upon the ability of servants to pass themselves off as gentlefolk, usually to promote their masters' rather than their own interests. Waitwell, Mirabell's servant in Congreve's *The Way of the World*, poses as Sir Rowland, his master's uncle, in order to court Lady Wishfort. Martin, Harcourt's servant, even impersonates a peer, Lord Apemode, in James Miller's *The Man of Taste*. Harcourt remarks: 'The coxcomb is so impudent . . . that he often takes it into his head to pass for a man of quality. He pretends to gallantry, and has such a contempt for others of his own condition, that he calls 'em all meer brutes.'[75] The rather involved plot of William Popple's *The Double Deceit; or A Cure for Jealousy* revolves around the impersonation of Courtlove and Gaylife by their men Jerry and Frank, and that of Harriet and Fanny Richly by their maids Rose and Jenny. Consequently Courtlove and Gaylife woo Harriet and Fanny thinking they are maids, while Jerry and Frank court Rose and Jenny, each pair of servants being under the illusion that the other is genteel. The ludicrous situations that ensue underscore the notion that gentlefolk and servants are interchangeable.

A jarring note is struck, however, when both maids and men decide to cheat their employers. The mutual impersonations had originally been embarked upon by the gentlemen to get their servants to make the initial overtures of courtship to the ladies in order to sound out their eligibility for marriage, an unlikely device rendered even more so by the ladies changing roles on the same ground, hence the 'double deceit' of the play's title. However, both sets of servants plot to woo in earnest, in the hope of marrying above their station. As Jerry says to Frank, 'Is not your state mean enough to run any risque to get out of it?'[76]

Similar comments crop up occasionally in Augustan drama.

Charles Johnson's *The Village Opera* features a gardener, Lucas, who instructs Colin, a fellow-labourer, to take his spade and work, observing: 'Don't let us idle away our lives like those creatures thay call gentlefolks, who seem to be born only to eat, and drink and sleep and do nothing.'[77] The point is sharpened, moreover, by being addressed to a gentleman in disguise. George Lillo in *Fatal Curiosity* depicted an apprentice forced to find his way in the world before finishing his time because his master has gone bankrupt. He asks:

> Whither shall I wander
> And to what point direct my views and hopes?
> A menial servant! – NO – what shall I live
> Here in this land of freedom, live distinguished
> And marked the willing slave of some proud subject
> And swell his useless train for broken fragments
> The cold remains of his superfluous board?[78]

The most explicit criticism of the subordination of servants to masters was made by James Miller in *Art and Nature*. The main contrast in the play is that between the nature of a savage, Julio, whom Truemore has brought back from the West Indies, and the artifice of civilisation. At one point Truemore tries to explain the use of money to Julio:

Truemore: There are among us two sorts of people, the rich and the poor; the rich have all the money, and the poor none.

Julio: A very equal distribution truly.

Truemore: They are under a necessity of working for the rich, who give them money in proportion to their labour.

Julio: And pray what do the rich do, whilst the poor work for 'em?

Truemore: Eat, drink, sleep and dress, and pass their whole time in diversions and entertainments.

Julio: This indeed is very happy for the rich.

Truemore: There's no living here without money, and those that han't it got ready to their hands, must submit to take pains for it, for the poor can have nothing for nothing.

Julio: How! And because I have got none of this trumpery

stuff shall I be obliged like those wretches to slave for my living?

Truemore: Ay Julio you must.

Julio: Why then did you draw me out of my own country to teach me that I am poor? In my native woods I had known neither riches nor poverty. I had done every office for myself, been at once master and servant, king and subject; from this stage of happiness and freedom you have drawn me to teach me, that I am only a miserable slave.[79]

Such attacks on the distribution of wealth between masters and servants are rarely heard in plays of the period, presumably because playwrights were on this issue sensitive to their audiences. Drama was unique, after all, in being addressed to audiences which included both masters and servants. As Fielding observed in *Tom Jones*, the upper gallery of theatres was 'a place in which few of our readers ever sit'.[80] They were in fact frequented by footmen in attendance on their masters who sat in better seats. How sensitive they could be to comments about their occupations on stage appeared at the end of our period, when James Townley's *High Life Below Stairs* (1759) provoked a riot among the footmen for portraying servants as utterly dishonest rogues. At the same time to depict them as downtrodden and exploited would not have appealed to their employers who made up a substantial part of theatre audiences. Dramatists doubtless played it safe by showing a harmony of interests between them. Even Dodsley, who wrote a play as well as a poem with the title *The Footman* (1732), reinforced the comic stereotype of the servant by depicting them as having ideas above their station. The comedy involves the activities of a dozen servants who ape their masters in everything, even down to modes of address, so that Charles, servant to Lady Gaylove, is actually called 'Lord Gaylove' by his colleagues.

If we can rarely draw on literature to discover what the lower orders were really like, it throws a great deal of light on the attitudes of their superiors towards them. Furthermore, despite the fact that a Court Whig like Defoe and a Country Tory like Swift held similar views on servants, literary sources document ideological differences between writers in their social attitudes. The basic disagreement was over the extent to which the masses could be regarded as rational. Some Augustans thought that they were little better than savages or brute beasts, completely swayed by their passions. Insofar as they possessed the faculty of reason at all it merely served to rationalise their self-interest and made them prone to evade responsibility, practise deception and ultimately indulge in vice and crime. Others claimed that all men, even the lowest, had some rational faculties, and that these could be developed to inculcate social sentiments, raising them above the level of brutes. Although, as we shall see, these attitudes combined too many strands of philosophy and religion to be categorised into two clear schools of thought, for convenience those who took the first can be called pessimists, and those who adopted the second can be termed optimists.

The leading pessimist of the period was surely Swift. His scepticism about the rationality of man pervades his works, and he explicitly denied that man was a rational animal, since he believed that men were only capable of reason. This belief is elaborated in the fourth voyage of Gulliver, on which he met the Houyhnhnms and the Yahoos. These represent respectively the opposite poles of Reason and Passion, the Houyhnhnms having no passions to control, while the Yahoos have no rational faculties at all. Swift is sometimes said to have presented the Houyhnhnms as an ideal, and made it utterly unattainable, a point emphasised by having them appear in the form of horses rather than as men. In opposition to this it is claimed that he was advocating a *via media* between them and the Yahoos, and that Gulliver, who has both reason and passions, is the recommended compromise. Even if we subscribe to the second interpretation, however, it does not get us off Swift's hook. The use which Gulliver and his kind have made of reason persuades his Houyhnhnm host that they are even worse than Yahoos, for men have rationalised their inclination towards evil: 'We made no other use [of reason] than by its assistance to aggravate our natural corruptions, and to acquire new ones which Nature had not given us.'[81]

Where Gulliver's host indicts all mankind, the sorrel nag

detects a distinction between Gulliver and the Yahoos which gives the advantage to the human. When Gulliver is banished the nag calls after him: 'Take care of thyself, gentle Yahoo.' The difference between them is thus seen to be not so much intellectual as social, the Captain possessing a gentility which the Yahoos lack. They have more in common with the masses, of whom Swift had no high opinion, than with the 'gentle reader' whom he explicitly addresses.

Other pessimists tended to agree with Gulliver's host that reason made men even more inclined to evil than did ignorance. 'To be Stupid and Ignorant is seldom the Character of a Thief', insisted Bernard Mandeville. 'Robberies on the High-way and other bold Crimes are generally perpetrated by Rogues of Spirit and a Genius, and Villains of any Fame are commonly subtle cunning Fellows.' Anybody who doubted it, and laid the blame on 'Ignorance, Stupidity and Dastardness', he invited to

> examine into the Lives, and narrowly inspect the Conversations and Actions of ordinary Rogues and our common Felons, and he will find the reverse to be true, and that the blame ought rather to be laid on excessive Cunning and Subtlety, and too much Knowledge in general, which the worst of Miscreants and the Scum of the Nation are possess'd of.[82]

He was therefore opposed to the charity-school movement, on the grounds that the ignorance of the masses was bliss, and that they would be educated to be discontented with their lot and prone to vice and crime. John Trenchard agreed that

> No education ought to be more discountenanced by a state, than putting chimera's and airy notions into the heads of those who ought to have pickaxes in their hands; than teaching people to read, write, and cast accompt, who, if they were employed as they ought to be, can have no occasion to make use of these requirements, unless it be now and then to read the Bible, which they seldom or never do.[83]

Optimists, on the other hand, welcomed the movement as

one which would make the labouring poor better citizens. The contributors to the *Spectator* thought charity schools were 'the greatest instances of publick spirit the Age has produced'.[84] Defoe agreed, extolling 'the blessing, and advantages of a sober and well govern'd education' and observing 'how much publick schools and charities might be improved to prevent the destruction of so many unhappy children, as, in this Town, are every year bred up for the Gallows'.[85] Isaac Watts also asserted that charity schools, so far from breeding criminals, rescued poor children from a life of crime. 'Human nature rude and untaught is the more prone to wickedness,' he declared, and recommended instruction in 'the virtues of the civil life' in the schools,

> to train them up in all the good qualities of the social life, and to guard them against those vile and pernicious practices, against that sloth, that falsehood, and lying, that thievery and drunkenness, rage and malice, which abound among the ignorant rabble of mankind, who never enjoyed the blessing of education, nor the benefit of a school, where their manners might be formed to virtue and goodness.[86]

Those who took a pessimistic view of the intelligence of the masses tended to be indulgent about their alleged proneness to immoral and licentious behaviour, since they could not be expected to do much about it. Optimists, on the other hand, were inclined to take a harsher view of their apparent failings, since they had sufficient reason to distinguish and choose between right and wrong. A striking example of this is in their differing attitudes towards the problem of gin-drinking. Mandeville took a charitable view of this, arguing that gin was among other things 'a Lethe of Oblivion, in which the wretch immers'd drowns his most pinching Cares, and with his Reason all anxious reflection on Brats that cry for Food, hard Winters Frosts and horrid Empty Home'.[87] Hogarth took a much sterner line. His 'Gin Lane' is often regarded as an indictment of environmental conditions which gave rise to the consumption of cheap spirits, but nothing could be further from the truth. The moral is not that Gin Lane produces gin-drinking, but the very reverse: drinking gin produces the squalor of Gin Lane. Indeed, the consideration of the print in isolation from its partner 'Beer Street' has obscured Hogarth's message. The lower orders had a choice: to drink beer and be hale and hearty, or to drink gin and be diseased and poverty-stricken.

This distinction between those who felt that the poor lacked the capacity to control their behaviour, and those who insisted that they could choose how to behave, can be discerned even in writings which agree that they were idle and insubordinate. It was a commonplace, as we have seen in the case of servants, for Augustans to claim that the labouring poor were prone to idleness and insubordination. Pessimists, however, argued that this was because they followed the example set by their superiors, while optimists insisted that it was through choice. According to the pessimistic argument, men would only act virtuously and eschew vice if they achieved some advantage thereby. Instead, society was so organised, from top to bottom, that the vicious prospered and the virtuous were unsuccessful. The only way to alter this state of affairs was by a thorough reformation, starting at the top. Swift's *Project for the Advancement of Religion and Reformation of Manners* appealed to Queen Anne to stop promoting vicious and corrupt ministers and to admit only good men into her counsels. This example would then percolate down to the lower reaches of society. Bernard Mandeville remorselessly pointed out that the whole of society flourished on the exploitation of the seven deadly sins. The knaves in the 'grumbling hive' only turned honest when Jove forced them to be so, 'From the great Statesman to the Clown'.[88] If the elite behaved as traditional patriarchs, practising piety and treating the poor charitably, the lower orders would respond appropriately. If, on the other hand, the employing classes behaved extravagantly and viciously, those they employed would act similarly.

Optimists did not see lower-class mores as a mimesis of elite morals but as the conscious exercise of choice. The way to condition their behaviour was not to set a good example from above but to alter the criteria. Gin-drinking could be controlled, for example, not by eliminating drunkenness among the upper classes but by pricing gin beyond the means of the lower orders. Idleness could be discouraged not by getting the elite to perform their duties but by making it unprofitable. The insolence of servants could be curbed, according to Steele, if their masters stopped paying them board wages. These gave them a financial independence which meant that they could afford to be impertinent. Begging, too, for instance, should not be rewarded with indiscriminate donations, since this merely encouraged the poor to beg and not to work. Almsgiving, indeed, was a question on which Augustans were very much divided. John Gay, walking the streets of London, observed how

> Proud Coaches pass, regardless of the Moan
> Of Infant Orphans, and the Widow's Groan;
> While Charity still moves the Walker's Mind,
> His lib'ral Purse relieves the Lame and Blind.
> Judiciously thy Half-pence are bestow'd,
> Where the laborious Beggar sweeps the Road.
> Whate'er you give, give ever at Demand,
> Nor let Old-Age long stretch his palsy'd Hand.[89]

Sir Andrew Freeport deplored such advice. 'The very Alms they receive from us, are the Wages of Idleness,' he informed Mr Spectator after having been importuned by beggars 'with the usual Rhetoric of a sick Wife or Husband at Home, three or four helpless little Children all starving with Cold and Hunger' until they were 'forc'd to part with some Money to get rid of their Importunity'.[90] Defoe agreed with Sir Andrew that

> The begging, as now practic'd, is a scandal upon our charity, and perhaps the foundation of all our present grievance — How can it be possible that any man or woman, who being sound in Body and Mind, may as 'tis apparent they may, have wages for their work, should be so base, so meanly spirited, as to beg for Alms for God-sake — Truly the scandal lies on our charity; and people have such a notion in England of being pitiful and charitable, that they encourage vagrants; and by a mistaken zeal do more harm than good.[91]

Robert Dodsley satirised the hard line in *The Blind Beggar of Bethnal Green* when the hero asks two passers-by to 'Pray remember the Blind!' One says: 'I have nothing for you friend. One cannot stir a step without being plagu'd with the cant of beggars.' The other agrees that 'Tis an infamous thing in a trading country that the poor are not some way or other employed.'[92]

Perhaps the greatest optimists were the members of the societies for reformation of manners, who thought that they could eliminate from the lower orders such vices as drunkenness, swearing and whoring by literally making them not worth while. They prosecuted people who practised such activities, pressing for heavy fines. Their prosecutions were so patently brought against the humble and obscure, however, that even writers like Defoe, who might have been expected to share their philosophy, objected to this discrimination. 'Your annual lists of criminals appear,' he wrote, referring to the black lists of those prosecuted every year, 'but no Sir Harry or Sir Charles is there.'[93] Pessimists like Mandeville thought the whole enterprise absurd. His *Modest Defence of Publick Stews,* which he dedicated to the gentlemen of the societies, claimed that under their vigilance prostitution was pruned rather than lopped.[94]

When dealing with the relations between the rich and the poor in their society Augustan writers hardly ever attacked the distribution of wealth between them. On the contrary, it was a commonplace that 'God is pleased to place different persons in different stations; and every one is to accommodate themselves according to their station; it would as well befit a hedger to wear a velvet coat, as a courtier to wear a leathern one.'[95] Isaac Watts agreed that 'The Great God has wisely ordained in the Course of his Providence in all Ages, that among Mankind there should be some Rich, and some Poor.'[96] The same sentiment was expressed by Pope:

> ORDER is Heav'n's first law; and this confest,
> Some are, and must be, greater than the rest.[97]

There was also a widespread feeling that the poor were not content to accept their lot, and that this was undermining the traditional hierarchy.

Behind this consensus, however, there was a significant disagreement over the causes of the discontent among the lower orders. Pessimists blamed the bad example set by the elite and urged them to return to traditional patriarchal values in order to inculcate proper deference in their subordinates. Optimists blamed precisely those outmoded values for encouraging the poor to shirk their obligations. As we have seen, they held indiscriminate almsgiving responsible for idleness. Defoe attributed the insubordination of servants to the softness of the employers whose misplaced sympathies led them to give even the most insolent a good reference on changing jobs. 'The miserable circumstance of this country is now such', he complained, 'that, in short, if it goes on, the poor will be rulers of the rich, and the servants be governors of their masters, the plebeii have almost mobb'd the patricii.'[98]

Most pessimists had a gloomy view of human nature. Many were influenced by the philosophy of Thomas Hobbes, who argued that men pursued pleasure and avoided pain, both defined in terms of their immediate consequences. Much of Swift's writing is tinged with Hobbesian psychology, while that of John Trenchard and Bernard Mandeville is steeped in it. Trenchard quoted with approval Hobbes's notion that the state of nature was a state of war and concluded that 'The making of laws supposes all men naturally wicked.'[99] Mandeville developed Hobbes's views on human motivation throughout his works. In *A Search into the Nature of Society* he denied altruism of any kind, insisting that 'Be we Savages or Politicians it is impossible that Man, mere fallen Man should act with any other View but to please himself whilst he has the Use of his Organs, and the greatest Extravagancy either of Love or Despair can have no other Center.' The problem of accounting for the fact that such an egoist had been reconciled to society he resolved by attributing the reconciliation to fear and pride. 'The only useful Passion then that Man is possess'd of towards the peace and quiet of a Society', he concluded in *The Fable of the Bees*, 'is his Fear.' In *An Enquiry into the Origin of Moral Virtue* he claimed that men were persuaded to subdue their antisocial passions by skilful politicians who appealed not to their reason or their altruism but to their pride:

> To introduce moreover an Emulation amongst Men, they divided the whole Species in two Classes, vastly differing from one another: The one consisted of abject, low minded

> People, that always hunting after immediate Enjoyment, were wholly incapable of Self-denial, and without regard to the good of others, had no higher Aim than their private Advantage; such as being enslaved by Voluptuousness yielded without Resistance to every gross desire, and made no use of their Rational Faculties but to heighten their Sensual Pleasures. These vile grov'ling Wretches, they said, were the Dross of their kind, and having only the Shape of Men, differ'd from Brutes in nothing but their outward Figure. But the other Class was made up of lofty, high-spirited Creatures, that free from sordid Selfishness esteem'd the Improvements of the Mind to be their fairest Possessions; and setting a true value upon themselves, took no delight but in imbellishing that Part in which their Excellency consisted; such as despising whatever they had in common with irrational Creatures, opposed by the help of Reason their most violent Inclinations; and making a continual War with themselves to promote the Peace of others, aim'd at no less than the Publick Welfare and the Conquest of their own Passions.

By working on man's pride the politicians were able to flatter him that he belonged to the second class, and thus made him a sociable creature.[100]

Pope's *Essay on Man*, which addressed itself directly to these issues, is usually considered to be an optimistic poem. So it is, in the sense that Pope considered the pursuit of happiness to be a worthy human goal and even held that it was possible to attain it. In the sense in which it is being used here, however, to define attitudes towards human nature, the *Essay* is not particularly optimistic. Rather there is a strong vein of pessimism running through it. Pope agreed with Hobbes that

> Self-love, the spring of motion, acts the soul.

Moreover, although reason could regulate self-love, the latter was stronger. Unrestrained by reason, men sought happiness in wealth, greatness and fame, which, Pope warned his reader, were vain pursuits:

If all, united, thy ambition call,
From ancient story learn to scorn them all.
There, in the rich, the honour'd, fam'd and great,
See the false scale of Happiness complete!

True happiness was to be found in 'health, peace, and competence'. This truth could only be realised if man stopped pursuing his own immediate gratification and reflected on his place in God's overall plan for the universe. Then he would come to realise

That true SELF-LOVE and SOCIAL are the same.

The adjective is vital. Most men, lacking the insights of Pope and his 'guide, philosopher and friend' Bolingbroke, had a false idea of where their interests lay, which clashed with those of society.[101]

Optimists were divided on the subject of whether man was by nature a selfish rather than a social animal. The contributors to the *Spectator* were influenced by the benevolent views of John Locke and the third Earl of Shaftesbury, who insisted that men were capable of altruistic and well as egoistic behaviour. While greed and lust were destructive passions, charity, love and pity held together families, societies and states. These instincts were innate. As the *Spectator* asserted:

Good nature is generally born with us. Health, prosperity and kind treatment from the world are great cherishers of it where they find it, but nothing is capable of forcing it up, where it does not grow of it self. It is one of the Blessings of a happy constitution which Education may improve but not produce.[102]

The implication here is that not all men are blessed at birth with good nature. Mary Collyer was more optimistic than this, believing that all people were innately good:

If we impartially survey the first impressions of nature, we shall find that all those propensities which are not acquired are on the side of virtue. . . . Even before reason can take place . . . he feels within him an internal and moral sense, which distinguishes between virtue and vice, beauty and deformity, harmony and dischord.[103]

According to the *Spectator*, good nature required education to bring it out:

> I consider an human soul without Education like marble in the quarry, which shews none of its inherent beauties till the skill of the polisher fetches out the colours, makes the surface shine, and discovers every ornamental cloud, spot and vein that runs through the body of it. Education, after the same manner, when it works upon a noble mind, draws out to view every latent vertue and perfection, which without such helps are never able to make their appearance. . . . The Philosopher, the Saint, or the Hero, the Wise, the Good, or the Great Man, very often lie hid and concealed in a Plebean, which a proper Education might have disinterred, and brought to light.[104]

This belief that education could benefit even the labouring poor was shared by Defoe and Isaac Watts, which is why they can be considered as optimists, even if, as Dissenters, they accepted Calvin's view that since the Fall man was universally depraved. Calvinism was almost diametrically opposite to benevolism, and its devotees were optimistic only in the sense that they believed man could be educated out of his depravity.

The ideologies behind these positions were complex. Pessimists tended to be influenced by Hobbesian ideas and were for the most part in the Country tradition. An exception to this was Bernard Mandeville, who, though a disciple of Hobbes, was very much on the side of the Court Whigs. He was a maverick anyway, since he geared his pessimistic psychology to a very optimistic economics. In his view consumer demand, stimulated by the gratification of the passions and indulgence in vice, buoyed up an expanding economy

> To such a Height, the very Poor
> Lived better than the Rich before.[105]

Country writers deplored this divorce of ethics from economics. To their way of thinking patriarchal values were most beneficial economically. Although Pope was prepared to concede to Mandeville that by Timon's conspicuous consumption

the Poor are cloath'd, the Hungry fed;
Health of himself, and to his Infants bread
The Lab'rer bears: What his hard Heart denies,
His charitable Vanity supplies,

nevertheless he insisted that a better use of Timon's resources would have been to grow wheat on the land he had landscaped:

Another age shall see the golden Ear
Imbrown the Slope, and nod on the Parterre,
Deep Harvests bury all his pride has plann'd,
And laughing Ceres re-assume the land.[106]

Optimists were more inclined to separate economic from ethical values and to argue that the poor fared best when left to fend for themselves. Although they reached these conclusions from widely different premises, ranging from Calvinism to the philosophies of Locke and Shaftesbury, they tended to subscribe to the same political views. Addison, Steele, Defoe and Watts were all Court Whigs.

The attitudes of writers towards the lower orders were therefore to a considerable extent based on ideological assumptions. Their writings tell us precious little about the reality of life as it was experienced by domestic servants and wage-earners. It is impossible to document from literature whether they were deferential or insubordinate, lazy or hardworking. Literary allegations about such characteristics, however, tell us a great deal about the ideologies of their superiors.

3
The Wheel of Fortune

That the World is a lottery, what man can doubt?
When born we're put in, when dead we're drawn out;
And tho' tickets are bought by the fool and the wise
Yet 'tis plain there are more than ten blanks to a prize.

The Lottery: a farce (1732)

That the World, 'tis agreed
Is a lottery indeed
Where one in a Thousand scarce draws a good prize.
Blame not Fortune, nor Chance
But this Maxim advance,
They who lucky wou'd be, must be Honest and Wise.
Luck and Chance, it is plain
Are things fancy'd and vain,
For our Fortunes alone on our Actions depend.
In Love still be steddy,
In Honour be ready,
And we shall draw prizes enough in the end.

Robert Dodsley, *The Footman* (1732)

They say, Sir, marriage and hanging go by Destiny, Heaven help us.

Theophilus Cibber, *The Lovers* (1730)

Although Augustans considered that Providence had ordained a fixed social hierarchy, they were well aware that some people did not remain in the place to which their birth had apparently allotted them. Indeed, the movements up and down the ladder of society fascinated and at the same time disturbed them.

Defoe, who had himself experienced many vicissitudes in his career, seems to have been particularly intrigued by those of his fictional characters. Robinson Crusoe starts out as a mere mariner, becomes a merchant, spends years on a remote island, and ends as a substantial planter. Moll Flanders, as the title-page of the novel informs us,

was born in Newgate, and during a life of continued variety,

> for threescore years, besides her childhood, was twelve years a whore, five times a wife (whereof once to her own brother), twelve years a thief, eight years a transported felon in Virginia, at last grew rich, lived honest, and died a penitent.

Similarly, the title-page of the first edition of *Colonel Jack* conveyed the information that he was

> born a gentleman, put 'prentice to a pickpocket, was six and twenty years a thief, and then kidnapp'd to Virginia. Came back a merchant, married four wives, and five [*sic*] of them prov'd whores; went into the wars, behav'd bravely, got preferment, was made Colonel of a regiment, came over and fled with the Chevalier, and is now abroad compleating a Life of Wonders, and resolves to dye a General.

Roxana's life, first as a wife of a spendthrift brewer left penniless with five children when he went bankrupt and abandoned her, then as the kept mistress of a German prince, as a courtesan at the Restoration court and finally as the wife of a thrifty Dutch merchant, was certainly one of a 'vast variety of fortunes'.

Fortune played a critical role in the careers of Defoe's heroes and heroines. The full title of *Moll Flanders* refers to her 'Fortunes and Misfortunes'. It becomes clear that he did not employ the idea casually, to mean mere fate or chance, for he used it interchangeably with Providence. The destiny of his characters is therefore ultimately dependent not upon the whims of the blind goddess but on the will of an all-seeing God. God intervenes constantly in the life of Robinson Crusoe to warn him of the dire consequences of his impiety and imprudence. He likewise checks Roxana's progress along the primrose path, for instance with the storm at sea which causes both her and Amy momentarily to feel contrite, and with the injury sustained by her prince in a boar hunt, which leads him to repent and thus end her hopes of becoming a princess. Defoe's own attitude comes out clearly in the preface to *Colonel Jack*:

> The various turns of Fortune in the world, make a delightful field for the reader to wander in; a garden where he

> may gather wholesome and medicinal plants, none noxious or poisonous; where he will see virtue and the ways of wisdom every where applauded, honoured, encouraged, rewarded; Vice and all kinds of wickedness attended with misery, many kinds of infelicities, and at last sin and shame going together, the persons meeting with reproof and reproach, and the crimes with abhorrence.

Attributing a positive role to Providence raises the question of how far people were responsible for their own fates. Defoe was particularly ambiguous on the subject. He loads the dice against Moll Flanders, Colonel Jack and Roxana by placing them in desperate situations, the first born in Newgate and brought up by gypsies, the second 'a dirty glass bottle house boy, sleeping in the ashes', the third left destitute by her bankrupt husband. This seems to make their subsequent vicious or criminal activities inevitable and therefore excusable. As the motto Defoe was fond of citing, and which Moll Flanders quoted as 'the wise man's prayer', put it, 'Give me not poverty lest I steal.'[1] The death of her banker husband leaves her in such dire straits that she blames it for her decision to commit the first crime in her criminal career. Similarly, Defoe claimed in *Colonel Jack* that 'circumstances form'd him by necessity to be a thief'.

Yet the circumstances he appears to have had in mind were educational rather than economic. 'If he had come into the world with the advantage of education,' Defoe continued, 'and been well instructed how to improve the generous principles he had in him, what a man might he not have been.' It was ignorance rather than poverty which led Jack to become a thief, for 'He set out into the world so early, that when he began to do evil, he understood nothing of the wickedness of it.'[2] Neither Moll Flanders nor Roxana had this excuse, both being given a sound grounding in morality. They are consequently morally autonomous, choosing their own destiny. Moll makes this quite explicit when the son of her first employer seduces her, admitting that 'I rather wished for that ruin than studied to avoid it.' While she blames poverty for compelling her to begin stealing, she confesses that 'As poverty brought me into the mire, so avarice kept me in, till there was no going back.'[3] Roxana, too, tries to put the blame upon 'the Devil and that greater Devil of Poverty' which, she claims, prevailed over 'a virtuous Education and a sense of Religion'. Yet while this might conceivably condone her agreeing to become the jeweller's mistress, it scarcely excuses what Samuel Holt Monk has called 'that glance into hell, which he [Defoe] allows us when Roxana puts her maid to bed with her lover and plays the *voyeuse* while Amy is debauched'.[4]

Defoe himself, while clearly intrigued by the limitations on choice which environmental conditions dictated, in the end brought the scale down on the side of individual responsibility. He did not approve Moll Flanders's or Roxana's excuses for their deviancy, as their subsequent fates indicate.

Providence in Defoe's fictional world, therefore, is a moral force which ultimately visits retribution on sinners, though it also gives impressive rewards to those who, like Crusoe and Moll, repent. Only Roxana, whose sins are too dark and whose repentance is too late, suffers pangs of conscience in the end and has to live with remorse, albeit in the material comfort of marriage to her rich Dutch merchant. It seems that Defoe, as a committed Dissenter, saw the real world in similar terms. When dealing with business failures in *The Compleat English Tradesman* he put them down quite firmly to some personal defect, and not to adverse economic circumstances:

> There must be some failure in the tradesman, it can be no where else; either he is less sober and less frugal, less cautious of what he does, who he trusts, how he lives, and how he behaves, than tradesmen used to be; or he is less industrious, less diligent, and takes less care and pains in his business, or something is the matter.[5]

Other writers were less certain than Defoe that the world rewarded moral worth, or even that there were such direct metaphysical sanctions for morality. An anonymous adaptation of *Moll Flanders* came out in 1730 with the title *Fortune's Fickle Distribution*. Jane Barker told the story of a tradesman's daughter who married a wealthy merchant rather than the lawyer's clerk to whom she had been betrothed. Seven years later her husband went bankrupt and had to become a labourer, while she became a nurse. Meanwhile the rejected lawyer had prospered. This led her to philosophise on her fate: 'Whether this ruin proceeded from losses by sea and land to which great dealers are obnoxious [*sic*], or from the immediate hand of Heaven, for my breach of vow to my young lawyer, I know not.'[6]

What disturbed some Augustans was that the deserving did not get their just deserts, at least on this earth, but that the undeserving seemed to thrive instead. The discrepancy was brought out vividly in an allegorical satire, *Fortune's Tricks in Forty-Six*. In this curious play Reason, Justice and Merit plead with Jupiter for permission to leave the world, where they have become mere cyphers: 'There is scarce one transaction in a thousand but what abounds with absurdity: not one trial in twenty is decided without manifest partiality; not one preferment in a hundred bestow'd where worthlessness is not the apparent motive.' Reason blames Fortune for this lamentable situation, saying to her:

> 'Tis you have introduced a general dissolution of manners into the world, banish'd virtue from our senates, religion from our churches, rooted luxury in all our youth, and like weeds to land, by choking the growth of their Reason, let in a torrent of ostentation, ignorance, self-sufficiency, pride and arrogance, leaving no room in the human breast for that generous social sensation, which was designed as a counterbalance to the unavoidable disparity and subordination that must ever subsist among mankind.[7]

The notion that Fortune was upsetting the social hierarchy seemed to receive powerful confirmation from the South Sea Bubble. The ruin of many families in the collapse of the South Sea Company, and the rise of others who speculated successfully in its stock, captured the imagination of a generation. 'The world is turned upside down, topsie turvy,' remarked Charles Gildon; 'those who had plentiful fortunes are now in want, and those that were in want, have now got plentiful fortunes.' Gildon was one of the few observers who considered the upheaval to have been beneficial, as the title of his play implies, *All For the Better; or The World Turned Upside Down.*[8] Most writers held it to have been a disaster. Swift, in *The Bubble*, compared it to a turbulent sea:

There is a gulph where thousands fell,
  Here all the bold Advent'rers came,
A narrow Sound, though deep as Hell,
  'Change-Alley is the dreadful Name;

Nine times a day it ebbs and flows,
  Yet he that on the surface lyes
Without a Pilot seldom knows
  The time it falls, or when 'twill rise.

Subscribers here by thousands float,
  And jostle one another down,
Each padling in his leaky Boat,
  And here they fish for Gold and drown.[9]

The very name 'bubble' meant a confidence trick or swindle in this period, a meaning endorsed by Swift, who blamed the company's directors for the débâcle. John Trenchard and Thomas Gordon were moved to write *Cato's Letters* by the Bubble, in which they called for those responsible to be brought to justice, including corrupt politicians as well as officials of the company. 'Shall a poor pick pocket be hanged for filching away a little loose money,' they demanded, 'and wholesale thieves who rob nations of all that they have be esteemed and honoured?'[10] This rhetorical question made the equation between criminals and cabinet ministers which was to inspire a host of similar comparisons, the most celebrated being Gay's *Beggar's Opera* and Fielding's *Jonathan Wild*.

The role of Fortune in generating social mobility up and down the ladder is a major theme in Fielding's novels. He expressed his own views on the subject most directly in *Amelia*:

> The various incidents which befel a very worthy couple after their uniting in the state of matrimony will be the subject of the following history. The distresses which they waded through were some of them so exquisite, and the incidents which produced these so extraordinary, that they seemed to require not only the utmost malice, but the utmost invention, which superstition hath ever attributed to Fortune; though whether any such being interfered in the case, or, indeed, whether there be any such being in

> the universe, is a matter which I by no means presume to determine in the affirmative. To speak a bold truth, I am, after much mature deliberation, inclined to suspect that the public voice hath in all ages done much injustice to Fortune, and hath convicted her of many facts in which she had not the least concern. I question much whether we may not, by natural means, account for the success of knaves, the calamities of fools, with all the miseries which men of sense sometimes involve themselves, by quitting the directions of Prudence, and following the blind guidance of a predominant passion; in short for all the ordinary phenomena which are imputed to Fortune; whom, perhaps, men accuse with no less absurdity in life, than a bad player complains of ill luck at the game of chess.
>
> But if men are sometimes guilty of laying improper blame on this imaginary being, they are altogether as apt to make her amends by ascribing to her honours which she as little deserves. To retrieve the ill consequences of a foolish conduct, and by struggling manfully with distress to subdue it, is one of the noblest efforts of wisdom and virtue. Whoever, therefore, calls such a man fortunate, is guilty of no less impropriety in speech than he would be who should call the statuary or the poet fortunate who carved a Venus or who writ an Iliad.[11]

Although Fielding here makes men the authors of their own destinies, in his fiction Fortune intervenes to push them in the direction in which he wishes them to go. This is illustrated in miniature by the biographies of Mr Wilson in *Joseph Andrews* and the Man of the Hill in *Tom Jones*, which, so far from being digressions from the main themes of the novels, as they are often represented, present in microcosm the moral view of the world which Fielding is elaborating through the principal plots.

Mr Wilson's descent from being the son of a gentleman to a debtors' prison seems to be entirely his own fault. He chose to break the terms of his father's will in order to enjoy the estate immediately, and used it to run up extravagant debts and lead a dissipated life in London, as Parson Adams says, below the existence of a brute beast, scarce better than a vegetable. Yet the death of his father when Wilson was only sixteen also influenced his choice. Indeed, he himself stated that 'To this early introduction into life, without a guide, I impute all my future misfortunes.' His good fortune came when a lottery ticket he had purchased won a prize of £3000. Once again death providentially intervened in his affairs, this time favourably. He had sold the ticket to a wine merchant, who would never have let him benefit from it. Thus his initial reaction upon hearing the news that it had drawn a prize was to lament that it 'was only a trick of Fortune to sink me the deeper', while the acquaintance who brought the news told him: 'I was one whom Fortune could not save if she would.' However, the merchant died on the very day the lottery was drawn, and his daughter used the prize to get Mr Wilson out of jail. Eventually he married her, and they left the wine trade to live in the country. Fortune had not rewarded the worthless, for Mr Wilson learned from his experience and lived in married bliss. Like Defoe, Fielding seems to have used the words Fortune and Providence interchangeably, for when Parson Adams says to Mr Wilson: 'Fortune hath, I think, paid you all her debts in this sweet retirement,' he answers: 'I am thankful to the great Author of all things for the blessings I here enjoy.'[12]

The Man of the Hill had an even more chequered career. Born the younger son of a gentleman farmer in Somerset, he received a good education, but was led astray at Oxford without even Mr Wilson's excuse that he lacked parental guidance. Left destitute, he took to gambling in 'Fortune's temples', i.e. the casinos, for two years, during which he 'tasted all the varieties of fortune; sometimes flourishing in affluence, and at others being obliged to struggle with almost incredible difficulties. Today wallowing in luxury, and tomorrow reduced to the coarsest and most homely fare.' Fortune then intervened by bringing about a providential meeting with his father in the streets of London, and like the prodigal son he returned home.

Instead of his retreat from London to the country providing a happy ending, however, as it did for Mr Wilson, the Man of the Hill becomes a wanderer when, upon the death of his father, his elder brother inherits the estate. This makes the rest of his story less satisfactory, as though Fielding himself conceded that life did not always resolve its problems as neatly as it does in the microcosm of the novel. The continuation of the Man of the Hill's story, however, does enable him to make a direct link with the major theme of *Tom Jones*, and again it is provided by the idea of Fortune. After leaving the family estate he joined in Monmouth's rebellion, being persuaded that under James II 'the danger to which the Protestant religion was so visibly exposed' was such 'that nothing but the immediate interposition of Providence seemed capable of preserving it'. This prompts Tom Jones to inform him that the '45 rebellion was then raging in favour of the son of James II, at which the Man of the Hill expresses incredulity. He himself was captured after the battle of Sedgemoor, but Fortune took pity on him, and he escaped, to lie low until the Glorious Revolution.[13] Thus Fielding shows how the same Providence which intervenes in the affairs of nations also keeps watch over those of men.

Despite Fielding's disclaimers at the outset of the novel, it also intervenes in the lives of the Booths in *Amelia*. Initially their apparent misfortune is indeed the result of Captain Booth's allowing the predominant passion of vanity to overcome prudence. Having successfully adapted to farming after a military career, he imprudently took on an additional farm, which proved a bad bargain, and extravagantly lived above his means. He acquired a coach as a status symbol, which led other tenant farmers and 'neighbouring little squires' to dislike his social pretensions and to call him 'the Squire Farmer'. It also led him so far into debt that he fled to London to escape his creditors, who nevertheless pursued him until like Mr. Wilson he found himself in a debtors' prison. He himself blames Fortune for his predicament, saying that 'Our happiness was, perhaps, too great, for Fortune seemed to grow envious of it, and interposed one of the most cruel accidents that could have befallen us by robbing us of our dearest friend the doctor.' This alludes to the departure of Dr Harrison as tutor to a peer's son on the Grand Tour. Although Amelia's husband blames the 'want of my sage counsellor' for his misfortune, it is clear that Fielding holds Booth responsible. He is also ironical when Booth succumbs to Miss Matthews's charms by inviting the reader 'to weigh attentively the several unlucky circumstances which concurred so critically, that Fortune seemed to have used her utmost endeavours to ensnare poor Booth's constancy'.

Yet for Amelia herself Booth's predicament appears to be a genuine misfortune. As Fielding observes:

> Fortune had attacked her with almost the highest degree of her malice. She was involved in a scene of the most exquisite distress and her husband her principal comforter torn violently from her arms; yet her sorrow, however exquisite, was all soft and tender, nor was she without many consolations. Her case, however hard, was not absolutely desperate, for scare any condition of fortune can be so. Art and industry, chance and friends, have often relieved the most distressed circumstances, and converted them into opulence. In all these she had hopes on this side the grave, and perfect virtue and innocence gave her the strongest assurances on the other. . . . Hence, my worthy reader, console thyself, that however few of the other good things of life are thy lot, the best of all things, which is innocence, is always within thy own power; and, though Fortune may make thee often unhappy, she can never make thee completely and irreparably miserable without thy own consent.

In this passage Fielding does appear to be conceding that Fortune played a role, however limited, in Amelia's destiny if not in her husband's. In the end it rescues both from their predicament by the literally providential news that Amelia had been cheated of her mother's estate by the forgery of her will, and that she has at last been restored to her rightful inheritance. When Dr Harrison informs Booth of this he exclaims: 'Your sufferings are all at an end and Providence hath done you the justice at last which it will, one day or other, render to all men.' It is highly significant that the news comes immediately after Booth's conversion to Christianity. The novel concludes with Fielding observing that 'As to Booth and Amelia, Fortune seems to have made them large amends for the tricks she had played them in their youth.'[14]

This *deus ex machina* has always seemed a desperate contrivance of Fielding's to give *Amelia* a happy ending. Yet it is in keeping with all his novels that in the end virtue should triumph. It is the equivalent of Mr Wilson's winning lottery ticket and the Man of the Hill's meeting his father in London. Fielding was more aware than the next man that the world rewarded rogues and punished the worthy, and yet he seems to have craved for one in which the deserving prospered and the wicked were punished, even to the extent of collecting anecdotes about discovered murders in a pathetic attempt to prove that Providence at least brought murderers to their just ends. In his fiction he created such a world. In the short run his heroes and heroines might be exposed to all sorts of vicissitudes, but in the end they triumph. At first it seems that a dyed-in-the-wool villain like Blifil is going to get the better of Tom Jones, who, however impure in mind and body, is always pure in heart. Again Fortune initially helps Blifil, since he is providentially enabled to intercept and suppress the message from his dying mother about Jones's true parentage. At last, however, Jones's impurities having been purged in the fire of experience, during which process he learns to curb passion with prudence, he thwarts Blifil of both his estate and his intended bride.

Jones's triumph is not that of the underdog in the sense of Fortune favouring one of the lower orders in his struggle with a social superior. Fortune is not a leveller in his novels. It is vital that Tom Jones was the son of Allworthy's sister by a clergyman, rather than of Jenny Jones, so that he should be socially as well as morally worthy of marrying Sophia, a country gentleman's daughter. For all that he disapproved of Squire Western's tyrannising her over the choice of a husband, Fielding was not prepared to let her love for Tom triumph completely over the conventional view of what sort of marriage was suitable for her.

Marriage is the most obvious and ready way in which characters change their fortunes for better or for worse, for richer or for poorer. It is also the one decision in which individuals appear to have some control over their own destiny, and yet at the same time is conditioned by so many considerations outside their control. The conflict between matrimonial conventions and freedom of choice is at the heart of the early novel.

Samuel Richardson was particularly concerned with the tensions which this conflict produced in *Pamela* and above all in *Clarissa*. He is sometimes held to have been criticising traditional marriage patterns in favour of more freedom of choice, but his attitude was more complicated than that. In many ways he was very conventional, and subscribed to the view that wedlock not only united individuals but was an alliance between families. The arrangements surrounding marriage should therefore be made with respect to the interests of both. He warned on the title-page of *Clarissa* against 'the distresses that may attend the misconduct both of parents and children in relation to marriage'.

The traditional pattern of uniting families by marriage reinforced the social hierarchy, and there were quite clear conventions governing who could marry whom. It was important not to demean the family by arranging an unsuitable match. Men could marry women of inferior rank, since the wife took the husband's status. But by the double standard which prevailed it was out of the question for a woman to marry beneath her family's station in society. Richardson stressed this convention in *Pamela* when Lady Davers remonstrates with Mr B for taking a servant girl as his wife. When she asks: 'Where can the difference be between a beggar's son married by a lady, or a beggar's daughter made a gentleman's wife?' he replies as follows:

> The difference is, a man ennobles the woman he takes, be she *who* she will; and adopts her into his own rank, be it *what* it will: but a woman, though ever so nobly born, debases herself by a mean marriage, and descends from her *own* rank, to that of him she stoops to marry. . . . When the broken-fortuned peer goes into the city to marry a rich tradesman's daughter, be he duke or earl, does not his consort immediately become ennobled by his choice? And who scruples to call her duchess or countess? . . . Now, Lady Davers, do you not see a difference between *my* marrying my mother's deserving waiting-maid, with such graces of mind and person as would adorn any rank; and *your* marrying a sordid groom, whose constant train of education, conversation, and opportunities, could

> possibly give him no other merit, than that which must proceed from the vilest, lowest taste, in his sordid dignifier?[15]

For all that Fielding despised the morality of *Pamela* he accepted the conventions within which it operated. It was far more absurd for Lady Booby to consider marrying Joseph Andrews, a mere footman, than it was for Mr B to marry his maidservant.

Clarissa, by contrast, appears to be an attack upon the conventionally arranged marriage in favour of a union based on love; yet Richardson's objective was not so simple. What he was attacking was the degrading of the arranged marriage for financial considerations. The traditional use of matrimony to ally families was essentially concerned with social status. In the early eighteenth century, however, it was alleged that this convention was being abused to raise the family fortune. Brides were being put on the marriage market and sold to the highest bidders, even if they were socially inferior. In this context Clarissa is right to object to Solmes, not only on the individualistic grounds that she detests him, but also on the conventional grounds that she would demean herself by becoming his wife. The Harlowes are well-established landed gentry, a cut above the *nouveau riche* Solmes. Miss Howe sees clearly that Clarissa's family are trying to sell her when she tells her:

> You are all too rich to be happy, child. For must not each of you, by the constitutions of your family, marry to be *still* richer? People who know in what their *main* excellence consists, are not to be blamed (are they) for cultivating and improving what they think most valuable? – Is true happiness any part of your family view? – So far from it, that none of your family but yourself could be happy were they *not* rich. So let them fret on, grumble and grudge, and accumulate; and wondering what ails them that they have not happiness when they have riches, think the cause is want of more; and so go on heaping up, till Death, as greedy an accumulator as themselves, gathers them into his garner.

Ironically Lovelace, scion of an aristocratic family, is socially if not morally a much more suitable traditional match for

Clarissa. As she herself insists, 'As to the advantage of birth, that is of his side, above any man who has been found out for me.' Solmes, by contrast, was a 'prosperous upstart, mushroomed into rank'.[16]

Other Augustan authors also objected to this allegedly new and pernicious practice whereby parents negotiated marriages not for social but for purely economic considerations. A stock dramatic situation in comedies is one in which an heiress wishes to marry one suitor, usually young but impoverished, but is under pressure from her family to marry another, generally old but rich. It is inevitably resolved in the triumph of love and youth over age and riches, the only variation being the contrivances whereby this is accomplished. Abraham Langford provided a sixty-year-old suitor, Matchwood, for Harriet, aged sixteen, in *The Lover His Own Rival* (1736). Clerimont, whom she prefers, gains her by disguising himself as Matchwood and successfully tricking her drunken father into consenting to their immediate wedding, hence the title of the play. Audiences watching *The Female Advocates* (1713) got two such situations for the price of one. Captain Stanworth and Heartly were betrothed to two sisters, but after their father's death a guardian, Sir Charles Transfer, arranges marriages for them to Sir Ralph Brute and Sir Feeble Dotard. Stanworth and Heartly, needless to say, outwit Brute and Dotard. In James Miller's *The Coffee-House* (1737) a widow plans to marry her daughter to Harpie the scrivener, though she herself prefers Hartley. Hartley succeeds in gaining her with the aid of Colley Cibber, a part played by the celebrated comedian himself in the first production.

These plays by and large are not asserting the primacy of romantic love over the arranged marriage. Rather they are criticising, not the traditional pattern of matrimonial alliances, but what was quite literally a marriage market.

Comedies were generally careful not to undermine the traditional assumptions. Susannah Centlivre's *The Artifice*, for example, used the stock situation of a daughter, Olivia, who wished to marry one man, Sir John Freeman, when her father, Sir Philip Moneylove, insists on her marrying another, Freeman's brother Ned. Of course she eventually becomes Sir John's wife. The twist in the plot which enables her to do this, however, is that Sir John is the elder son, who has been disinherited by his Tory father because of his Whig principles. Olivia romantically accepts this, offering to run away with Sir John and live in poverty. 'For my part I can make purses by day and sing ballads by night,' she tells him. 'Now if you can grind knives or turn tinker I'm yours.'[17] This fate is averted when Ned marries his Dutch mistress and gives the estate to his brother, thereby removing Sir Philip's objections. Thus romantic love and matrimonial convention are reconciled in the happy ending, as they are in *Tom Jones*.

The mercenary marriage, on the other hand, was constantly criticised on the Augustan stage. Sir Timothy Careful in Henry Ward's *The Happy Lovers* typifies the parental attitude under attack when he announces bluntly:

> How happy shall I be, if I can but prevail upon my daughter to marry Mr Modish; he has four thousand a year of his own, which, with a little good management, may make 'em live extreamly happy together; but then I know my daughter detests him; but I'll make her marry him for all that, or I will never give her a shilling. . . . I'll try first what soft persuasions will do with her to make her comply, and if that won't do with her, force shall.[18]

'In a marriage made by the cold prudence of parents', declares a character in John Baillie's *The Married Coquet,* 'Hymen generally carries, instead of a lighted torch, a weighty money bag.'[19] 'They marry not but sell their daughters', declaims Horatio in *The Rival Nymphs*, 'who have regard to settlements alone, and value more their outward grandeur than their real happiness.'[20]

The mercenary marriage was to some extent seen as superseding matches based on romantic love. 'Marrying for love is quite out of fashion,' declares Sir Timothy Careful. 'I'll allow such things have been practis'd some two or three centuries ago, but now it is quite forgot.'[21] As the epilogue to James Thomson's *Edward and Eleanora* put it:

> Of old, they say, a husband was a lover:
> But, thank our stars! these foolish days are over:
> To such substantial Prudence are we come,
> We wed not heart to heart – but Plumb to Plumb.

At the same time it is also presented as a threat to the traditional pattern, and therefore subversive of the social hierarchy. This is stressed in Leonard Welsted's *The Dissembled Wanton; or My Son, Get Money*. Sir Humphrey Staple, an unscrupulous merchant, endeavours to arrange a marriage between his son Toby and Lord Severne's ward Emilia, who prefers Colonel Severne, her guardian's son. Staple explains his view of the situation to Beaufort: 'I understand the case thus – Here is a commodity to be disposed of; you, I, another are alike at liberty to bid for it, and the fairest bidder has in course, the best claim.' Beaufort ripostes: 'With your leave, Sir Humphrey, beauty is not the common merchandise, to be sold by cant and auction, or to be put up by inch of candle. That is for African slaves, not free born British ladies.' This is a double rebuke to Staple, for he had earlier offered his own daughter to Beaufort for 'fifty thousand pounds in money, or money's worth', telling him: 'My daughter is as my merchandise, and I'll not part with her upon credit; something for something and nothing for nothing, as I often say, is our family wisdom.'[22] The implication is that it was not the conventional wisdom, in which social considerations prevailed over economic advantage.

Those who criticised the mercenary marriage insisted that a couple yoked purely for financial reasons would inevitably be unhappy together. This widely held view was graphically illustrated in Hogarth's *Marriage-à-la-mode*. A model of modish or modern marriage was frequently depicted on the stage, usually amongst the people of quality at the fashionable end of town. These were portrayed living entirely separate existences, often with the wives running an extravagant social life which jeopardised their own virtue and their husbands' pockets. This stock situation was realised in such couples as Sir Thomas and Lady Willit in Gay's *The Distressed Wife*, Lord and Lady Townley in Vanbrugh's *The Provok'd Husband*, Worthy and Moderna in *Chit-Chat*, Mr and Lady [*sic*] Ombre in *The Masquerade*, Sir George and Lady Modern in *The Modern Wife*, and Lord and Lady Modeley in *The Modish Couple*. The Modeleys 'neither eat of the same dish, drink of the same bottle, nor lie in the same bed'.[23] Separate beds were regarded as the height of modernity in these comedies.

Melinda in John Baillie's *The Married Coquet* asks Sir Charles Modish: 'Do you count matrimony so gross?' He replies: 'As it is in vulgar practice, rot me, the very grossest thing in the universe. That the same sheets should for a whole night together imbibe the vapours of two creatures; which from their heterogeneous qualities must fret most exceedingly.' When she points out that 'There is such a thing as separate beds,' he declares himself 'a most passionate admirer of the quality fashion of separate beds'.[24] In *The Humours of Oxford* Victoria admits: 'My notions of life don't quite tally with the prevailing opinions of the world – I am so old fashioned as to think that by marrying a man I distinguish him from the rest of his sex, to contract the most intimate friendship with,

> To make the pleasing partner of my fortune
> And a belov'd companion for life.'

To this Clarinda replies: 'Mere poetry, perfect blank verse – companion for life! You have a mighty odd notion of life, I find, child – why, a husband nowadays is the only person that never can be one's companion for life. . . . For after the first moon, 'tis the most unfashionable thing in the world, either to eat, drink or lie together.'[25]

The point is emphasised that this allegedly new pattern of wedlock is confined to the aristocracy and upper levels of the gentry who possess town houses at the court end of town. When a character in James Miller's *The Man of Taste* asks: 'Would you have 'em perpetually at one's elbow, as if we were really yoked together?' another says: 'No, leave that to the insipid vulgar; people of taste and sensibility have a higher relish for life. Separate tables, separate apartments, separate coaches and separate pleasures – Those are the peculiar privileges of quality.'[26]

Fielding painted a dire picture of those who defied the conventions to negotiate the allegedly novel mercenary marriage in *The Modern Husband*. The marriage of Mr and Mrs Modern is entirely mercenary, to the point where the husband is prepared to prostitute his own wife for monetary gain. The point is made that such matches are the inevitable consequences of socially ambitious parents forcing their children into them when Mrs Modern protests that she was 'forced to marry . . . by the commands of my parents'.[27] A similar fate awaits Sophia if she does not stand up to the pressure of her father and even more of her aunt, for where Squire Western and his sister agree that she should marry Blifil, Di Western would have her accept the proposal of the odious Lord Fellamar, 'a nobleman of the first rank and fortune', to marry whom would be 'the highest honour' to Sophia's family. Western, however, though a stickler for the traditional arranged marriage, is not prepared to accept the modern mercenary match and refuses to sell his daughter to the peer, saying: 'I hate all lords; they are a parcel of courtiers and Hanoverians and I will have nothing to do with them.'[28] This associates the mercenary marriage with the Court values criticised by Country writers. Fielding underlines this when Mr Modern threatens his wife with returning to the country if she does not fall in with his schemes. When he mentions the country she protests: 'Racks and tortures are in that name.'[29] Colonel James and his wife in *Amelia* lead a life very similar to the Moderns. He also threatens to send her into the country until she agrees to assist him in his scheme to seduce Amelia. There are respectable characters in *The Modern Husband*, such as Mrs Bellamant and Emilia; but they are constantly pining to leave town and return to rural bliss.

Examples of happy marriages in literature occur chiefly amongst the gentry and the urban middle classes. Pamela's marriage to Mr B turns out happily once his affair with a countess ends in his conversion to Christianity. An anonymous continuation of *The History of Tom Jones* 'in his married state' shows him and Sophia enjoying wedded bliss. 'Would they but correct their depraved taste, moderate their ambition and place their happiness upon proper objects,' opines Jones, speaking of husbands and wives, 'felicity, in a married state, would not be found such a wonder, as it now seems to be, especially amongst persons of distinction and fortune.' Allworthy agrees that 'Could the wedded pair but habituate themselves, for the first year, to bear with one another's faults, they would find but little difficulty afterwards. They that begin this state of life, without jars at their setting out, arrive, within a few months, at a pitch of benevolence and affection, of which the most perfect friendship is but a faint likeness.'[30] Although Fielding himself did not follow his hero's matrimonial career, he did portray some happily married couples in his novels, including the Heartfrees in *Jonathan Wild*, the Adamses and the Wilsons in *Joseph Andrews* and, despite the husband's shortcomings, the Booths in *Amelia*.

Where matrimony among the middling sort appears in literature to be happy in comparison with the *marriage à la mode* of the upper classes, amongst the lower orders it is frequently represented as far from a union of equals. On the contrary, husbands often appear as tyrants who beat their wives. Charles Coffey's *Merry Cobbler* beats his, saying:

> He that governs a wife
> Must, like me, sincerely
> For the ease of his life
> Strap her late and early.
> This is the sov'reign pill
> If she's proud and scorning
> Cures her of every ill
> Taken night and morning.[31]

Two separate plays by Charles Johnson and Christopher Bullock, both called *The Cobbler of Preston* and both based on the induction scene in *The Taming of the Shrew*, also present their heroes as wife-beaters. The tanner in John Arthur's *The Lucky Discovery; or The Tanner of York* likewise threatens his wife with 'lawful correction'. When she asks him: 'What law is that which gives a man such privilege over women that he should use his wife like his spaniel?' she is told 'that law that gave you to me, made you my vassal; my boot, to pull on, or put off, as my ease, or pleasure, requires'.[32] Ned Ward set one of his *Nuptial Dialogues* 'between a squeamish cotting mechanick and his sluttish wife in the kitchen'. He upbraids her slovenliness thus:

> Therefore, I say, I'll have my fish well drest,
> After such manner as shall please me best,
> Or, Hussy, by this ladle, if I han't,
> I'll make you show good reason why I shan't.[33]

Literary sources therefore seem to document Professor Lawrence Stone's thesis that the eighteenth century witnessed different patterns of marriage amongst various social groups. The traditional arranged marriage was characteristic of the aristocracy, whilst among the lower orders the husband exercised despotic authority. In both the upper and lower sections of society dependants of the head of the household were treated very much as inferiors who had to submit to his will. Amongst other groups, and especially the bourgeoisie and the gentry, the period was marked, according to Stone, by the rise of affective individualism, with companionate marriages where spouses were equal, and where children were raised on more liberal principles and given more freedom of choice, especially when choosing husbands and wives. As he goes on to argue, 'Together the upper bourgeoisie and the squirearchy . . . formed the elite which not only dominated political, social and economic life in the eighteenth century, but which served as the carrier of these new cultural values in personal and family life.'

Since literature apparently illustrates Stone's thesis copiously, it is not surprising to find the eighteenth-century passages in his *The Family, Sex and Marriage* liberally sprinkled with quotations from contemporary authors. He is well aware that their works document their ideas more than any objective reality. Thus, when dealing with those which discuss marriages, he concludes that

> This literary evidence shows that there was a prolonged public argument during the late seventeenth and eighteenth centuries about a child's freedom of choice of a marriage partner, with more liberal views slowly but steadily becoming more common among authors catering both to the middling ranks of commercial and professional people, and also to the wealthy landed classes.

Only occasionally does he succumb to the temptation to use contemporary literature more directly. For instance, when dealing with 'lower middle-class circles' he falls into the trap of referring to a fictitious character as though she had been a real person: 'Defoe's Moll Flanders, who moved in these circles', he writes, soon came to the sad conclusion that 'marriages are here the consequence of politic schemes, for forming interests, carrying on business', and that love had no share or very little in the matter. After a bitter experience she decided that 'money only made a woman agreeable . . . the money was the thing'. In other words, in terms of marriage, a woman in the late seventeenth and eighteenth centuries was still regarded in these circles less as a companion or a sex object than as property, and to some extent also as a status object.

By and large, however, when dealing with practice rather than theory, Professor Stone turns to more objective sources where these are available. For the lower orders, unfortunately, there are precious few a historian can use, and he had perforce to fall back on the literature of low life. He has already conceded that this can be a travesty of reality, written for the most part by writers placed above the lowest rungs of the social ladder, whose observations often betray little first-hand knowledge and much social prejudice.[34]

Professor Trumbach, however, dealing with the family life of the aristocracy in the eighteenth century, claims that literary sources are equally biased against the upper ranks of society. As he puts it, 'Satirical depiction of aristocratic family life was so often in the eighteenth century the first means of middle-class aggression.'[35] His research on the surviving private papers of the peerage led him to conclude that the very changes which Professor Stone detected as first occurring amongst the bourgeoisie and gentry were taking place in the aristocracy also. The forty families he investigated married increasingly for love rather than for family advantage and demonstrated growing affection for their offspring.

Once again there is a conflict between the evidence of literary sources and that provided by surviving private papers. Just as Macaulay was misled by literary representations of the gentry in the late seventeenth century, to be corrected by later scholars with access to their archives, so modern historians could be led astray by the dramatic depictions of modern marriages amongst the elite at St James's into concluding that aristocratic unions were totally devoid of affection or companionship. As Trumbach has shown, less biased sources painted a rather different picture.

Most of the attacks upon the mercenary marriage were based less on sociological observations than on ideological preconceptions. They were aimed at an allegedly degenerate Court aristocracy by writers for the most part imbued with the Country attitude that courtiers were degenerate. The modish couple, like the booby squire, were more a political stereotype than a social reality. Whether or not the people of quality who frequented the court end of town in the season were really as decadent as they were represented by Country writers cannot be documented from literary sources. What they do establish is that, in Country ideology, the wheel of fortune was held to have brought to the top of society a corrupt and dissolute elite of upstarts, who were overturning the traditional marriage patterns in order to achieve their own sordid ends.

4
The City and the Country

Resolved at length, from Vice and London far,
To breathe in distant fields a purer air.
Samuel Johnson, *London* (1738)

Contrasts between the City and the Country provide a permanent theme in European literature. Dr Johnson's uncharacteristic attack upon his beloved London in the poem of that name was consciously modelled on the third satire of Juvenal, and he was pleased with the way he translated the classical satirist's criticisms of ancient Rome into Thales' censure of the English capital. Thus he turned Juvenal's observation that there was not enough iron for ploughs, because it was being made into fetters for prisoners, into a complaint that there was not enough rope for rigging ships since it was in such demand by the hangman. One must take care, therefore, not to apply the poem too literally to Augustan London. It was not true, for instance, that houses there were as prone to collapse as those in ancient Rome, though historians unaware of the neo-classical conceit could use the poem as evidence that buildings might suddenly cascade about the ears of the unwary walker in the eighteenth century.

Similarly, idyllic representations of the countryside as 'Arcadia' drew on a long tradition of pastoral literature which originated in classical antiquity. The most celebrated English contribution to the genre was Spenser's *The Shepherd's Calendar*, which John Gay burlesqued in *The Shepherd's Week*, a poem in six pastorals modelled on Theocritus' eclogues. Ambrose Philips peopled his *Pastorals* with such Arcadian shepherds as Lobbin, Cuddy and Hobbinol.

Yet in many literary works of the period Arcadia and

Rome are replaced by recognisably English countryside and a quite specific London. Augustan writers showed an appreciation of particular locations, mentioning English counties when referring to the country, and even naming wards, streets and individual buildings when dealing with sites in London. As Macaulay observed of Restoration comedy, 'The scene is laid in some place which is as well known to the audience as their own houses, in St James's Park or Hyde Park or Westminster Hall. The lawyer bustles about with his bag, between the Common Pleas and the Exchequer. The Peer calls for his carriage to go to the House of Lords on a private bill.'[1] In those few comedies where the action occurs outside London it usually takes place in a recognisable location, like the Bath of Thomas Durfey's *The Bath; or The Western Lass* or the Lichfield of George Farquhar's *The Recruiting Officer*. Early novels, too, are often located in a precise English setting, urban or rural. Thus Defoe's intimate knowledge of the seamy side of London makes the environment play an active part in *Moll Flanders*. One of the most vivid of Moll's criminal exploits is the theft of a necklace from a little girl, which takes place in 'a paved alley that goes into Bartholomew Close'. The thought of actually murdering the child even crosses Moll's mind, but fear suppresses it. She then escapes by

> another passage that goes into Long Lane, so away into Charterhouse Yard and out into St John Street; then crossing into Smithfield, went down Chick Lane, and into Field Lane, to Holborn Bridge, when, mixing with the crowd of people usually passing there, it was not possible to have been found out.[2]

Fielding had Tom Jones stay at the Bell in Gloucester, where George Whitefield's brother was landlord. Such concern for time and place give Augustan plays and novels an air of realism. Yet this can be misleading, for writers could manipulate topography for ideological purposes.

There were in fact two quite distinct Londons in Augustan literature. One was the city proper, the centre of business and commercial life, inhabited by merchants and tradesmen. The other was the court end of town, frequented by the aristocracy and gentry who visited the capital for the season. These symbolised different sets of values. William Taverner dramatised the distinction in two plays, *The Artful Husband* and *The Artful Wife*. In the first Lady Upstart observes that 'Hampshire and London are not so far asunder as the City and St James. Here we are à la mode de Paris, there they are à la mode de champagne.' In the second Sir Francis Courtal and Lady Harriet, who are residing in Westminster, show their disdain for Mrs Ruth, who lives in the city. 'The women at this end of town are hideous to her,' says Sir Francis, 'and the men Devils incarnate. She believes there's no manners, virtue or religion but within Temple Bar. . . . She'll make an excellent wife for a banker, a haberdasher of small wares, a Norwich factor or a wholesale cheesemonger.' Lady Harriet agrees:

> May I die, if she has not been praising the dear air of Moorfields, the pleasant walks of Hogsdon, the retir'd situation of Islington, and the polite inhabitants of Hackney, Clapton and Humerton; and that the gentile part of the world live in Coleman Street, Billeter Square, Mark Lane, Mincing Lane, Crouched Fryars, Tower Hill and Thames Street. . . . She can't endure the thoughts of the Mall, Hyde Park, St James's, the Bath, Tunbridge and Epsom.

Mrs Ruth for her part tells Lady Harriet:

> You may despise the citizens, but they know how to thrive and get money, as well as the people at this end of the town know how to throw it away. But when you want wherewith to supply your follies, you are glad to cringe to 'em with your jewels, plate, and estates to pawn, discharge honourable debts, as you call 'em, or supply your extravagant play and exorbitant pride.[3]

Sir Testy Dolt, a brewer in William Burnaby's *The Ladies' Visiting Day*, moved from Threadneedle Street to St James's at his wife's instigation, and rued it. 'What a pox made me leave Threadneedle Street?' he complains. 'My right vertuous wou'd have it so; she must be near St James's Park and White's chocolate house.'[4] Old Lady Languish and her daughter-in-law argue about the merits of the city as opposed to the court end of town in John Mottley's *The Widow Bewitched*. Young Lady Languish gives her opinion that standing behind a counter 'is but one degree beyond the standing in a pillory', at which her mother-in-law chides her: 'Don't you know, Madam, that the younger branches of many ancient families are bred to trade? Sir Lawrence, your husband's father, had two brothers tradesmen, who made no small figure in the City.' Young Lady Languish replies: 'I never heard of the creatures, or if I have I've forgot them: besides to be talking of making a figure in the City! What signifies what is done in the dark dirty lanes of the City?'[5]

When writers contrasted London with the country they usually juxtaposed with a rural setting not the 'dark dirty lanes of the City' but the St James's end of the town. They frequently compared the allegedly innocent diversions to be found in the countryside with the notorious assemblies, balls, coffee-houses, gambling dens, masquerades and theatres located in Westminster. Mottley's Old Lady Languish preferred simple country pastimes such as 'reading of riddles, acting of proverbs, playing at questions and commands, and moulding cockledee bread' to a masquerade, 'that midnight assembly, that scene of nonsense and debauchery'.[6] Lady Willit in John Gay's *The Distressed Wife* took a contrary view:

> Surely nothing can be more shocking than knowing the day of one's death, except knowing the day one is to be buried in the country! There to stick and to have a new suit every spring like a tree, for the benefit of the birds of the air and the beasts of the field; to be gaz'd at every Sunday at church by ploughmen and their cubs, and draw the envy of their wives and daughters.[7]

Clarinda in James Miller's *The Humours of Oxford* similarly disdained the 'West Country way of living':

> to be cooped up in an old melancholy cottage like a pullet in a pen, with nothing to do but to feed – to rise in a morning because tis light; and go to bed at night because you have no where else to go; to have no diversion but raising pies and reading weekly journals – not a soul to converse with but an old Grannum . . . not a creature to visit but the vicar's wife.

She prefers the delights of London, 'the toilet, the tea table, the park for the day; and for the evening, that noon of pleasure – operas, masquerades, assemblies, china houses, playhouse'.[8] Lady Francis in *The Masquerade* is another who cannot bear the thought of returning to Shropshire 'to raise paste and whip syllabubs instead of punting at Basset or playing parties at Picket'. She protests to her husband:

> Do I not this moment lose, do I not give up all the gay sweet politer pleasures of a Court, no dancing, no masquerading, no more assemblies, no more tallying, no more punting, no parties at play of any sort. . . . In the country . . . you and I my dear shall sit and play parties together for sixpence at picquet and yawn at one another in a cold parlour by a wood fire in a long tedious winter evening. . . . Oh the joyless, insipid, full, nauseous imagination.[9]

Most of these plays in fact are satirising those who prefer the pleasures of St James's to the pastimes of the countryside, and are by implication advocating the values of the country over the city. Pope's *Epistle to Miss Blount on her Leaving the Town* is rather more ambiguous. It appears to be sympathising with Zephalinda, who 'with sighs withdrew':

> She went, to plain-work, and to purling brooks,
> Old-fashioned halls, dull aunts, and croaking rooks;
> She went from Op'ra, park, assembly, play,
> To morning walks, and pray'rs three hours a day;
> To pass her time 'twixt reading and Bohea,
> To muse, and spill her solitary Tea,
> Or o'er cold coffee trifle with a spoon,
> Count the slow clock, and dine exact at noon;
> Divert her eyes with pictures in the fire,
> Hum half a tune, tell stories to the squire;
> Up to her godly garret after sev'n,
> There starve and pray, for that's the way to heav'n.

Yet Pope seems to have been teasing Miss Blount, for he describes himself as 'vext to be still in town'.[10] There is no such ambiguity about the similar experience of Euphelia in Dr Johnson's essays in the *Rambler*, which described a visit to her aunt in the country:

> I unhappily told my aunt in the first warmth of our embraces that I had leave to stay with her ten weeks. Six only are yet gone, and how shall I live through the remaining four? I go out and return; I pluck a flower, and throw it away; I catch an insect, and when I have examined its colours, set it at liberty; I fling a pebble into the water and see one circle spread after another. When it chances to rain, I walk in the great hall and watch the minute hand upon the dial. . . . I am confident that a thousand and a thousand ladies who affect to talk with ecstasies of the pleasures of the country, are in reality, like me, longing for the winter and wishing to be delivered from themselves by company and diversion.[11]

Zephalinda deserves more sympathy than Euphelia, for she was dragged into the country by her mother. Dr Johnson is partly mocking the idealism of the thousands of ladies who romanticise the attractions of the countryside. At the same time he was not, like Pope, vexed to be in town. On the contrary, he showed his own preference for living in London quite clearly. As Boswell observed, 'His love of London life was so strong, that he would have thought himself in exile in any other place, particularly of residing in the country.' Why then did he write an attack upon the town shortly after his arrival there? *London*, as has been noted, is a neo-classical exercise. Yet it is more than that. Boswell said of it: 'We find in Johnson's "London" the most spirited invectives against tyranny and oppression.'[12] It is indeed a political poem.

In the poem Thales, leaving Greenwich on a wherry bound for St David's, pours out his spleen against the corruptions of the capital to a friend who is bidding him farewell. London's vice and crime he attributes to a vicious and criminal court, presided over by Orgilio, one of Walpole's many literary pseudonyms. The main reason why 'A single Jail, in Alfred's golden reign / Could half the Nation's criminals contain', while under George II so many were being hanged at Tyburn that there was scarce enough rope left to rig the fleet, was that the virtuous court of Alfred set a good example, while the corrupt ministry of Walpole presided over an orgy of vice and crime. Thales declaims:

Here let those reign, whom Pensions can incite
To vote a Patriot black, a Courtier White.

This is the ideology of opposition, as is the observation

Could'st thou resign the Park and Play content,
For the fair Banks of *Severn* or of *Trent*;
There might'st thou find some elegant Retreat,
Some hireling Senator's deserted Seat;
And stretch thy Prospects o'er the smiling Land,
For less than rent the Dungeons of the Strand.

It is significant that the only locations in London actually mentioned are the Strand (twice) and Tyburn, both at the court end of the town, as was the Haymarket, where 'warbling Eunuchs fill a licens'd Stage'.[13]

John Gay wandered all over London, visiting both ends of the town, in *Trivia*. Yet while his topography betrays no particular political bias, his sociology is loaded with ideological comment. The very fact that he is giving advice on 'the art of walking the streets of London' indicates that he is not addressing persons of quality, who would not be seen dead on foot and who are conveyed in coaches and sedan chairs. Whenever these are mentioned they are rebuked:

Let Beaus their Canes with Amber tipt produce
Be theirs for empty show, but thine for use.
In gilded chariots while they loll at ease,
And lazily insure a Life's Disease;
While softer Chairs the tawdry Lord Convey
To Court, to White's, Assemblies, or the Play:
Rosie-complexion'd Health thy steps attends,
And Exercise thy lasting Youth defends.

The political implication of such observations is made clear in the lines

See, yon bright Chariot on its Harness swing,
With *Flanders* Mares, and on an arched Spring;
That wretch, to gain an Equipage and Place,
Betray'd his Sister to a lewd Embrace. . . .
This next in Court Fidelity excells,
The Publick rifles, and his Country sells.[14]

Where Johnson's criticism of the court confines *London* to the fashionable end of town, while Gay's is conveyed in those passages of *Trivia* which condemn people who do not walk but are conveyed through the streets, Alexander Pope used the environs of the city itself to attack the government in the *Dunciad*. Again, though, he does not associate the court with the business life of the capital, but with the seamier parts of the city. In the *Dunciad Variorum* it is linked with Smithfield and Bartholomew Fair, and in the *Dunciad in four books* it is identified with Moorfields and Bedlam. Pat Rogers has demonstrated how the dunces frequent districts with low or dubious associations, the resorts of criminals and whores. They play their aquatic games in the Fleet Ditch, whose 'disemboguing streams'

> Rolls the large tribute of dead dogs to Thames,
> The King of Dykes! than whom, no sluice of mud
> With deeper sable blots the silver flood.

Above all, they inhabit Grub Street, where cheap lodgings could be rented in a neighbourhood renowned for vice and crime. Besides being a real street it was also used as a collective designation to signify the gutter press. The dunces got no further west in their progress than the Strand and did not penetrate the court end of town at all; nevertheless, they succeeded in bringing 'the Smithfield muses to the ear of kings', and in so doing caused the purlieus of St James's to become identified with the most squalid districts of London.[15]

In contrast to the vicious city, the countryside was regarded as the seat of virtue. Penelope Aubin wrote about 'a French lady who lived in a cave in Wales about fourteen years undiscovered' – surely the most inaccessible of all rural retreats in the period – whose daughter said to her:

> How often have you recounted to me the miseries and dangers that attend a life led in crowded cities and noisy courts. . . . Our homely cell, indeed, is nothing like the splendid places I have heard you talk of; but then, we are not half so much exposed to the temptations you have warned me of.[16]

The idyllic innocence of the rustic farmers and agricultural workers was a commonplace of pastoral literature. Vanbrugh drew on it in his play *Aesop*, which was partly translated from Boursant. Roger, a substantial village farmer, solicits a place at court from Aesop, such as 'secretary of state or butler'. Upon being asked if he lacks anything in the country, however, he replies: 'Nothing 'fore George.' The following dialogue then ensues:

> *Aesop*: You have good drink?
> *Roger*: 'Zbud the best i' th' parish. (*singing*) And dawne it merrily goes, my lord, and dawne it merrily goes.
> *Aesop*: You eat heartily?
> *Roger*: I have a noble stomach.
> *Aesop*: You have honest neighbours?
> *Roger*: Honest? 'Zbud we are all so, the tawne round. We live like breether; when one can sarve another he does it with all his heart and guts; when he have anything that's good, we eat it together, holidays and Sundays we play at ninepins, tumble upon the grass with wholesome young maids, laugh 'till we are sleepy, then swap into bed and snore 'till we rise to breakfast.
> *Aesop*: And all this thou woud'st leave to go to Court?

He then warns Roger against the move by telling him the traditional story of the town and country mice.

Vanbrugh was a Court supporter, and in an earlier exchange with two tradesmen Aesop had justified high taxes on the grounds that 'If the king had no money, there cou'd be no army, and if there were no army, your enemies would be amongst you; one day's pillage wou'd be worse than twenty years' taxes.'[17] Yet even he subscribed to the myth of rustic innocence and bliss. Indeed, so compelling was the Country myth that many Court writers paid lip-service to it, even if they patently preferred to live in town. Ambrose Philips prefaced his *Pastorals* with the observation

> When I see a little country-dwelling advantageously situated amidst a beautiful variety of hills, meadows, fields, woods and rivulets, I feel an unspeakable sort of satisfaction, and cannot forbear wishing my kinder fortune would place me in such a sweet retirement.[18]

He nevertheless spent most of his life in Dublin and London. Matthew Green, who devoted his career to the London custom house, expressed a similar wish in *The Spleen* (1737):

> May my humble dwelling stand
> Upon some chosen spot of land;
> A pond before full to the brim,
> Where cows may cool, and geese may swim;
> Behind, a green like velvet neat.
> Soft to the eye and to the feet.[19]

This is close to the sentiments of John Pomfret's *The Choice* (1700), a very popular poem of the period:

> Near some fair Town I'd have a private seat
> Built uniform, not little nor too great.
> Better, if on a rising ground it stood
> Fields on this side, on that a neighb'ring wood . . .
> A little Garden, grateful to the Eye,
> And a cool rivulet run murmuring by,
> On whose delicious Banks a stately Row,
> Of shady Lymes, or Sycamores, shou'd grow.[20]

Green, however, was not content to live in rustic retirement. Where even Pomfret wanted to be 'near some fair Town', he was far more specific, requiring 'a farm some twenty miles from town', in order to make

> trips to town, life to amuse
> To purchase books, and hear the news,
> To see old friends, brush off the clown . . .

The customs official did not want to vegetate in the country. Country writers by contrast made a virtue out of rusticity. Robert Dodsley in *The King and the Miller of Mansfield* and its sequel *Sir John Cockle at Court* contrasted not only the virtues of the countryside with the corruption of the city but also the honesty of the miller, John Cockle, and the hypocrisy of courtiers. In one scene the king tests his honesty by disguising himself and asking Cockle to use his interest at court to get him a place, offering him a bribe for his services. The miller stoutly refuses to accept it.

In *The Seasons* James Thomson contrasted

The happiest he! who far from public rage
Deep in the vale, with a choice few retired
Drinks the pure pleasures of the rural life

with courtiers who

Wreathe the deep brow, diffuse the lying smile,
And tread the weary labyrinth of State.

The most striking contrast is between the way villagers and city-dwellers divert themselves in winter. When 'the village rouses up the fire' its inhabitants gather round to tell ghost stories or harmless jokes, steal kisses and dance, so that 'jocund fleets with them the winter-night'. Meanwhile in the city

the sons of riot flow
Down the loose stream of false inchanted joy
To swift destruction. On the rankled Soul
The gaming fury falls; and in one gulph
Of total ruin, honour, virtue, peace,
Friends, families, and fortune headlong sink.

This is not the city of the merchant and the business man, but of 'the glittering Court'.

Although *The Seasons* is set in the countryside, it was addressed to those 'who live in luxury and ease, in pomp and pride'. These were exhorted not to

Think these lost themes unworthy of your ear:
Such themes as these the rural Maro sung
To wide-imperial Rome, in the full height
Of elegance and taste, by Greece refined.
In ancient times the sacred plough employed
The kings and awful fathers of mankind;
And some, with whom compared your insect-tribes
Are but the beings of a summer's day,
Have held the scale of empire, ruled the storm
Of mighty war; then, with victorious hand,
Disdaining little delicacies, seized
The plough, and greatly independent scorned
All the vile stores corruption can bestow.

Thus even farm labour is transformed into a Country virtue in the ideological sense. This gives Thomson's description of reaping an added resonance:

> Before the ripen'd field the reapers stand
> In fair array; each by the lass he loves,
> To bear the rougher part and mitigate
> By nameless gentle offices her toil.
> At once they stoop and swell the lusty sheaves;
> While thro' their chearful band the rural talk,
> The rural scandal, and the rural jest
> Fly harmless to deceive the tedious time
> And steal unfelt the sultry hours away.[21]

Stephen Duck painted a less idyllic picture:

> The morning past, we sweat beneath the Sun;
> And but uneasily our work goes on.
> Before us we perplexing Thistles find,
> And corn blown adverse with the ruffling wind.

But then Duck had experienced the hard work of harvesting at first hand and was under no illusions about rural life being bliss. Quite the reverse, as a thresher he knew 'The Sweat, the Dust, and suffocating Smoke'.[22] The Country ideology had no charms for him, but when he was offered a place at court he took it, accepting a pension and an apartment at Kew from Queen Caroline. Not for him the moral of the town and country mice which Vanbrugh's *Aesop* had used to deter Roger from seeking preferment.

Soame Jenyns was another Court poet who found little to recommend in the country. He conceded that in the remote past country life might have been happy and

> free from wickedness and strife!
> Then each man liv'd upon his farm
> And thought and did no mortal harm . . .
> But now, whatever poets write
> 'Tis sure the case is alter'd quite,
> Virtue no more in rural plains
> Or innocence, or peace remains.

Sex and violence, political and religious discord, had disturbed rural tranquillity. Jenyns, however, expressed disinterest in them, claiming to 'equally detest the strife and usual joys of country life'. Amongst the usual joys he detested was country house hospitality. He describes with obvious distaste a dinner given by a neighbouring knight which ended with the drunken host damning all ministers and taxes. The stereotype of the booby squires, 'who hunt all day and drink all night', was thus associated with Country values in the more explicitly political effusions of Court writers.[23]

Where some Court writers disparaged the myth of rural bliss, others praised the glories of London. Daniel Defoe extolled its greatness in his *Tour through the Whole Island of Great Britain*. He was particularly impressed with the way the city had expanded in his own lifetime. Not only had the district destroyed in the fire of 1666 been rebuilt, but the urban area itself had grown. In Westminster especially 'the increase of the buildings . . . is really a kind of prodigy'. After recounting the growth of the suburbs in the north and west, including Piccadilly, Hanover Square, 'and that new city on the north side of Tyburn Road called Cavendish Square and all the streets about it', he concluded that 'This last addition is, by calculation, more in bulk than the cities of Bristol, Exeter and York, if they were all put together; all which places were, within the time mentioned, mere fields of grass, and employed only to feed cattle as other fields are.' He then enthused about the new buildings, and how many were more magnificent than any which had existed before. He was particularly lavish in his praise of St Paul's, describing it as 'beautiful, magnificent, and beyond all the modern works of its kind in Europe, St Peter's at Rome only excepted'. Even St Peter's excelled it only because it was lavishly decorated in a way which would have been inappropriate in a Protestant church.

Defoe strove to demonstrate that the two ends of the town were not distinct communities, but were connected by 'a constant communication of business'. Where before the Revolution there might have been tension between them, 'now we see the Court itself the daily instrument to encourage and increase the opulence of the City, and the City again, by its real grandeur made not a glory only, but an assistance and support to the Court'. This stress on 'a perfect good understanding between the Court and the City', which 'contributes greatly to the flourishing circumstances of both', was a direct response to the claims of Country writers that the two ends of town represented different sets of values.

They would certainly disagree with his own description of 'the Court end of the town', which was almost abjectly sycophantic:

> The king's palace, though the receptacle of all the pomp and glory of Great Britain, is really mean, in comparison of the rich furniture within; I mean the living furniture, the glorious Court of the King of Great Britain: the splendour of the nobility, the wealth and greatness of the attendants, the economy of the house, and the real grandeur of the whole royal family.[24]

This was pure Court propaganda.

So too, in many respects, was his *Journal of the Plague Year*. Indeed, Isaac Kramnick has called it 'his most enduring piece of propaganda for Walpole'.[25] Defoe paints a grim picture of London as a frightening and threatening environment, quite at odds with the optimistic bustle and energy of the city's depiction in the *Tour*. It has been claimed that this reflected the author's vision of the capital, and that 'it requires only the slightest shift in focus to see these states of mind present in the normal city as well'.[26] Yet the circumstances in which the *Journal* appeared indicate that H.F.'s vivid memoirs were meant to contrast the then healthy state of the city with the diseased condition into which it had fallen in 1665 – and might fall again if preventive measures were not taken to avert it.

The bubonic plague, absent from England for fifty-five years, broke out in the Mediterranean ports in 1720, and by 1721 was ravaging southern France. Fears that it would reach Britain from the continent led the government to make draconian contingency plans, including a Quarantine Act which empowered the authorities to seal off affected areas and to compel those suspected of being in contact with it into lazarets, death being the penalty for those who resisted. These measures were widely resented as infringements on

English liberties, and a petition from the city of London protesting against them was presented to parliament in December. Although the petition was dismissed, some of the offending clauses in the act were repealed early in 1722.[27]

Defoe, as a ministerial propagandist, devoted himself to demonstrating what the alternatives to the precautions would be if the plague arrived. In 1721 he wrote articles in *Applebee's Weekly Journal* and the *Daily Post* describing the progress of the plague in France. Then in March 1722 he published the *Journal of Plague Year*, which, as Alfred Henderson pointed out, was 'intended to be used as an aid to the administration in diverting the minds of Londoners from a possible establishment of a despotism to the more fearful horrors of the more probable invasion of pestilence and death'.[28] The very title-page reminded people what had happened 'during the *last* great visitation in 1665'. The opulent, crowded metropolis had been transformed into a nightmare ghost town. People fled in panic, which was 'a very terrible and melancholy thing to see'.[29] The court moved to Oxford, while so many left the other end of town that H.F. 'began to think there would be really none but magistrates and servants left in the City'.[30] Those who did remain suffered agonies of apprehension before the real torments of the disease, the symptoms of which are illustrated in almost morbid detail. Reason collapsed before its horrors, giving way to superstition and crazed delusions, fed by astrologers and mountebanks.

To prevent the complete collapse of order the authorities were obliged to make the most stringent regulations, shutting up shops and even houses, confining their occupants, and appointing officials to ensure that they stayed there. Notwithstanding these precautions, the mortality continued unabated, until thousands of bodies were buried in communal graves. For all his journalistic skill Defoe was conscious that 'It is impossible to say anything that is able to give a true idea of it to those who did not see it, other than this; that it was indeed *very, very, very* dreadful, and such as no tongue can express.'[31] Quite apart from the plague, the breakdown of order led to a great increase in crime, with thieves everywhere looting warehouses and shops. The economy also collapsed, leaving thousands of citizens destitute and dependent upon hastily improvised charities, without which there might have been a mass uprising.

Besides chilling the blood of his contemporaries with these horrific visions, Defoe emphasised the fact that the city had been completely unprepared for the outbreak, and he drew lessons from the experience which would be useful 'in case of the approach of a like visitation'.[32] He particularly stressed that advance precautions were vital, since preventive measures such as shutting up houses were useless once the plague had broken out. It was also pointless to segregate the healthy from the diseased, since he thought that people were contagious before the actual symptoms appeared, though in fact bubonic plague is spread by parasites and not by physical contact. Amongst his proposals, therefore, was the compulsory evacuation of the city, to break up the great crowds of people there and thus lessen the risk of mass contagion.[33] This would have required powers to be granted to the authorities just as arbitrary as those in the Quarantine Act, if not more so. The implied justification for them was that any strong preventive action by the government was preferable to the horror of another plague year.

Although Defoe's usual view of London was far more optimistic than that which he painted for propaganda purposes in the *Journal of the Plague Year*, he did not deny that the capital was a more vicious environment than a country village. Unlike opposition writers, however, he did not attribute the capital's crime to the bad example set at court. Whereas he was ambiguous on the question of whether people took to crime through choice or circumstances, other ministerial writers had no doubt that criminals chose a life of crime. Bernard Mandeville tried to make it a less attractive choice by increasing the deterrent effect of capital punishment. In his *Enquiry into the Causes of the Frequent Executions at Tyburn* he claimed they no longer deterred, owing to the carnival atmosphere in which they took place. 'All the way from Newgate to Tyburn is one continued fair,' he complained. The condemned man was given a hero's farewell, his courage kept up by alcohol and the applause of the crowd. Mandeville recommended that executions should fulfil the purpose for which they were originally intended. Those condemned to death should be kept in solitary confinement on a diet of bread and water. This would induce proper dread of the gallows, which should be erected inside the prison and not at a place of popular resort. Those let in to witness the hanging in such a sombre atmosphere would be struck into similar dread by the sight of a sober convict meeting a proper end. Where many condemned criminals had the death penalty commuted to transportation to the colonies, Mandeville favoured instead exchanging them for English sailors in captivity 'on the Coast of Barbary', because the deterrent of being transported had been weakened by the fact that many found their way back to England.[34]

Mandeville typically turned vice to the advantage of the city. Although he wrote in the preface to *The Fable of the Bees* that 'No body can doubt but before the stinking Streets of London, I would esteem a fragrant Garden, or a shady Grove in the Country,' the whole work is such a celebration of the city that it is impossible to take this seriously. Like Yorkshiremen, Mandeville appreciated that where there's muck there's brass. He contrives to make the very stink in the streets advantageous, observing that

> There are, I believe, few People in London, of those that are at any time forc'd to go a foot, but what could wish the Streets of it much cleaner than generally they are; whilst they regard nothing but their own Cloaths and private Conveniency; but when once they come to consider, that what offends them is the result of the Plenty, great Traffick and Opulency of that mighty City, if they have any Concern in its Welfare, they will hardly ever wish to see the Streets of it less dirty.

This observation is a metaphor for the paradox Mandeville is advocating, summed up in the subtitle of the work, *Private Vices, Publick Benefits.* The very vices of London contributed to its greatness. It could not be both great and virtuous. The choice was between the simple economy of a virtuous village and the expanding economy of a vicious city. Any other combination was chimerical:

> T' enjoy the World's Conveniences,
> Be fam'd in War, yet live at ease

> Without great Vices, is a vain
> Eutopia seated in the Brain.

He demonstrated the truth of his paradox by claiming that Luxury

> Employ'd a Million of the Poor,
> And odious Pride a Million more.

It was particularly the luxury and pride of the people at the top of society, the inhabitants of the St James's end of the town, whose demand for buildings, furniture, equipages and clothes stimulated the urban economy.[35]

In this debate on the respective merits of the City and the Country there can be little doubt that Fielding preferred rural values. As Max Byrd has observed, 'In all of his fiction the great city appears as corrupt and corrupting, the country for all its flaws as wholesome.'[36] All levels of London society, from the *beau monde* of Lady Bellaston to the underworld of Jonathan Wild, are inhabited by beasts of prey who feed off the misfortunes of their fellow-citizens. The Man of the Hill in *Tom Jones* and Mr Wilson in *Joseph Andrews* both find London a vicious place by bitter experience. *Amelia* is in many ways the most sombre of Fielding's novels because much of its action takes place there.

Yet the main target of Fielding's criticism, as with other attacks inspired by Country ideology, was not the city proper, the business part of the capital, but the St James's end of the town. *The Modern Husband* is located there, as Mr Bellamant stresses when he says: 'He would be as much laughed at, who preferred his love to his interest, at this end of the town, as he who preferred his honesty to his interest at the other.'[37] Mr Wilson and the Man of the Hill both experience their downfalls in the fleshpots of the West End. Tom Jones makes his way there after his arrival in London, by a route across town which provides Fielding with an opportunity to indulge in some very heavy sarcasm upon its inhabitants:

> Jones, as well as Partridge was an entire stranger in London; and as he happened to arrive first in a quarter of the town, the inhabitants of which have very little intercourse with the householders of Hanover or Grosvenor Square (for he

> entered through Gray's-Inn Lane) so he rambled about some time, before he could even find his way to those happy mansions, where Fortune segregates from the vulgar, those magnanimous heroes, the descendants of ancient Britons, Saxons, or Danes, whose ancestors being born in better days, by sundry kinds of merit, have entailed riches and honour of their posterity.

The denizens of 'those terrestrial Elysian fields' are in fact cynical and materialistic debauchees, as Jones soon discovers.[38] He falls for the charms of Lady Bellaston after attending a masquerade at the Haymarket opera house.

The Haymarket also features in *Amelia*, while the heroine is invited to a masquerade at Ranelagh with potentially even more fateful results than Jones's liaison with Lady Bellaston. Mrs Atkinson fortunately tells her in time that the noble lord who invited her there had used a similar invitation to debauch herself and destroy her first marriage. Amelia finds herself within easy reach of the diversions at the St James's end of town because her own husband, to evade his creditors, takes lodgings in Spring Gardens, within the verge of the court, which gave debtors a tenuous sanctuary. Once a week Booth leaves their apartment to walk in Green Park.

Like Jones, Booth finds that the purlieus of Piccadilly are infested with predatory humans. Colonel James, as well as the noble peer, plots to seduce Amelia. Captain Trent had set himself up in 'a house at the polite end of town' by prostituting his own wife to the licentious lord. Although Booth rarely ventures out, and then endeavours to remain close to Green Park, he falls victim to the temptations of the district. In the King's Arms he loses heavily to two sharpers who lived in Grosvenor Square. The furthest he ventured from Spring Gardens were Hyde Park, where he fought the duel with Colonel James; Monmouth Street, where he apprehended the maid, Betty, who had stolen some of Amelia's clothes; and Gray's Inn Lane, where he was twice confined after being arrested. Although Gray's Inn Lane, as Tom Jones had discovered, was remote from the fashionable end of town, it was equally remote from the business district of the city.

Neither Tom Jones nor the Booths therefore came close to Heartfree's jewellery shop. Although Fielding does not mention its address, it is clear that it is in an unfashionable part of the town. When Jonathan Wild and Count la Ruse plot to cheat Heartfree they take 'a handsome house ready furnished in one of the new streets', i.e. around Hanover Square. By fitting it out with servants and equipage 'and all the insignia of a large estate' they are able to convince the jeweller that the count is creditworthy. When Heartfree discovers that he has been duped by the count Wild expostulates with him: 'I thought the part of the town where he lived sufficient caution not to trust him.'[39] In *Jonathan Wild* Fielding associated the West End with the crime and vice of his 'hero', and the city with the solid virtues of the Heartfrees.

The contrasts between the Country and the City made by Augustan writers were not just exercises in the timeless clash between rural and urban values, but were reflections of their own experience. Raymond Williams has shown how literary treatments of the two themes responded to changes in economic circumstances over four centuries in his brilliant work *The Country and the City*. Even in the more restricted time-scale of this study one can detect a similar response.

The great chorus of complaint about the corrupting effects of luxury which is a feature of the period 1700-60[40] coincided with an increase in agricultural production which outstripped a slight increase in population. It has been estimated that the yields of wheat, barley and oats increased from 14,770,000 quarters in 1700 to 16,468,000 by 1760. Agricultural production overall increased from £20,000,000 to £28,900,000 in 1700 prices over the same period.[41] The most authoritative investigation of demographic trends in the Augustan period has concluded that the growth in population which set in during the sixteenth century came to a halt around the middle of the seventeenth. Between 1656 and 1686 the number of people in England and Wales actually declined from 5,281,347 to 4,864,762. Thereafter a slow increase occurred, though it was not until 1721 that the total surpassed that of 1656. Moreover, an increase in the death rate in the late 1720s again reduced the population to a level below that of James II's reign. By 1731 the figure was 5,263,374. From then on the demographic trend went up unchecked, to reach 5,772,415 at mid-century.[42] Even so, this growth was modest compared with the population explosion which occurred in the second half of the eighteenth century.

One result of bountiful agricultural produce and no great increase in the number of mouths to feed, even though they might have eaten more, was a fall in food prices. In the first half of the eighteenth century wheat prices in England declined by about 16 per cent. This created a depression in some rural areas producing food for the market, and at the same time improved real incomes in town. Many landlords had difficulties finding tenants for their farms and often had to write off arrears of rents to cushion tenant farmers against the low prices which their products received. Farmers tried to cut costs by improving productivity, so that the progress of the so-called agricultural revolution was spurred on by adversity and a squeeze on profit margins rather than by the promise of high returns on capital investments. Meanwhile town-dwellers had a margin of income over expenditure on mere subsistence which they spent on what had previously been regarded as luxury goods. Even the poorest had a surplus to spend on gin, and it was in these years that the orgy of gin-drinking in London reached its height. Significantly, there does not appear to have been any noticeable increase in the consumption of spirituous liquors in rural areas. More affluent inhabitants of London and other towns could afford a range of consumer goods from cheap cutlery and crockery to fine clothes, more servants, new furnishings, coaches and better accommodation. Demand for such products stimulated growth in manufacturing towns such as Stoke-on-Trent, Sheffield and Birmingham. Increased affluence also enabled citizens to spend on leisure, stimulating activities to cater for it, such as the development of the spa towns of Bath, Scarborough and Tunbridge Wells, other urban centres which benefited from the improved terms of trade between town and country. These centres experienced a building boom in these years which has led one historian to talk in terms of an urban renaissance in the period.[43] Thus the contrast between rural and urban economies was particularly acute at the very time that literature was much concerned with the distinction between the Country and the City.

At the same time Augustan writers were not merely reflecting these changes; they were also responding to them ideologically. It was axiomatic in this period that the state of the economy was influenced by constitutional and political considerations. This equation was vividly symbolised in the slogan 'popery and wooden shoes', an equation which propagandists for the Protestant succession regularly exploited. It summed up the argument that Roman Catholicism went hand in glove with absolutism, and that under Catholic regimes the people were poverty-stricken. By contrast, commerce was held to prosper where liberty prevailed. As *A Tract of the National Interest* put it in 1757:

> Riches, trade and commerce are nowhere to be found but in the regions of freedom, where the lives and properties of the subjects are secured by wholesome laws. Nowhere else, in no other soil can they grow or subsist: oppression and slavery being weeds the most obnoxious and ever deemed the greatest enemies to industry, art and science.[44]

This argument pervades Richard Glover's poem *London; or The Progress of Commerce*, which versifies a potted history of the goddess from her birth, the result of a liaison between Neptune and Phoenice, to her arrival in England around 1650. Commerce had been forced to move constantly over the centuries from the Mediterranean to the North Sea, and finally to London, in order to escape tyranny. She was welcomed by the Rump, a liberal government in Glover's eyes, but threatened by the tyrant Cromwell.

Glover's poem was published in 1738, the same year as Johnson's *London*, but unlike that Juvenalian condemnation of the capital, it extols the 'illustrious City'. Commerce is reported to be

> pleased with thee,
> Thou nurse of arts, and thy industrious race;
> Pleas'd with their candid manners, with their free
> Sagacious converse, to inquiry led,
> And zeal for knowledge, hence the opening mind
> Resigns its errours, and unseals the eye
> Of blind opinion; Merit hence is heard
> Amidst its blushes, dawning arts arise

The gloomy clouds, which ignorance or fear
Spread o'er the paths of virtue, are dispell'd
Servility retires and every heart
With public cares is warm'd.

Despite these differences, Glover shares with Johnson an essentially Country attitude towards London. Although Commerce has made her seat there, he observes that

London late hath seen
(Thy lov'd, thy last retreat) desponding care
O'ercloud thy brow.

The reason is that the Court is not protecting her. On the contrary, it is threatening her prosperity, by not defending her interests abroad, especially against Spanish depredations, and by menacing them at home, for instance with a standing army, the maintenance of which had always been hostile to trade. Glover advocated Country policies to rescue Commerce from her plight. The navy should be employed, as Blake's was by the Rump, to challenge threats to English trade from foreigners. The army should be disbanded, so it could not be used by a potential Cromwell. Instead there should be a citizen militia, such as the trained bands which saved the city from advancing Royalist forces at Newbury in the Civil War. Were these policies to be implemented, then

liberty, security and fame
Shall dwell for ever on our chosen plains.[45]

Literary treatments of the City and the Country, therefore, document the ideological conflict between Court and Country. Court writers defended the government's economic role. They denied that the regime was hostile to commerce, insisting that it fostered its growth. They celebrated the government's connections with the financial world of London and disparaged the countryside for being backward and resistant to progress. Country writers attacked not the city proper but the court end of town. They held it to be responsible for upholding corrupt values which were contaminating the city and even poisoning the countryside, previously the domain of liberty and virtue.

5

Henry Fielding and the Historian

It is by falling into Fiction therefore, that we generally offend against this Rule, of deserting Probability, which the Historian seldom if ever quits, till he forsakes his Character, and commences a Writer of Romance.

Henry Fielding, *Tom Jones* (1749)

Henry Fielding's works are so often quarried by historians for illustrative materials that they present a prime instance of the advantages and disadvantages of using imaginative literature as a prime historical source. Because the fictitious world which he created in his novels is so vivid, he is widely regarded as a social realist. 'His work gives a peculiar impression of solidity and reality,' observed Sir Leslie Stephen.

> We have the conviction that the man has given an absolutely faithful portrait of all that came within his sphere of vision. He has drawn the men and women of his land so faithfully that we learn more from him of the true character of his contemporaries than we learn even from a direct observation of the men themselves. An accurate picture of eighteenth-century society may of course be constructed from the memoirs and letters and the various annals of the time. . . . But in Fielding's novels we find the work already done to our hands; the essential fact is presented to us in a social picture.

A. R. Humphreys agrees that Fielding created 'not merely diversions but accurate panoramas of something real, a permanent furnishing of the mind with impressions adequate to the large subject of Hanoverian national life'.[1]

Fielding's apparent realism can, however, be deceptive. As with other Augustan writers, he observed reality through ideological spectacles. Before citing his work as evidence, therefore, the historian needs to allow for this bias. This chapter consequently seeks to establish his ideology before examining his observations on social structure in its light.

Bertrand Goldgar rightly points out that 'Those who regard the literary figures opposed to Walpole as motivated by fixed principles or operating from a common ideology . . . have great difficulty with the career of Henry Fielding.'[2] Although Fielding came to be associated with George Lyttelton in the 1730s, he cannot be ascribed comfortably to the ranks of the opposition during that decade. Even the plays which he produced about this time, and which seem to be most clearly directed against the Great Man and his ministry, are not unequivocally Country in their orientation.

Many literary critics regard four plays which were produced between 1731 and 1737 as opposition pieces: *The Welsh Opera*, *Pasquin*, *The Historical Register for the year 1736* and *Eurydice Hissed*. Certainly the Court is criticised in them all. *The Welsh Opera*, which Fielding renamed *The Grub Street Opera*, concerns a household headed by Sir Owen Apshinken, his domineering wife, and a corrupt butler, Robin, who had purloined silver spoons, glasses and beer for his own advantage. These characters are clearly recognisable as the king and queen and Walpole. *Pasquin* has a sequence about an election in a parliamentary borough, where 'the candidates on the Court side are my Lord Place and Colonel Promise, the Country candidates are Sir Henry Fox-chase and Squire Tankard'. Place and Promise attempt to secure their elections by downright bribery and offers of preferment at court. In *The Historical Register* five politicians display their hopeless incompetence in all affairs of state except the raising of fresh taxes, while a character Quidam, whom everybody recognised as Walpole, blatantly bribes his opponents. The prime minister also appears as Pillage in *Eurydice Hissed*. Pillage, the manager of a playhouse, is trying to secure a favourable reception for a play by packing the audience with his cronies, since he cannot get a single honest man to promise his applause. Unfortunately even his friends desert him during the performance, and the play is damned. Although it appeared four years after the event this was, in Lord Egmont's words, 'an allegory on the loss of the Excise bill'.[3]

And yet the first three at least of these plays also carry reflections on the opposition. *The Grub Street Opera* has an air with these words:

> The worn-out rake at pleasure rails,
> And cries, 'tis all idle and fleeting;
> At Court, the man whose interest fails,
> Cries, All is corruption and cheating:
> But would you know
> Whence both these flow;
> Though so much they pretend to abhor 'em?
> That rails at Court,
> This at love's sport,
> Because they are neither fit for 'em.

It also includes William the coachman, 'enemy to Robin', who is obviously Pulteney. He is accused of having stolen curtains to make a waistcoat, and buckles to sell to the son of the household for his shoes. Owen, the son, presumably intended to represent the Prince of Wales, is a despicable womaniser who forges the handwriting of two letters, an action on which the plot revolves. Parson Puzzletext found it 'a difficult matter to determine which deserves to be hanged most' and concluded that 'If Robin the butler hath cheated more than other people, I see no other reason for it, but because he hath had more opportunity to cheat.'[4] The Country candidates in *Pasquin* are as guilty of bribery as their opponents, Sir Harry buying vast quantities of wine, clothing and bricks from the local tradesmen when making interest. Besides the inept politicians in *The Historical Register* there are four patriots: a 'noisy patriot who drinks and roars for his Country and never does either good or harm in it'; a cautious patriot; a self-interested patriot, who clamours for war because he is a sword-cutler; and an indolent patriot.[5] All allow themselves to be bribed by Quidam.

None of these works, therefore, can be described as opposition plays pure and simple. Fielding is criticising both Court and Country in them. His targets are not just the corrupt politicians either, but the venal burgesses who shout

'Liberty and property and no excise' in *Pasquin*, and the general corruption of the age in *The Historical Register*, which depicts an auction where the auctioneer can sell 'a most curious remnant of political honesty' for only five pounds and cannot get anyone to bid for 'a most delicate piece of Patriotism', whereas 'a very considerable quantity of interest at Court' sells for £1000.[6] Only *Eurydice Hissed* is an unqualified attack upon Walpole.

After Walpole's fall in 1742 the opposition was demoralised and divided by the subsequent realignments. As Maurice Goldsmith concluded from a survey of the literary response to these events:

> The ideological consequences of Walpole's decline and fall were firstly, disillusionment – some of those who had been true patriots of the Country party lost their faith: secondly, cynicism – especially with regard to the motives of those who might aspire to office . . . thirdly, scepticism – both about the doctrines of the Country ideology and about the possibility of a virtuous, patriotic government doing away with 'influence' or 'corruption'.[7]

Among the cynical was Henry Fielding. He is usually said to have changed his politics at about this time, and to have gone over from opposition to government, having become disillusioned with the motives of Country politicians. According to Pat Rogers, there was an even more compelling motive for the transition: 'He changed sides, it appears, less on account of ideology than in order to pay his bills.'[8]

Indeed, in many ways he did not have to change his views at all. As we have seen, there is criticism of both Court and Country in his 'political' plays, and he continued to censure both. *The Opposition: A Vision* was a swingeing attack upon the patriots published at the very end of 1741, while *Jonathan Wild the Great*, much of which was written during the last year of Walpole's ministry, though it did not appear until 1743, was an even more rigorous onslaught on the Court. Between the two he produced *Joseph Andrews*, which, like his plays, wished a plague on both houses.

Nevertheless, the ferocity of *The Opposition: A Vision*, which even mentions Walpole favourably, is so unexpected after his previous political sorties that it cannot merely be explained by his impecuniousness, or explained away by reconciling it with his constant attitude towards politics and politicians. He depicts the opposition as passengers in a wagon who disagree which direction it should take, while it has become bogged down in filth and cannot be made to budge by the asses which are trying to pull it along. One of the passengers complains that he was bespattered with mud by the last motion which the wagon made, which indicated that Fielding considered the opposition had lost all sense of direction, and had consequently ground to a halt, when it lost a motion of censure against Walpole in February 1741.

The motion, which called upon the king to dismiss the prime minister and not to employ him again, had in fact been a fiasco. It was completely mishandled in the House of Commons by Samuel Sandys, who moved it, and by William Pulteney, who seconded it. They did not properly consult their supporters to organise it, and when it was raised in parliament many of Walpole's opponents considered it to be too extreme. Tories and even some Country Whigs demonstrated their displeasure with it by not voting at all, while a few even voted against the motion, so that Walpole easily defeated it. It seemed to many that a great opportunity for which they had waited years had been lost by the total disorganisation of the opposition. Among them apparently was Fielding, who stopped contributing to the *Champion* soon if not immediately afterwards. In *The Opposition: A Vision* he vented his spleen on the failure of the 'patriots' to unite on this issue, attributing it partly to the different politics of the Tories and Whigs who made up the Country coalition, and partly to the motives of their leaders. Thus he noted that some of the passengers in the wagon wore white roses, others wore red roses, while several wore no roses at all. This alludes to the Jacobites, Hanoverians and republicans who allegedly made up the rank and file of the opposition. As for the leaders, while pretending to be making their way forward in the Country interest, they were in reality concerned with replacing Walpole by themselves in order to gratify naked ambition. Thus the wagon is turned towards St James's when fresh Cornish and Scottish asses are harnessed to it. This alludes to the results of the general election of 1741, which improved the position of the Country coalition, but, ironically for 'patriots', only by the suspect use of influence in the narrow constituencies of Cornwall and Scotland. Reinforced by members from those parts of the realm, the 'patriots' head towards St James's, but then find the way blocked by a coach and six in which rides the bluff and genial figure of Walpole.

The asses in Fielding's *Vision* he identified as those writers who had borne the heat and burden of the day for the opposition only to find themselves betrayed by its leaders. Among them he saw himself as the leanest and most worn ass of all. The opposition leaders only intended to feed them on thistles anyway, whereas Walpole takes pity upon them and turns them into a meadow where they can munch lush grass. By this Fielding virtually admitted that he preferred the fruits of patronage to the thistles of opposition. His justification was that the Country leaders were hypocrites who jumped on the opposition bandwagon to advance themselves. In his eyes hypocrisy was the most deadly of all sins. As he put it in the preface to his *Miscellanies*:

> In my Essay on the Knowledge of the characters of men I have endeavoured to expose a . . . great Evil, namely, Hypocrisy; the Bane of all Virtue, Morality, and Goodness. . . . I believe a little Reflection will convince us, that most mischiefs (especially those which fall on the worthiest part of mankind) owe their original to this detestable vice.[9]

'Of True Greatness', one of the poems in the collection, argued that it was not to be equated with wordly reputation but with goodness. The contrast between wordly greatness and goodness was most sharply made in the third volume of the *Miscellanies* (*The Life of Mr Jonathan Wild the Great*). 'Indeed,' Fielding observed of the totally unscrupulous gang leader,

> while GREATNESS consists in power, pride, insolence, and doing mischief to mankind – to speak out – while a GREAT MAN and a great rogue are synonymous terms, so long shall Wild stand unrivalled on the pinnacle of GREATNESS.

Given Fielding's views on hypocrites, it is not surprising to find that 'The character which he [Wild] most valued himself upon, and which he principally honoured in others was that of hypocrisy.'[10]

It is usual to draw a parallel between Wild and Walpole, who was generally referred to as the 'Great Man'. Certainly the equation of criminals and cabinet ministers is as implicit in the novel as it is in Gay's *Beggar's Opera*. It is often made quite explicit, as when Wild asserts that 'In civil life, doubtless, the same genius, the same endowments, have often composed the statesman and the prig: for so we call what the vulgar name a thief,' and when Fielding notes how the thieves 'have the words honesty, honour and friendship as often in their mouths as any other men', which 'may appear strange to some, but those who have lived long in cities, courts, jails, or such places, will perhaps be able to solve the seeming absurdity'.

Wild undoubtedly served as a Walpole figure, but during his stay in Newgate he also appears to symbolise Pulteney, or some other patriot who benefited from the prime minister's fall. Upon his arrival there he finds one Roger Johnson, 'a very Great Man' who 'had long been at the head of all the prigs in Newgate'. Wild makes a party against him by claiming that he had violated the liberties of Newgate, until the prison 'resounded with WILD for ever, JOHNSON for ever. And the poor debtors re-echoed the liberties of Newgate, which, in the cant language, signifies plunder, as loudly as the thieves themselves.'[11] When Wild eventually triumphed he refused to share the booty among the prisoners, but kept it for himself, making specious excuses similar to those which Pulteney had made for not rewarding all his followers when he finally overcame Walpole.

Corrupt courtiers and hypocritical patriots are both reproached in *Joseph Andrews* too. Beau Didapper, one of the more contemptible characters in the novel, is associated with the court, for 'tho' he was born to an immense Fortune, he chose, for the pitiful and dirty Consideration of a Place of little consequence, to depend entirely on the Will of a Fellow, whom they call a Great-Man'. The odious Bellarmine in the 'History of Leonora' admits that 'Before I had a Place, I was in the Country Interest, he, he, he! but for myself, I would see the dirty Island at the bottom of the sea, rather than wear a single rag of English work about me.' He is thus discredited by being associated with William Pulteney and other 'patriots' who betrayed the Country interest by accepting places on Walpole's fall. Pulteney and his colleagues are also rebuked in the passage where Parson Adams rescues Fanny from a ravisher, for before she recognises him she 'began to fear as great an Enemy in her Deliverer. . . . She suspected he had used her as some very honest Men have used their Country; and had rescued her out of the hands of one Rifler, in order to rifle her himself.'[12]

Adams, of course, is a model of exemplary behaviour, and in the chapter 'wherein that gentleman appears in a political light', although Country politicians are again displayed as broken reeds, he endorses true patriot principles. Fielding himself was to enlarge on that theme in a weekly newspaper, *The True Patriot*, which appeared between November 1745 and June 1746. Two of the numbers actually contained letters purporting to come from Parson Adams. In one he blamed the early successes of the Jacobite rebellion, against which the paper was directed, upon the luxury and vice which had overwhelmed the nation and were now being punished by Providence.

It was during the course of writing *The True Patriot* that Fielding was finally reconciled to the ministry. He began by dissociating the paper from self-styled 'patriots' who had used the Country coalition for their own ends:

> We have now Men among us, who have stiled themselves Patriots, while they have pushed their own Preferment and the Ruin of their Enemies at the manifest Hazard of the Ruin of their Country. . . . This Paper is not writ on the Principles, or with the Purposes of modern Patriotism.

He even observed in no. 14, for 28 January to 4 February 1746, that 'Ministers of State . . . are generally the Worst and Wickedest of Men.' But only three issues later he was describing the ministry as

> that glorious Body of Men who have shown that the highest

> Dignity and Property in this Kingdom are accompany'd with the highest Honour; and that the Administration is in the Hands of Men who esteem Power and Preferment of no Value any longer than they can be preferred with a strict Adherence to the True Interest of the Country.

What had happened in the interim to produce this *volte-face* was that the Duke of Newcastle, his half-brother Henry Pelham, and most of their ministerial colleagues had forced the king to choose once and for all between their ministry and the counsels of the Earls of Bath and Granville, as the former 'patriots' Pulteney and Carteret were by then titled. The showdown took the form of a mass resignation of the Pelhamites, an abortive attempt to form a ministry led by the two earls, which lasted two days, and the reinstatement of their rivals on their own terms. Fielding appears to have believed quite genuinely that this bold gesture was a remarkable instance of statesmanship, one which showed that the Pelhams and their colleagues were the true patriots his paper supported. Where he was heavily sarcastic about the two-day ministry, he extolled the virtues of the two brothers not only in the leading article of no. 17 but also in the column headed 'The Political History of Great Britain', which claimed that

> The Administration of Affairs is now in the Hands of Men who have given such Proofs of their Integrity, that have at once convinced us we are free Men, and may depend on being so under their Protection. It is indeed the rare Blessing of the Public, in the present Age, to be convinced that their Friends are in Power; that the greatest Men in the Kingdom are at the same time the honestest; that the very Person to whose councils it is to be attributed, that the Pretender hath not been long since in Possession of this City, is at the Head of the Ministry; and that the greatest Enemies of the People are disabled from any longer hurting or oppressing them. Indeed it is now known in our streets, to whom we owe the Preservation of this Kingdom, by the timely bringing our Troops from Flanders, and who they were who opposed and delayed that measure.
>
> It is now therefore that Opposition is really and truly

> Faction; that the Names of a Patriot and Courtier are not only compatible, but necessarily conjoined; and that none can be any longer Enemies to the Ministry, without being so to the Public.[13]

Although Fielding considered the opposition to be insignificant when he was writing *The True Patriot*, during the general election of 1747 he thought it worthy of refutation in a pamphlet he wrote in support of the ministry's electoral campaign, *A Dialogue between a Gentleman of London, Agent for Two Court Candidates, and an Honest Alderman of the Country Party*. The whole aim of the pamphlet was to denigrate the Country party, 'as it is absurdly called', as an unholy alliance of Jacobites and discontented Whigs.[14] Despite the fact that the failure of the '45 rendered threadbare the old charge that the Tories were Jacobites, Fielding reiterated it rather tediously in the *Jacobite's Journal*, which appeared weekly between December 1747 and November 1748. This was the nearest he ever got to becoming a ministerial hack.

It was at about this time that he became High Steward to the Warden of the New Forest, John Russell, fourth Duke of Bedford. Bedford was also a Secretary of State, and his patronage doubtless helped to obtain for Fielding his positions as a commissioner of the peace for both Middlesex and Westminster. How far this association with the duke contributed to his defence of the ministry in print is difficult to establish. Certainly contemporary critics accused him of having sold out to the government. As we have seen, however, Fielding was converted to the Pelhams during the crises of the Jacobite rebellion and their showdown with the king in 1746, while he did not apparently receive any favours from Bedford before 1747. Unless fresh evidence establishes that he benefited from his association with the duke while he was writing *The True Patriot*, therefore, he should be acquitted of the charge that he was bought off by the ministry. It seems more likely that his appointments were a reward for services rendered rather than the price of his independence.

At all events, in spite of his writings on behalf of the ministers, Fielding never altogether dropped his former Country stance. On the contrary, it remained basic to his political philosophy, being implicit throughout *Tom Jones* and *Amelia*. In the latter novel he made it absolutely explicit with the chapter on 'Matters Political' (XI, 2). Dr Harrison, hoping to renew Booth's full commission in the army, waited on a nobleman to request his intercession with the ministers 'at that time', the novel being set in Walpole's heyday. The peer agreed to do so only if the clergyman would support the candidature of a Colonel Trompington, who was standing for mayor in his town. Harrison declined, having already undertaken to support Trompington's opponent, Mr Fairfield. Moreover, this was far from being the only consideration, for, as he tells the peer, 'I should do so if I was acquainted with both the gentlemen only by reputation; the one being a neighbouring gentleman of a very large estate, a very sober and sensible man, of known probity and attachment to the true interest of his country; the other is a mere stranger, a boy, a soldier of fortune, and, as far as I can discern from the little conversation I have had with him, of a very shallow capacity, and no education.' The conversation then developed from a consideration of the individual merits of Booth, Trompington and Fairfield to the question of qualifications for office in general. 'Do you think it is possible', the peer asked, 'to provide for all men of merit?' To this the Doctor replied that it would be easy if those who had none were not preferred, a suggestion dismissed as utopian by the peer. When Harrison defended it on the grounds that in classical antiquity there were periods when merit was rewarded in Greece and Rome, the peer agreed, but insisted that 'all those notions are obsolete and long since exploded'. England was now 'as corrupt a nation as ever existed under the sun', and it was impossible to govern it by strict principles of honesty and morality. Even religion was no longer a consideration in the conduct of politicians. This so shocked Dr Harrison that he launched into a lecture on the ill effects of denying men of merit preferment and giving it to those who did not deserve it. It was unjust to individuals and to the public, and tended to destroy all virtue and all ability in a people, and would in the end create discontent and grumbling. 'And do you really think', the nobleman riposted, 'that any minister could support himself in this country upon such principles as you recommend?' In reply Harrison outlined a programme whereby governments could be supported on his principles. If a minister would

> consider the true interest of his country, and then only in great and national points; if he will engage his country in neither alliances nor quarrels but where it is really interested; if he will raise no money but what is wanted, nor employ any civil or military officers but what are useful, and place in these employments men of the highest integrity, and of the greatest abilities; if he will employ some few of his hours to advance our trade, and some few more to regulate our domestic government; if he would do all this, my lord, I will answer for it, he shall either have no opposition to baffle, or he shall baffle it by a fair appeal to his conduct.[15]

Dr Harrison's manifesto encapsulated the political creed of Henry Fielding. It is essentially a Country creed. Fielding may have persuaded himself that the Pelham ministry came up to his high ideals, though there is the uneasy feeling that he compromised them. Yet to the end he remained a moralist, about politics as well as society. Ideally, good government should reward merit. In reality most governments promoted the undeserving. His appreciation of the tension between the ideal and the real was to make him a great political as well as social satirist.

Fielding's view of social structure has been cited by E. P. Thompson in support of his own conclusion that eighteenth-century society was divided into two 'classes', the patricians and the plebs. The passage in *Joseph Andrews* quoted to illustrate the distinction is, however, ambiguous. It does indeed separate 'people of fashion' from 'people of no fashion', as Mr Thompson maintains.[16] But, having made the distinction, Fielding continues:

> These two parties, especially those bordering nearly on each other, to wit, the lowest of the high and the highest of the low, often change their parties according to place and time, for those who are people of fashion in one place, are often people of no fashion in another. And with regard to time, it may not be unpleasant to survey the picture of dependence like a kind of ladder, as for instance; early in

> the morning arises the postillion, or some other boy, which great families no more than great ships are without, and falls to brushing the clothes and cleaning the shoes of John the footman; who being drest himself, applies his hands to the same labours for Mr Second-hand, the squire's gentleman; the gentleman in the like manner, a little later in the day, attends the squire; the squire is no sooner equipped than he attends the levee of my lord; which is no sooner over, than my lord himself is seen at the levee of the favourite, who, after the hour of homage is at an end, appears himself to pay homage to the levee of his sovereign. Nor is there, perhaps, in this whole ladder of dependence, any one step at a greater distance from the other than the first from the second, so that to a philosopher the question might only seem whether you would chuse to be a great man at six in the morning, or at two in the afternoon.[17]

So far from documenting a two-class society, this could be said to illustrate a finely graded hierarchy.

Although Fielding moved in aristocratic circles, with the Duke of Bedford as his patron and Lord Lyttelton as his friend, peers are not portrayed sympathetically in his works. On the contrary, when they appear at all, which is not often, it tends to be in a very poor light. Lord Richly, Mrs Modern's lover in *The Modern Husband*, is cynical and vicious. Lady Bellaston and Lord Fellamar are also immoral. The 'noble peer' in *Amelia* who pretends to be concerned for Captain Booth's plight is really only interested in seducing his wife. Indeed, his insatiable womanising eventually leads him to 'become so rotten that he stunk above-ground'.[18] Like most peers in Augustan literature, those in Fielding's works are neither patriarchs nor patricians, but parasites frequenting the pleasure haunts of the court end of town. These characterisations indicate the extent to which he retained essentially Country attitudes even when he himself became attached to the Court.

He was also a Whig, and in his earlier works at least could perpetuate the stereotype of the booby squire which fellow-Whigs employed to castigate the Tory squirearchy. Thus Squire Badger, who appears in *Don Quixote in England*, is one of the grossest country gentlemen in Augustan drama, outrageously drunk on stage. The 'roasting squire' in *Joseph Andrews* also exhibits many characteristics of the stock character, especially his unrefined sensuality.

With the characters of Allworthy and Western, however, Fielding moved on from the stage squire to a more subtle delineation of the gentry. Although they live deep in the West Country, the heart of 'hick' England in Restoration comedies, they differ from the booby in several important respects. Western is nearer to the traditional stock character, with his love of hounds and drink, his sentimental Jacobitism and his dislike of London. Yet he generates fear and resentment as well as mirth, treating his hated wife like a servant, tyrannising over his daughter, and browbeating his servants. Where Western is a patrician, Allworthy, as his very name suggests, is a model patriarch. In Paradise Hall he appears as a God-like figure presiding over a veritable Garden of Eden. He earns the respect of his family and of his neighbours with his hospitality, his liberal dispensations of charity and his wise exercise of authority as a justice.

The fourth chapter of *Tom Jones*, in which the reader is introduced to Allworthy at his country seat, is almost a reversal of Pope's visit to Timon's villa. So far from being exposed to a keen northern wind, his house 'stood on the south-east of a hill, but nearer the bottom than the top of it, so as to be sheltered from the north-east by a grove of old oaks'. Instead of artificial symmetry there is much 'artful wildness', so that the stream is 'not carried down a regular flight of steps' but tumbles 'in a natural fall over the broken and mossy stones'. Where Timon appears 'with a majestic mien, / Smit with the mighty pleasure, to be seen', Allworthy is presented as 'a human being replete with benevolence, meditating in what manner he might render himself most acceptable to his Creator, by doing most good to his creatures'.

Almost immediately we witness Allworthy exercising his jurisdiction as a magistrate when he deals with Jenny Jones, who has confessed to being the mother of the foundling left in his bed. Although 'it was universally apprehended that the house of correction would have been her fate', she is let off with a grave admonishment and given the opportunity of a fresh start in life, since he agreed to bring up the child while she is encouraged to leave the neighbourhood. This contrasts markedly with Squire Western's determination to send Mrs Honour, his daughter's servant, to Bridewell merely for insulting his sister, a resolve only prevented by his clerk, who advised him that he could not legally commit anyone there 'only for ill-breeding'.[19]

Again, unlike Western, Allworthy expresses no overt political preference. Yet there are at least strong hints of his politics. In *Tom Jones* Fielding admired the country seats of Ralph Allen, Lord Cobham, George Bubb Dodington, the Earl of Pembroke and Henry Pelham.[20] Politically this was a very mixed bag. Allen, despite being a government contractor for the cross-country mail, was independent in his politics; Cobham was a leading opposition Whig; Dodington was associated with the party of Frederick, Prince of Wales; Pembroke and Pelham were Court Whigs, the latter being prime minister in 1749, the year when the novel was published. The action was set during the time of the Jacobite rebellion of 1745-6, when Fielding was finally reconciled to the ministry. It could be that his inclusion of Pelham's house at Esher, which would not feature on everybody's short list of the period's greatest houses, was little more than flattery. Yet Pope had also expressed some regard for it, referring to 'Esher's peaceful Grove' in the second *Epilogue to the Satires*, while it is noteworthy that Fielding does not mention Woburn, the house of his patron the Duke of Bedford.[21] Moreover, Prior Park, Stowe, Eastbury and Wilton, the seats of the other four, would rank high in any estimation of domestic architecture in the eighteenth century. Fielding's observations, therefore, probably reflect his aesthetics rather than his politics. At the same time his preference for Prior Park, home of his friend Ralph Allen, suggests philosophical as well as artistic priorities:

> Here nature appears in her richest attire, and art dressed with the modestest simplicity, attends her benignant mistress. Here nature indeed pours forth the choicest treasures which she hath lavished on this world; and here human nature presents you with an object which can be exceeded only in the other.[22]

It is therefore significant that, as has been generally agreed, Fielding modelled Allworthy on Allen. He represents not just an aesthetic or a moral ideal but a political philosophy of sturdy independence, which is in contrast with both the mindless opposition to the Court of Squire Western and the blind adherence to it advocated by Western's sister. Squire Western had been 'twice a candidate in the Country interest at an election', and 'had rather be anything than a Courtier, and a Presbyterian and a Hanoverian'. He even drank to the king over the water, the hallmark of the sentimental Jacobite, and was apprehensive that his sister might accuse him of complicity in a plot. Di Western, on the other hand, 'had lived about the court, and had seen the world'. She had read 'most of the political pamphlets and journals published within the last twenty years' and 'prided herself on her knowledge and understanding of politics', which she used to defend the Court against her brother's criticisms. She once described him as 'one of those wise men whose nonsensical principles have undone the nation: by weakening the hands of our government at home, and by discouraging our friends and encouraging our enemies abroad'. Allworthy does not get involved in political disputes, but we can surely detect his influence in Tom Jones's declarations 'I love my King and country' and 'The cause of King George is the cause of liberty and true religion.'[23] These were almost certainly Allworthy's sentiments, and by the time he came to write *Tom Jones* those of Fielding too.

Fielding showed an acute awareness of the border-line between the upper classes and the middling sort. In *Joseph Andrews* Mr Wilson, who was 'descended of a good family, and was born a gentleman', distinguished between the 'polite circles' and those whose birth and fortune placed them just outside these, by which he meant 'the lower class of the gentry and the higher of the mercantile world'.[24] Mr Wilson expresses contempt for them, and it is likely that Fielding too had not much time for them. Certainly not many appear in his novels, and those that do are not developed sympathetically. One of the few substantial merchants he described was old Mr Nightingale in *Tom Jones*, who turned banker after amassing a fortune in trade and who 'conversed so entirely with money, that it may be almost doubted whether he imagined there was any other thing really existing in the world. . . . At least . . . he firmly believed nothing else to have any real value.'[25] On the other hand, Fielding could be sympathetic towards merchants who were not plutocrats. Indeed, one of the few admirable characters in *Jonathan Wild* is the jeweller Thomas Heartfree, who was 'good natured, friendly and generous to a great excess'.[26]

While there are hardly any business men in Fielding's major novels, they teem with members of the professions. His doctors, lawyers and soldiers show little advance on the stock dramatic characters which he had himself used in his own plays. By contrast, his treatment of Parson Adams and Dr Harrison marked a significant advance on the representation of clergy in fiction.

The physicians who attend at the death of Captain Blifil in *Tom Jones*, whom Fielding, 'to avoid any malicious applications', identified as Dr Y and Dr Z, could have stepped straight off a stage. So could the surgeons who attended Joseph Andrews after he had been assaulted by robbers, and Tom Jones after his fight with Ensign Northerton. The first told Parson Adams that Joseph's case was 'that of a dead man. – The contusion on his head has perforated the internal membrane of the occiput, and divellicated that radical small minute invisible nerve, which coheres to the pericranium.'[27] 'Of wounds, indeed, it is rightly and truly said, *nemo repente fuit turpissimus*,' the second begins. 'I was once, I remember, called to a patient who had received a violent contusion in his tibia, by which the exterior cutis was lacerated, so that there was a profuse sanguinary discharge; and the interior membranes were so divellicated, that the os or bone very plainly appeared through the aperture of the vulnus or wound.' Once launched on this previous case, his description becomes more and more obscured with quack jargon until those there confess they cannot understand a word. Meanwhile Jones is left unattended. Not content with exposing the surgeon as a charlatan once, Fielding introduces him again on a return visit to his patient, when he says that food his patient had eaten would 'corrode the vascular orifices, and thus will aggravate the febrific symptons'.[28] As for apothecaries, Fielding's low opinion of them is indicated by his inclusion of one, significantly called Mr Arsenic, in *Amelia*.

Not all medical men are condemned in the novels, however. Those who display honesty and integrity are praised, such as Dr Thompson, a real contemporary who had treated Fielding himself, and who is introduced into *Amelia* to cure the Booths' small child after incompetent treatment by a quack had been to no avail. Partridge, too, who gravely informs Tom Jones that he is a barber-surgeon, which 'is a profession, not a trade', uses common sense to treat him following the absurdities of the quack surgeon.[29] So indeed does Parson Adams, who advises Joseph Andrews to 'be chearful, for that he plainly saw the surgeon, besides his ignorance, desired to make a merit of curing him, tho' the wounds in his head, he perceived, were by no means dangerous; that he was convinced he had no fever, and doubted not but he would be able to travel in a day or two'.[30]

Fielding distinguishes between honest competence and corrupt incompetence amongst lawyers too. Thus he describes Lawyer Scout in *Joseph Andrews* as

> one of those fellows, who without any knowledge of the law, or being bred to it, take upon them, in defiance of an act of parliament, to act as lawyers in the country, and are called so. They are the pests of society, and a scandal to a profession, to which indeed they do not belong; and which owes to such rascallions the ill-will which weak persons bear towards it.[31]

Another such was the self-styled lawyer of Lidlinch who appears in *Tom Jones*. 'This fellow', says Fielding,

> stiled himself a lawyer, but was indeed a most vile petty-fogger, without sense or knowledge of any kind; one of those who may be termed train-bearers to the law; a sort of supernumeraries in the profession, who are the hack-neys of attornies, and will ride more miles for half a crown than a post-boy.[32]

By contrast with these there is the Horatio who features in the 'History of Leonora' told by the lady to divert her fellow coach passengers in *Joseph Andrews*. Horatio 'was a young gentleman of a good family, bred to the law, and had been some few years called to the degree of a barrister'. He appears as a sterling character.[33]

Yet the bad lawyers far outnumber the good. When Partridge tells Allworthy of his own dealings with the legal profession, although he acknowledges that some of its members who had employed him were admirable, he reveals that he had been sent to prison because of 'a parcel of the confoundest lies' told about him by a lawyer employed by a neighbour who sued him for letting a pig trespass on his property. Another had contrived to double the debt he owed by way of law charges, which led Fielding to add a footnote:

> This is a fact which I knew happen to a poor clergyman in Dorsetshire, by the villainy of an attorney, who not contented with the exorbitant costs to which the man was put by a single action, brought afterwards another action on the judgement, as it is called. A method frequently used to oppress the poor, and bring money ino the pockets of attorneys, to the great scandal of the law, of the nation, of Christianity, and even of human nature itself.[34]

The worst lawyer of all in Fielding's novels was 'one Murphy, an attorney' in *Amelia*. At his first appearance he tries to bamboozle Miss Matthews with legal jargon. When she expresses her ignorance of the law, he answers:

> It can't be expected you should understand it. There are very few of us who profess it that understand the whole, nor is it necessary we should. There is a great deal of rubbish of little use, about indictments, and abatements, and bars, and ejectments, and trovers and such stuff, with which people cram their heads to little purpose. The chapter of evidence is the main business; that is the sheet-anchor; that is the rudder, which brings the vessel safe *in portum*. Evidence is, indeed, the whole, the *summa totidis*, for *de non apparentibus et non insistentibus eandem est ratio*.

Towards the end he is discovered to be 'the greatest rogue . . . now in the world'. He contrived with Betty Harris to alter her mother's will so that her sister Amelia, instead of receiving the whole fortune less one thousand pounds, obtained a mere ten pounds. The last we hear of Murphy is that he 'was brought to trial at the Old Bailey, where, after much quibbling about the meaning of a very plain act of parliament, he was at length convicted of forgery, and was soon afterwards hanged at Tyburn'.[35]

There are relatively more good soldiers than there are good lawyers in the novels, perhaps because Fielding was partial towards the profession of arms since his own father was a military man. In this respect it is interesting to observe that army officers form the largest single category of any social grouping in his novels, there being no fewer than twelve named individuals with commissions in *Tom Jones* and *Amelia*. To be sure, the soldiers Tom Jones meets on their way to suppress the Jacobite rebellion of 1745 are for the most part a somewhat disreputable crew. Ensign Northerton, undoubtedly the worst, deliberately seeks a quarrel with Jones by insulting Sophia, and then floors him with a bottle aimed at his head. Yet even among these men there is the lieutenant who 'was a religious, honest, good-natured man; and had behaved so well in his command, that he was highly esteemed and beloved, not only by the soldiers of his own company, but by the whole regiment'. His promotion had only been blocked because his wife refused to 'purchase his preferment at the expence of certain favours which the colonel required of her'.[36]

While officers appear only incidentally in *Tom Jones*, they play a crucial role in *Amelia*, for the heroine's husband is a captain. We even encounter him in action at the siege of Gibraltar in 1727, where his courage was conspicuous. When he returned to England he was reduced to half pay, amounting to £40 a year, which leaves the couple in straitened circumstances. Although Captain Booth has his faults, which help to aggravate their condition, he is on the whole represented as a credit to his profession. This contrasts with rogues like Captain Trent, whose advancement is entirely due to villainy, in Trent's case ranging from his absconding with £50 from his mother's escritoire to his conniving at his wife's seduction by a peer.

The juxtaposition of honourable and disreputable professional men is most marked in the contrast between Parson

Adams on the one hand and Parsons Barnabus and Trulliber on the other. Again, by having the admirable type outnumbered by the reprehensible, Fielding implies that the ideal is more honoured in the breach than in the observance. Indeed, besides Adams, as Martin Battestin observes, 'there are no fewer than six clergymen in *Joseph Andrews*. . . . All six are corrupt or incompetent, unworthy of their order.'[37]

Battestin also demonstrates that Parson Adams exemplifies the commonsense Christianity of the latitudinarians. Adams particularly admires Benjamin Hoadly, saying of his *Plain Account of the Nature and Sacrament of the Lord's Supper* that it was written 'with the pen of an angel'. Now Hoadly was not just a latitudinarian but a Low Church Whig divine, who earned notoriety by his ascent up the ladder of preferment after the accession of the House of Hanover, becoming successively Bishop of Bangor, Hereford, Salisbury and Winchester. He became the butt of every critic of the Hanoverian Church who accused it of promoting timeservers, for it was notorious that Hoadly only once visited Bangor and never set foot in Hereford. High Church clergymen complained, when their own route to advancement was blocked after George I came to the throne, that the Whig regime preferred clergymen on political rather than on religious grounds. This is perhaps why Barnabus criticises the *Plain Account* as being equivalent to the works of Moslems, atheists and deists, though he admits that he has never read it himself. Adams indicates his subscription to Whig principles elsewhere too, by expressing the opinion that he 'never heard of any plays fit for a Christian to read, but *Cato* and the *Conscious Lovers*'.[38] Both Addison's classical tragedy and Steele's somewhat sombre comedy upheld Whig principles.

Fielding was very anxious to rescue the clergy from the contempt in which many contemporaries held them. The worst offenders in this respect were anticlerical Whigs who tended to denounce all clergymen as High Church Tories if not Jacobites. By making Adams a staunch Whig, therefore, he was asserting that some of the clergy at least were loyal to the Protestant succession. At the same time Adams is no timeserving Court Whig – unlike Parson Williams, the hard-drinking, pipe-smoking lover of Shamela, who tells his mistress 'that the Court-side are in the right on't, and that every Christian ought to be on the same with the Bishops'.[39]

Some clergymen blamed the government for the disrespect in which they were held, claiming that the state should protect the priestly order from criticism. The young deacon who accompanied Dr Harrison to Vauxhall, where they were insulted by two anticlerical rakes, aired the opinion that 'It is a scandal to the government that they do not preserve more respect to the clergy, by punishing all rudeness to them with the utmost severity.'[40] Harrison, however, considered divine sanctions for such disrespect to be more appropriate, and also expressed the opinion that some of their order brought the whole profession into disrepute by their scandalous behaviour. The notion that the Church should command respect by the example of its members rather than enforce it by the power of the state was one which Low Churchmen had used in argument with High Churchmen on the issue of whether Dissenters should be tolerated or persecuted. Dr Harrison, like Adams, holds views in line with the Low Church thinking, which Fielding is clearly advocating. Clerical status could only be enhanced by the clergy themselves, not by decree.

Fielding was more concerned with the status of the clergy than he was with that of other professional men. His doctors and lawyers for the most part appear as parasites, dependent upon wealthy hosts and despising the poor. The commissioned officers, on the other hand, pride themselves upon their independence. As a landlady of an inn observes, 'There is narrow a one of all those officer fellows, but looks upon himself to be as good as arrow a squire of £500 a year.'[41] The clergy, however, are represented as occupying an intermediate status between the two. Ideally, their function in society required them to be independent, and to some extent in theory they were. As Dr Harrison, the paragon of priestly virtue in *Amelia*, observes, 'The lowest clergyman in England is in real dignity superior to the highest nobleman.' Yet their poverty frequently forced them to be clients of more affluent men and brought them into ridicule and contempt. Dr Harrison considered that dependence upon a patron was incompatible with the spiritual obligations of the clerical profession. He tells a junior colleague:

> We are told we cannot serve God and Mammon. When we see a man sneaking about in courts and levees, and doing the dirty work of great men, from the hopes of preferment, can we believe that a fellow whom we see to have so many hard task-masters upon earth ever thinks of his Master which is in heaven?[42]

Inferior clergymen not fortunate enough to obtain the patronage of an aristocrat or a gentleman could be in dire straits. Many such appear in the pages of Fielding's novels. One of the most penurious is Parson Adams, who at the age of fifty was still only a curate in a living to which he had been presented by a bishop some thirty years previously, the revenues of which amounted to a mere £23 a year, on which he had to keep a wife and six children. Yet he contrives to be sturdily independent. He publicly rebuked Mr Booby and Pamela for laughing in church at the wedding of Joseph Andrews and Fanny Goodwill. When Mr Booby offered him a living of £130 a year he 'at first refused it, resolving not to quit his parishioners, with whom he hath lived so long', Fielding informs us at the end of the novel. 'But on recollecting he might keep a curate at this living, he hath been lately inducted into it.'[43] At the end of *Tom Jones* he takes the place of Thwackum in Allworthy's employment.

Very few of Fielding's clergymen are able to maintain themselves independently in comfort. One is Parson Trulliber, who does so by dint of keeping pigs in addition to his curacy, which means that he was only 'a parson on Sundays, but all the other six might more properly be called a farmer'.[44] His involvement with pigs, which he physically resembles, has made him so worldly that Adams rebukes him for being no Christian. Dr Harrison, by contrast, is a model Christian, and he enjoys a living worth over £600 a year, of which he charitably disposed of some £400. It is possible that Fielding wished all clergymen to be as financially independent as his hero Harrison, though even he had obligations to a patron, an earl whose son he accompanied on the Grand Tour.

Fielding's business and professional types expressed his political commitment. As we have seen, this oscillated between Court and Country, though it swung more towards the opposition than to the government standpoint. Yet he was consistently Whig. Parson Adams's admiration for the works of Benjamin Hoadly echoes Fielding's own subscription to the Lockean principles of that Low Church bishop.[45] His Whiggism led him to be more favourably disposed towards the middle classes than were other Country authors. To be sure, there are men who abuse their professional and business roles in abundance in his plays and novels. Yet these are offset by enough characters, such as Heartfree, Dr Thompson, Horatio, Adams and Harrison, to indicate that as far as Fielding was concerned the middle station of life was not beyond redemption.

Fielding's attitude towards the lower orders in his novels is very ambiguous. At one stage in *Tom Jones* he provides a definition for the reader:

> By the poor here I mean that large and venerable body which, in English, we call The Mob. Now whoever hath had the honour to be admitted in any degree of intimacy with this Mob, must well know that it is one of their established maxims, to plunder and pillage their rich neighbours without any reluctance; and this is held to be neither sin nor shame among them.[46]

Similar opinions are expressed in his discussion of the mob as the fourth estate of the realm in the *Covent-Garden Journal*, no. 47. Yet twenty issues earlier he had published an essay protesting that the rich had no right to claim to be 'the betters' of the poor, but that, on the contrary, the poor were in many respects better than the rich, being happier, more temperate, more modest, more chaste and more decent. Mrs Bennett likewise can exclaim in *Amelia*: 'I have myself, I think, seen instances of as great goodness and as great understanding too, among the lower sort of people as among the higher.'[47] When he picks out faces in the crowd Fielding can discern heroes as well as villains. Even his rogues, like Black George and Molly Seagrim, are not without their endearing features, while Fanny in *Joseph Andrews* is a positive saint. The poor people whom Joseph meets after being dismissed by Lady Booby tend to be more charitable than the more affluent. After he has been beaten up and left for dead the travellers in the stage-coach which passes by react very differently according to their ranks. The lady begs the coachman to drive on and leave him, while the postillion, who stopped the horses when he heard Joseph's groans, lends him his greatcoat, 'his only garment, at the same time swearing a great oath (for which he was rebuked by the passengers) "that he would rather ride in his shirt all his life than suffer a fellow-creature to lie in so miserable a condition" '.[48]

This ambiguity extends even to Fielding's view of the justice of the division between rich and poor. According to Homai J. Shroff, 'The necessity and logic of the class structure itself are never questioned by him. The purpose of the harsh satire is to recall the privileged classes to their duties and obligations, not to summon the downtrodden to seize and share their privileges.'[49] This might be true of *Joseph Andrews, Tom Jones* and *Amelia.* There is a passage in *Jonathan Wild*, however, which can be seen to be critical of the class structure, as well as of the failure of the upper classes to perform their duties. Wild, having got Bob Bagshot to rob Count la Ruse, insists that he himself should have the lion's share of the booty. He justifies the uneven distribution by drawing an analogy between their respective roles and that of an employer and employee:

> Your hire I shall not refuse you, which is all that the labourer is entitled to, or ever enjoys. . . . The ploughman, the shepherd, the weaver, the builder, and the soldier work not for themselves but others – they are contented with a poor pittance (the labourer's hire) and permit us the Great to enjoy the fruits of their labours. . . . It is well said of us, the higher order of mortals, that we are born only to devour the fruits of the earth; and it may be as well said of the lower class that they are born only to produce them for us. . . . Is not the cloth, or the silk, raught into its form, and variegated with all the beauty of colours, by those who are forced to content themselves with the coarsest and vilest part of their work, while the profit and enjoyment of their labours fall to the share of others? Cast your eye abroad, and see who it is lives in the most magnificent buildings, feasts his palate with

> the most luxurious dainties, his eyes with the most beautiful sculptures and delicate paintings, and clothes himself in the finest and richest apparel, and tell me if all these do not fall to his lot who had not any the least share in producing all these conveniences, nor the least ability so to do?[50]

There is no such ambiguity, however, in his social tracts. Fielding's *Proposal for Making an Effectual Provision for the Poor* clearly regarded them as a threat to their betters. Although he showed compassion for them ('they starve and freeze and rot among themselves'), he displays none of the sentimentality which pervades his novels ('they beg and steal and rob among their betters'). He was far more concerned here to stop them begging, stealing and robbing than to prevent them starving, freezing and rotting. Vagrancy itself was to be made a crime. All 'persons of low degree, who, after the hour of ten in the evening shall be found harbouring in any alehouse or victualling house' were to be arrested and held in prison until brought to trial. 'Poor persons' were only to be allowed freedom of movement if they travelled with a pass issued by a justice of the peace. All others who could not maintain themselves were to be placed in a workhouse with rules which would have been considered inhumane even by the farmers of the Poor Law Amendment Act, for not only were sexes to be segregated, but inmates were to work hard from six in the morning until seven at night.[51]

Readers charmed by the humanity of the novels find this hard to square with the harshness of Fielding's tracts. The connection is to be found, however, in his ideological attitude towards the lower orders. In the debate on human nature, and the role of reason in controlling behaviour, he came out on the side of the optimists, and this led him to take a stern view of human frailty.

There are many passages in Fielding's novels which address themselves, either directly or obliquely, to this debate. One of the attractions of the novelist is that, unlike philosophers and theologians, he is not dogmatic and can take an ambiguous stance on such issues. Indeed, he ridiculed dogmatism on both sides in the persons of Thwackum and

Square. Thwackum 'maintained that the human mind, since the Fall, was nothing but a sink of iniquity', whereas Square 'held human nature to be the perfection of all virtue, and that vice was a deviation from our nature in the same manner as deformity of body is'.[52] Both are shown in *Tom Jones* to have oversimplified the issue. Fielding clearly believed that some men were born good and some bad. 'Those who predicate of men in general, that he is an animal of this or that disposition, seem to me not sufficiently to have studied human nature,' he observed in *An Essay on the Knowledge of the Characters of Men*: 'for that immense variety of characters, so apparent in men even of the same climate, religion, and education . . . could hardly exist, unless the distinction had some original foundation in nature itself.'[53] Tom Jones himself, though he was said to have been 'born to be hanged', was blessed with a good heart, while Blifil seems to have been innately wicked. Fielding did, however, take issue with the hedonism of the pessimists, and particularly challenged Mandeville's assertion that pride and fear were the passions which most controlled behaviour. He emphasised that this denied the sentiment of love, and urged the pessimists 'to grant that there is in some (I believe in many) human breasts, a kind and benevolent disposition, which is gratified by contributing to the happiness of others'.[54]

He returned to this theme in *Amelia*, when Captain Booth rebukes Miss Matthews for following Mandeville, claiming that he

> hath represented human nature in a picture of the highest deformity. He hath left out of his system the best passion which the mind can possess, and attempts to derive the effects or energies of that passion from the base impulses of pride or fear. Whereas it is as certain that love exists in the mind of man as that its opposite hatred doth; and the same reasons will equally prove the existence of the one as the existence of the other.

Dr Harrison was even more emphatic on the subject, telling Amelia:

> The nature of man is far from being in itself evil; it abounds with benevolence, charity, and pity, coveting praise and

honour, and shunning shame and disgrace. Bad education, bad habits, and bad customs, debauch our nature and drive it headlong into vice.[55]

How far Fielding's own views agreed with those of Dr Harrison is not clear. The debate between Parson Adams and Joseph Andrews on the effects of a public-school education indicate that he had not worked out to his own satisfaction how far education could change behaviour. According to Adams, 'Public schools are the nurseries of all vice and immorality.' Joseph, however, begs to differ, pointing out that many who were educated at them were virtuous, while some who were taught at home were 'as wicked as if they had known the world from their infancy. I remember,' he continues, 'when I was in the stable, if a young horse was vicious in his nature, no correction would make him otherwise; I take it to be equally the same among men: if a boy be of a mischievous, wicked inclination, no school tho' ever so private, will ever make him good; on the contrary, if he be of a righteous temper, you may trust him to London, or wherever else you please, he will be in no danger of being corrupted.'[56] By the time he came to write *Tom Jones* Fielding had concluded that 'It is much easier to make good men wise, than to make bad men good.'[57]

Fielding's optimism about the innate capacity for good, and the benefits of sound education gave him a higher opinion of the civility of the lower orders than was held by even enlightened contemporaries. 'I know not', declares his hero Booth in *Amelia*,

> why we should be more surprised to see greatness of mind discover itself in one degree or rank of life than in another. Love, benevolence, or what you will please to call it, may be the reigning passion in a beggar as well as in a prince; and wherever it is, its energies will be the same.[58]

The refined Earl of Chesterfield found this hard to swallow, commenting: 'How can the low born be expected to have such sensitive or fine feelings as those of higher rank? Mr Fielding has here gone too far.' It was precisely because he had a high regard for the potential of the lower orders that Fielding was so harsh when condemning their failings.

6

Tobias Smollett and the Historian

> He values himself upon being entirely free from all national jealousy and prejudice; and altogether uninfluenced by that illiberal partiality which has disgraced the works of many English historians. He is soured by no controversy in religion: he is inflamed by no faction in politics. Truth is the object of his enquiry; and candid information the scope of his labour.
>
> Tobias Smollett, prefatory plan to *The Complete History of England* (1758)

Tobias Smollett was himself a historian as well as a novelist, and his *History of England* documents his political philosophy, which also pervades the novels. Despite his own disclaimers of partiality, it is usual to describe him as a Tory and even as a Jacobite historian. A close examination of his treatment of eighteenth-century British history, however, reveals that it would be more appropriate to call him a Country chronicler.

Donald Greene has shown that, if the *History* had a Tory bias, it was a curious kind of Toryism.[1] Smollett had little sympathy for the Jacobites or even for the High Church clergy. Moreover, when dealing with the events of Anne's reign he displayed no preference for the Tory ministry of 1710-14 over the Whig administration of 1708-10. Of those years he asserted that 'The history of England is disgraced by the violent conduct of two turbulent factions, that in their turn engrossed the administrative and legislative power.'[2] This is more in keeping with the anti-party spirit of Country ideology than with Tory partisanship. So too was his attitude towards the South Sea Bubble, which he placed in the context of an 'age of interested projects inspired by a venal spirit of adventure; the natural consequence of that avarice, fraud and profligacy, which the monied corporations had introduced'.[3] His description of the state of politics at the accession of George II reads like a Country manifesto:

> Dangerous encroachment had been made upon the constitution by the repeal of the Act for triennial parliaments; by frequent suspensions of the Habeas Corpus Act upon frivolous occasions; by repealing clauses in the Act of Settlement; by votes of credit; by habituating the people to a standing army; and above all, by establishing a system of corruption which at all times would secure a majority in parliament.[4]

The whole work was dedicated to William Pitt, and in the dedication Smollett informed 'the patriot', rather than 'the minister': 'I revere that integrity which you have maintained in the midst of corruption.'

Corruption, of course, was a Country watchword. It was seen as the main means by which the Court conspired to undermine the constitution. According to Country historiography, England had always enjoyed the blessings of constitutional monarchy, in which the powers of the Crown were limited by the Lords and Commons. This mixture of monarchical, aristocratic and democratic elements, if held in perfect balance, produced an ideal form of government which could be described as mixed monarchy. Such a polity avoided the excesses of monarchy, aristocracy and democracy on their own, which tended to degenerate respectively into tyranny, oligarchy and anarchy. Thus the Lords and Commons together checked the tendency of the monarch to become a tyrant; the King and Commons prevented the Lords becoming oligarchs; and the Crown and aristocracy resisted the Commons' propensity for anarchy. This happy state of affairs could only endure, however, provided that the perfect balance of the three elements was maintained. Unfortunately it was not a self-regulating mechanism. Each element strove to exert itself against the others, thereby upsetting the equilibrium. At various times in history, therefore, England had experienced tyranny, oligarchy and anarchy. The main trend had been for the Crown to exceed its due bounds, exerting arbitrary authority over the other two. The Norman kings, and the Tudors and Stuarts, had been particularly prone to do this, and had only been held in check by the reassertion of mixed monarchy, in constitutional conflicts which resulted in such definitive documents as Magna Carta and the Petition of

Right. The last monarch to challenge the traditional limitations had been James II. The ancient constitution of mixed monarchy had been temporarily overcome by tyranny, to be restored in the Glorious Revolution. Since 1688, however, the Crown's influence over the Lords and Commons had once more insidiously asserted itself through the agency of corruption.[5]

This historical account of the English constitution was denounced as legendary by Stuart apologists such as Robert Brady. They argued that the traditional system of government was one of absolute monarchy, and that any limitations on the powers of the Crown had either been granted by the king's grace, or had been wrested from it by force, and were not constitutional rights.[6] Court apologists under the early Hanoverians paradoxically drew on the more convincing historiography of royalist historians than on the Country notion of the ancient constitution. To them limited or mixed monarchy had not existed from time out of mind, but had been established by the Glorious Revolution. The perfect balance of King, Lords and Commons, which guaranteed the liberty and property of Englishmen, dated not from the mists of Anglo-Saxon times but from 1689.[7] The Revolution settlement had realised in practice the theoretical notion that government was a trust reposed in the ruler by his subjects, and if he betrayed that trust he forfeited his right to rule and could be replaced.

Smollett subscribed more to the views of Stuart and Court apologists than to Country historiography. He did not share the idea that there was an ancient constitution of limited monarchy which had been undermined by James II and restored in 1689. To him the historical relationship between King, Lords and Commons had been restored along with Charles II in 1660. Thus he attributed the rejoicings of the people at his restoration to the fact that

> They had been so long distracted by unrelenting factions, oppressed and alarmed by a succession of tyrannies, which threatened national anarchy and destruction, that they could not, without extravagant emotions of joy, behold their constitution restored without bloodshed; while the king remounted the throne of his an-

> cestors, and law, order, and subordination began to flow quietly in their ancient channels.[8]

Brady would have concurred with this explanation, which was in line with Tory thinking on the events of 1660. In his account of those occurring in 1688, however, Smollett went along with Court Whig notions. By the Revolution settlement, he claimed,

> the constitution of England had now assumed a new aspect. The maxim of hereditary, indefeasible right was at length renounced by a free parliament. The power of the crown was acknowledged to flow from no other fountain than that of a contract with the people.[9]

Where others were agreed that the Revolution settlement, whether it restored the ancient constitution or established a new one, was a guarantee of English liberties, however, Smollett begged to differ. 'Yet on this occasion', he wrote,

> the zeal of the parliament towards their deliverer seems to have overshot their attachment to their own liberty and privileges: or at least they neglected the fairest opportunity that ever occurred, to retrench those prerogatives of the crown to which they imputed all the late and former calamities of the kingdom. Their new monarch retained the old regal power over parliaments, in its full extent. He was left at liberty to convoke, adjourn, prorogue, and dissolve them at his pleasure. He was enabled to influence elections and oppress corporations. He possessed the right of chusing his own council; of nominating all the great officers of the state, and of the household, of the army, the navy and the church. He reserved the absolute command of the militia: so that he remained master of all the instruments and engines of corruption and violence.[10]

So, by a somewhat novel route, Smollett arrived at an essentially Country position. He did not share the adulation bestowed on the constitution in church and state by most English writers; perhaps his Scottish background made him more objective. Even Country propagandists paid at least lip-service to the notion that the constitution was theoretically the best possible, before going on to expose those in the executive whom they accused of undermining it. Smollett subscribed to the view that corruption was not solely due to the abuse of power by men intent on removing the checks and balances enshrined in the Revolution settlement, but also sprang from the very nature of the new constitution of 1689, which contained the seeds of its own destruction.

These seeds germinated and grew in the congenial soil of luxury and degeneracy which the Court sedulously fertilised. In Smollett's *Complete History of England* luxury is vividly portrayed as a tidal wave which swept in with the Revolution of 1688, and inundated the country under the Hanoverians, until by 1748 'an irresistible tide of luxury and excess' had 'flowed through all degrees of the people, breaking down all the mounds of civil polity, and opening a way for licence and immorality'.[11] This was a typical Country observation used to substantiate the charge that the Court was engaged in a conspiracy to undermine English liberty, since a people softened by luxury and vice were more readily enslaved than those who stayed frugal and virtuous. It is possible to detect a difference between Tories and Country Whigs on the origin of this development. Tories tended to date the deluge of luxury from the Revolution, while Country Whigs usually ascribed it to the decadence and immorality of the court of Charles II after the Restoration. On this question of dating, Smollett inclined towards the Tory rather than the Country Whig view, his denunciations of luxury in the *History* being much more noticeable in his narrative of the 1690s than in that of the 1660s. In later works, however, he seems to have changed his mind and to have held Walpole responsible for presiding over and encouraging the insidious growth of luxury and immorality. Whatever the preferred chronology, the denunciation of luxury and its association with the regime was essentially a Country concept. Country ideology thus informs Smollett's critique of luxury which, as John Sekora has shown, suffuses all his works.[12]

While these ideological considerations are particularly prominent in *Humphry Clinker*, which has been fully analysed by Sekora, they can also be detected in the earlier novels.

Roderick Random is himself a Country Whig, and his experiences in the world confirm his political philosophy. His Whiggism is emphasised in his conversation with a French soldier, who takes exception to his criticisms of Louis XV and absolute kingship:

> In vindication of my countrymen, I repeated all the arguments commonly used to prove that every man has a natural right to liberty; that allegiance and protection are reciprocal; that, when the mutual tie is broken by the tyranny of the king, he is accountable to the people for his breach of contract, and subject to the penalty of the law; and that those insurrections of the English, which are branded with the name of rebellion by the slaves of arbitrary power, were no other than glorious efforts to rescue that independence which was their birthright, from the ravenous claws of usurping ambition.

In the very next chapter he demonstrates his opposition to the ministry when deliberating upon what choice of career is open to him:

> Neither should I succeed in my endeavours to rise in the state, inasmuch as I could neither flatter nor pimp for courtiers, nor prostitute my pen in defence of a wicked and contemptible administration.[13]

His opinion of the government is confirmed by his treatment at the hands of Mr Cringer, a Scottish MP; of the Navy Office; and of a noble lord with interests at court. His reliance on Mr Cringer to find him a position as surgeon's mate on a man-of-war teaches him that 'there was nothing to be done with a member of parliament without a bribe', and that even with one their promises were mostly empty. He finds he also has to bribe the secretary of the Navy Office if he wishes to obtain a posting as second mate, which he cannot afford: 'Far from being in a capacity to gratify a ravenous secretary, [he] had not wherewithal to purchase a dinner.'[14] Much later, when Lord Strutwell undertakes to get the secretaryship of an embassy for him, he discovers to his cost that the promises are empty. He also discovers that Strutwell is a homosexual, which shocks and disgusts a Scot educated in Presbyterian principles and devoted to heterosexual practices. Unlike Roderick's encounter with the homosexual naval officer in the West Indies, this episode is not introduced by Smollett simply to confirm his hero's manly qualities. One of the complaints made in Country propaganda about the debilitating effects of luxury and vice on the constitution was that it inculcated effeminacy, which sapped the nation's ardour and valour, making it vulnerable to its more virile and vigorous foreign enemies. This view was expressed most emphatically by John Brown in his *Estimate of the Manners and Principles of the Times*, published in 1757. Smollett shared it, and vividly symbolised it by making Strutwell, the only real courtier Roderick Random encounters, a predatory homosexual.

The Country theme also holds together what otherwise can be regarded as a discursive, episodic novel. Roderick's travels involve four separate entries into England. On each occasion he meets different elements of English society, which confirm the basically pessimistic social aspects of Country ideology.

On his first visit he is an impoverished traveller making his way from Scotland to London, most of his journey through England being undertaken in a wagon. He and his companion Strap encounter the lower depths of London society. Some xenophobic Englishmen insult their nationality in an alehouse, which leads to a fight. They dive into a cellar for a meal, to find themselves 'almost suffocated with the steams of boiled beef, and surrounded by a company of hackney coachmen, chairmen, draymen and a few footmen out of place, or on board wages'. They lose their money to confidence tricksters in a public house. As Strap observes after this incident, 'we have not been in London eight and forty hours, and I believe we have met with eight and forty thousand misfortunes. – We have been jeered, reproached, buffeted, pissed upon, and at last stripped of our money; and I suppose by and by we shall be stripped of our skins.' Worse follows. Roderick is bilked in a brothel, and then accused of theft by the madam before a justice of the peace with whom she is in league. The justice even threatens Random with the gallows, claiming to recognise him as a felon convict returned illegally from transportation, until he is persuaded that he has mistaken Roderick's identity. Meanwhile Strap gets into another fight, which leads him to conclude 'that surely London is the devil's drawing-room'.[15] Random must have reached the same conclusion before his first visit to London ends in a chapter headed: 'I am reduced to great misery – Assaulted on Tower Hill by a Press-gang who put me on board a Tender.'

He next visits London after serving as a surgeon's assistant on board the *Thunder* in the expedition to Cartagena in 1741, and as a soldier in the French army at the battle of Dettingen in 1743. Once again he teams up with Strap, though on this occasion they are able to move in more polite circles, thanks to his companion's having been left a comfortable settlement by an English gentleman whom he had served as valet. They are therefore able to rent 'very handsome lodgings not far from Charing Cross', while Random resolves 'to introduce myself into a set of good acquaintance'.[16] He does not, however, become acquainted with any more reputable people than he had previously encountered in low life. A prostitute passes herself off as a lady, and a dancer, a fiddler and a Catholic priest purport to be a prince, an ambassador and a doctor. A real doctor, Wagtail, is exposed as a gullible pedant. The very names of those whom Random associates with on this visit indicate their characteristics: Bragwell, Banter, Chatter, Medlar, Ranter, Slyboot, Straddle and Swillpot. After an adventure amongst high society at Bath, which includes a duel fought with Lord Quiverwit, Random returns to London penniless, runs into debt, and finds himself in the Marshalsea prison. His uncle providentially comes to his rescue, and again he leaves the country by sea.

His third visit to London is in the company of his long-lost father, whom he has discovered living as a rich planter in Argentina. He is thus able to enter polite society on equal terms for the first time. When his former associates discover that he now has an independent fortune 'then the tables were turned, and our acquaintance courted as much as it had been despised'. He does not value their attentions, however, and leaves the town after a short stay to return with his father to Scotland, where he settles down.

London thus appears in *Roderick Random* as a jungle inhabited by beasts of prey. Everywhere the hero goes, from jail to court, from low alehouses to fashionable coffee-houses, he encounters cunning, deception, hypocrisy, malice and treachery. Such a grim view of the capital accorded with Country notions that the urban environment was corrupt and corrupting in comparison with rural virtues.

By contrast, Roderick sings 'the praises of a country life, as described by the poets whose works I had read'. Yet when he experiences the English countryside it does not live up to his expectations. Between his voyage to Cartagena and his participation in the Dettingen campaign he made another visit to England, this time being washed up on the Sussex coast in a lifeboat following a shipwreck. After an argument with his companions in the boat he is stripped of everything but his shoes, stockings, breeches and shirt, and abandoned on the beach. When he seeks succour from the local inhabitants they prove to be remarkably inhospitable. The country people, concerned that if he dies they will be at the expense of burying him, trundle him around in a wheelbarrow, passing him on from one to the other to avoid the trouble. Roderick complains that he 'was bandied from door to door through a whole village, nobody having humanity enough to administer the least relief to me, until an old woman, who was suspected of witchcraft by the neighbourhood, hearing of my distress, received me into her house, and having dressed my wounds, brought me to myself with cordials of her own preparing'.[17] Such rough treatment is painfully at odds with his romantic notion of rustic manners, and apparently with Country ideology.

An explanation of this apparent inconsistency in Smollett's political philosophy is provided by the conviction of Country writers that people behaved according to the example set by their betters. In London a corrupt court presided over a corrupted capital. In a country village the inhabitants would mimic the behaviour of the local landowners. Random found himself in a part of Sussex presided over by Sir Timothy

Thicket and Squires Bumper and Topehall. These were characteristic boobies, so brutalised by foxhunting and hard drinking that Topehall's own sister called him 'the Savage'. When Roderick incurs Sir Timothy's resentment the woman who succoured him encourages him to flee, since Thicket would seek revenge. 'Indeed I cannot see how you will be able to elude his vengeance,' she warns him; 'being himself in the commission, he will immediately grant warrants for apprehending you; and as almost all the people in this country are dependent on him or his friend, it will be impossible for you to find shelter among them.'[18]

Not all the dependants of the local Sussex squires are brutes, for one of them, Topehall's sister Narcissa, is such a paragon of beauty and virtue that she eventually becomes Random's wife. Moreover, they resolve to settle down in the country, albeit in Scotland rather than in Sussex, on his father's estate. Upon their arrival there they 'were met by a prodigious number of poor tenants, men, women and children, who testified their joy by loud acclamations, and accompanied our coach to the gate'. Although Smollett makes Random attribute their affection to the fact that 'there is no part of the world in which the peasants are more attached to their lords than in Scotland', the real difference between them and the country people he met in England is not that of nationality. In Sussex they lived under the sway of brutal patricians, while Roderick's father was a benevolent patriarch, who 'had always been their favourite, and now that he appeared their master, after having been thought dead so long, their joy broke out into a thousand extravagancies'. Orson Topehall is a more tyrannical patrician than Squire Western, incarcerating his sister for years to prevent her marriage to Roderick Random. Don Rodrigo, as Roderick's father is known after his sojourn in Argentina, is, by contrast, a patriarch in the mould of Sir Roger de Coverley and the Man of Ross. After his tenants had greeted him by kissing his hand or the hem of his garment 'he ordered some bullocks to be killed, and some hogsheads of ale to be brought from the neighbouring village, to regale these honest people, who had not enjoyed such a holiday for many years before'.[19]

The landowners who appear in *Roderick Random*, therefore, are no more, or less, representative of real landed proprietors of the time than are Squires Allworthy and Western. Like Fielding's creations, they are patrician and patriarchal stereotypes developed very much from a Country point of view.

Unlike Fielding, however, Smollett does not have a good word to say about army officers. Those whom Roderick Random encounters in England, from Captain Weazel in the wagon between Newcastle and London, to the captain in the coach to Bath, are arrogant braggarts revealed as cowards when put to the test. In the navy, on the other hand, although he meets monsters like Oakum, the ferocious and arbitrary captain of the *Thunder*, he also makes the acquaintance of sympathetic characters such as his own uncle Bowling. Smollett clearly preferred the Senior Service, perhaps because he himself had been on the Cartagena expedition and knew naval life at first hand. At the same time distrust of the army and reliance on the navy was a constant factor in Country thinking.

Three of the more whimsical characters in *Peregrine Pickle*, Commodore Hawser Trunnion, Lieutenant Jack Hatchway and Boatswain Tom Pipes, are also naval types. The association of the navy with Country politics is established at the very outset of the novel when Trunnion protests volubly at the promotion of worthless seamen under the present administration, and the neglect of the meritorious, in contrast with the practice during the reign of Queen Anne, when such able admirals as Sir John Jennings and Sir George Rooke rose to eminence. His choice of these two is interesting, for Jennings was a staunch Whig, while Rooke was a High Church Tory champion. Trunnion could have chosen a number of Whig admirals to associate with Jennings, notably Sir Cloudesley Shovel, who rose from being a cabin boy by personal merit alone and who was thus particularly relevant to his observation. Rooke in fact had been a controversial figure, being set aside as commander-in-chief by the Whigs when they came to control naval appointments in 1705, because of his involvement with High Church Tory politics. Trunnion's own sympathy for such political views is also reflected in his choice of

Jacob Jolter to be Peregrine's 'governor', 'to whom he allowed a very handsome appointment for that purpose'. Jolter, we are informed, 'being an highchurchman, and of consequence a malecontent, his resentment was habituated into an insurmountable prejudice against the present disposition of affairs which, by confounding the nation with the ministry, sometimes led him into erroneous, not to say, absurd, calculations'. There is even a hint that he might be a Jacobite. Peregrine, finding Jolter's journal on returning from Europe, inserted in it the words 'Mem., Had the pleasure of drinking myself into a sweet intoxication, by toasting our lawful king, and his royal family, among some worthy English fathers of the society of Jesus.'[20] Yet Jolter plays a key role in Peregrine's education, accompanying him while at Winchester and at Oxford, and on the Grand Tour.

Peregrine, a born rebel, resists his mentor's attempts to indoctrinate him. This is particularly apparent in their respective views concerning France. On their voyage thither

> Jolter, transported with the thought of a speedy landing, began to launch out in praise of that country for which they were bound. He observed, that France was the land of politeness and hospitality, which were conspicuous in the behaviour of all ranks and degrees, from the peer to the peasant; that a gentleman and a foreigner, far from being insulted and imposed upon by the lower class of people, as in England, was treated with the utmost reverence, candour and respect; that their fields were fertile, their climate pure and healthy, their farmers rich and industrious, and the subjects in general the happiest of men.[21]

Pickle responds to these sentiments on this occasion by rushing up on the deck to be sick, Smollett leaving it ambiguous whether this is due to the motion of the ship or the nauseating Francophilia of Jolter. He replies much less equivocally to his governor's later effusions on the subject of France. Jolter

> took an opportunity of imparting to his pupil the remarks he had made upon the industry of the French, as an undeniable proof of which he bad him cast his eyes around,

> and observe with what care every spot of ground was cultivated; and from the fertility of that province, which is reckoned the poorest in France, conceive the wealth and affluence of the nation in general.

Amazed and disgusted by these observations, Peregrine

> answered that what he ascribed to industry, was the effect of meer wretchedness; the miserable peasants being obliged to plough up every inch of ground to satisfy their oppressive landlords, while they themselves and their cattle looked like so many images of famine; that their extreme poverty was evident from the face of the country, on which there was not one inclosure to be seen, or any other object, except scanty crops of barley and oats, which could never reward the toil of the husbandmen; that their habitations were no better than paltry huts; that in twenty miles of extent, not one gentleman's house appeared; that nothing was more abject and forlorn than the attire of their country people; and lastly, that the equipage of their travelling chaises was infinitely inferior to that of a dung cart in England.[22]

It is obvious, without the verification of his own *Travels*, that Smollett shared the convictions of Pickle rather than those of Jolter. His disdain for the Tories' admiration of French culture is another indication that his opposition to the Whig ministries of the years 1714-60 was from a Country rather than from a Tory standpoint.

At the same time his Country ideology was not underpinned by an admiration for classical republicanism, unlike that of many Whigs who wrote in a republican tradition.[23] Among the latter was Mark Akenside, who features in the novel as a physician encountered by Peregrine and Jolter in Paris. Jolter and the physician engage in a dispute about the respective merits of High Church Toryism and republicanism. Smollett pours scorn on both in his account of the disputation, his very language being chosen with a view to ridiculing their positions:

> These gentlemen, with an equal share of pride, pedantry and saturnine disposition, were by the accidents of educa-

> tion and company, diametrically opposite in political maxims: the one . . . being a bigotted high churchman, and the other a rank republican. It was an article of the governor's creed, that the people could not be happy, nor the earth yield its fruits in abundance, under a restricted clergy and limited government: whereas in the doctor's opinion, it was an eternal truth, that no constitution was so perfect as the democracy, and that no country could flourish, but under the administration of the mob.

Yet as the argument proceeds Jolter scores several points off the doctor. For instance, he points out that

> The liberal arts and sciences had never flourished so much in a republick as under the encouragement and protection of absolute power; witness the Augustan age, and the reign of Lewis the fourteenth; nor was it to be supposed that genius and merit could ever be so amply recompensed by the individuals, or distracted councils of a commonwealth, as by the generosity and magnificence of one, who had the whole treasures at his own command.

At this, Peregrine 'observed that there seemed to be a good deal of truth in what Mr Jolter advanced'. The doctor replied by asking Jolter 'if he did not think that very power of rewarding merit, enabled an absolute prince to indulge himself in the most arbitrary licence over the lives and fortunes of his people?' Jolter's reply is most interesting. He

> affirmed that though supreme power furnished a good prince with the means of exerting his virtues, it would not support a tyrant in the exercise of cruelty and oppression: because in all nations, the genius of the people must be consulted by their governors, and the burthen proportioned to the shoulders on which it is laid. 'Else, what follows?' said the physician. 'The consequence is plain; (replied the governor) insurrection, revolt, and his own destruction: for it is not be to supposed that the subjects of any nation would be so abject and pusillanimous as to neglect the means which heaven hath put in their power for their own preservation.'

It was a strange form of High Church Toryism, especially after Jolter's assertion 'that monarchy was of divine institution, therefore indefeasible by any human power', which gave the subject the divine right to resist a tyrant.[24] Here surely the characters of Jolter and the doctor are laid aside, and Smollett refutes Akenside directly. If he was a Tory, his Toryism included an escape clause which justified resistance.

The fictitious debate resumes with the adversaries becoming incensed until Jolter loses his temper and leaves the room. Peregrine compliments the physician on his victory, though his praises are ironical. Again it is clear from Smollett's language that he shares his hero's real disdain for the doctor, who was

> so elevated by his success, that he declaimed a full hour on the absurdity of Jolter's proposition, and the beauty of the democratic administration; canvassed the whole scheme of Plato's republic, with many quotations from that ideal author; touching the To Καλον; from thence he made a transition to the moral sense of Shaftsbury, and concluded his harangue with the greatest part of that frothy writer's rhapsody, which he repeated with all the violence of enthusiastic agitation.[25]

To what extent Smollett identified himself with other attitudes adopted by Peregrine Pickle, however, is much less clear. His hero is far from being an admirable character in all respects. On the contrary, he is hot-blooded, quick to anger and resentment, violent, impulsive, arrogant, lecherous and prodigal. Smollett's attempts to offset these traits with virtues such as his affection for Trunnion, Pipes and Hatchway, his love for his sister and Emilia, and his boundless generosity, do not tip the balance in Pickle's favour, as the novelist himself realised when he suppressed or edited some of the more unsavoury adventures in the second edition. It seems that Smollett sympathised with his 'adventurer's' volatile passion more than did most readers. Certainly excess of language and extremes of violence are hallmarks of his early novels, making them characteristically coarser and more brutal than those of contemporaries such as Fielding and Richardson. At the same time one of the major themes in *Peregrine Pickle* concerns the development of the hero's character to the point where he is worthy of the hand of the fair Emilia, just as Fielding develops that of Tom Jones until he is acceptable as Sophia's husband. The transformation is harder for Pickle, however, since he begins with greater disadvantages, having more faults than Jones and fewer redeeming features. One of the characteristics which makes him hard to take is his delight in practical jokes, some of which show him up to be nothing but a bully. Yet Smollett takes such obvious delight in his pranks, in which Pipes and Hatchway frequently take part as accomplices, that he apparently sees them as an endearing trait in his hero. They actually make him into an anti-hero, or Lord of Misrule. It is the taming of his rebellious instincts by experiencing their unfortunate consequences, however, that finally brings Pickle to heel.

In this process political circumstances play a crucial role. Of all the brick walls Peregrine bangs his head against, the thickest is that of the court. His attempts to get preferment from courtiers are more persistent and more serious than those of Roderick Random.

His first application is made not on his own behalf but on that of Godfrey, Emilia's brother. Godfrey Gauntlett is unusual in these two novels in being a meritorious army officer – brave, honourable, a true gentleman. When Pickle first encounters him he is 'a needy volunteer, greatly inferior to himself in fortune'. It turns out that his father, a subaltern officer of marines, had been with Trunnion on the *Warwick*, a man-of-war, and had impressed the Commodore with his bravery. When Peregrine learns of Godfrey's situation he expresses 'innumerable execrations upon the ingratitude and injustice of the ministry, which had failed to provide for the son of such a brave soldier'. Peregrine makes up for the ministry's neglect by getting Trunnion to give Godfrey money, on the pretext that it was a debt he owed his father, and then by bribing an official in the War Office to obtain the young soldier a commission. Later Peregrine procures a captain's commission for Godfrey from a nobleman whose interest at court was very powerful, by waiving a gambling debt which the peer's son owed him. Although it seems at the time that justice has finally been done, it has in fact cost Pickle £2000 to obtain Godfrey's commission, since that was the amount he had won from the nobleman's son at cards.[26]

Nevertheless, Peregrine's success with this nobleman does not prepare him for the disappointment his own hopes receive from another court peer, and a member of the ministry, possibly the prime minister himself. The court peer acts as a father-figure to Pickle, who is virtually an orphan following the total disregard of him by his parents and the death of Commodore Trunnion. He persuades Peregrine to abandon his profligate life and to invest his remaining assets in seemingly safe securities. He also induces him to stand as a candidate in a general election, presumably that held in 1747, 'assuring him that if he could once procure a seat in the house, he might look upon his fortune as already made'.[27]

In fact the court peer's advice proves to be the final cause of Peregrine's ruin. His recommendations about investments are not disinterested, for his steward persuades Pickle to invest £10,000 in mortgages on his lordship's own estates. The election costs him a great deal of money, for he stands as a candidate in a borough where the prevailing interest is enjoyed by a duke who sides with the opposition. His grace spends so much that Peregrine, after spending £2000 of his own money, is obliged to borrow £1200 from the Treasury to keep up the contest. All his efforts are fruitless, however, for the ministry comes to an accommodation with the duke in which Pickle is prevailed upon to stand down. 'No other disappointment in life could have given him such chagrin as he felt at the receipt of this tantalising order,' Smollett observes, 'by which the cup of success was snatched from his lip, and all the vanity of his ambitious hope humbled in the dust. He curs'd the whole chain of his court connexions, inveighed with great animosity against the rascally scheme of politicks, to which he was sacrificed.'[28] Although he is promised another seat when it becomes vacant, this never materialises.

Notwithstanding his mortifying experience, Pickle continues to believe the promises of the courtiers, especially when he is taken under the wing of a leading minister, Sir Steady Steerwell. He does not realise that the court peer has procured this patronage not because he is concerned for Peregrine's fate but because he dare not risk knowledge of the mortgage transaction coming to light. Pickle fails to obtain a place, but does procure a pension, albeit of only £300 a year, which is a meagre return on the money he had invested in the election campaign. This temporarily lifts the gloom which had uncharacteristically affected him, and he even recommences the profligate way of life he had managed to renounce. Then the final blow of the court peer's death falls heavily upon him. He is financially ruined, for the heir to the estate repudiates the debt of £10,000. In a desperate attempt to redeem his shattered fortunes he turns writer, 'and, conscious of the little regard which is, in this age, paid to every species of poetic composition, in which neither satire, nor obscenity occurs, he produced an imitation of Juvenal, and lashed some conspicious characters, with equal truth, spirit, and severity'. It is perhaps this kind of composition which leads him to lose the last shred of favour from Sir Steady Steerwell. At all events, his pension is not renewed at the end of the year, and when he protests about this to the minister he is debarred from his house. 'This prohibition, which announced his total ruin, filled him with rage, horror and despair.'[29] He becomes so distracted, indeed, that when the peer who procured Gauntlett's commission intercedes with the minister on Pickle's behalf Sir Steady explains his refusal to see Peregrine by asserting that he appears to be insane.

Peregrine attempts to revenge himself on the minister by attacking him in print, saying: 'I will forthwith exhibit the monster to the public, in his true lineaments of craft, perfidy, and ingratitude.' The use of the word 'craft' echoes the title of the opposition periodical, the *Craftsman*. Pickle is now finally identified with the Country partisans, 'distinguishing himself in the list of those who, at that period, wrote against the administration'.[30] Unfortunately the minister retaliates by having him arrested for the non-repayment of the money he lent to him for his election expenses. He is then left to languish and rot in the Fleet.

Smollett rescues him from prison by the providential device of having his father die without making a will, so that he inherits the country house and a fortune estimated at £80,760. Peregrine's response to this shows how his experiences have led him to espouse Country values:

> This was a sum that even exceeded his expectation, and could not fail to entertain his fancy with the most agreeable ideas. He found himself immediately a man of vast consequence among his country neighbours, who visited him with compliments of congratulation, and treated him with such respect as would have effectually spoiled any young man of his disposition, who had not the same advantages of experience as he had already purchased at a very extravagant price. Thus shielded with caution, he bore his prosperity with surprising temperance; every body was charmed with his affability and moderation; and when he made a circuit round the gentlemen of the district, in order to repay the courtesy which he owed, he was caressed by them with uncommon assiduity, and advised to offer himself as a candidate for the county, at the next election, which, they supposed, would soon happen, because the present member was in a declining state of health.[31]

To become a knight of the shire would be the ultimate Country accolade, for county seats were regarded as much more prestigious than borough seats, while most of them were held by opposition MPs.

As if to reassure readers that in his conversion to Country values Peregrine was not opting for clownish rusticity, Smollett has him encounter a booby squire on his way back to London and marriage to Emilia. He is astonished to find that the squire's ancestral portraits, painted by Van Dyck, have been altered with the addition to each head of a ridiculous tye-periwig. The squire explains in a broad provincial accent that he commissioned the additions because 'I could not abide to zee the pictures of my vamily, with a parcel of loose hair hanging about their eyes, like zo many colts; and zo I employed a painter vellow from London to clap decent periwigs upon their skulls at the rate of vive shillings a head.' Peregrine Pickle's education and experience have prevented him from becoming 'such a barbarous Goth'.[32]

7

Augustan Writers and their Readers

Weekly essays, amatory plays and novels, political pamphlets and books that revile religion; together with a general hash of these, served up in some monthly mess of dulness, are the meagre literary diet of town and country.

John Brown, *An Estimate of the Manners and Principles of the Times* (1757)

To claim that Augustan literature documents not so much reality as ideology is to beg the question how far ideologies reflect social realities. Is literature part of a Marxist superstructure, rooted in a socio-economic substructure? Even literary historians who do not see it in quite such reductive terms have used Marxian phraseology to describe the relationship between society and literature in the eighteenth century. The novel, for instance, is often regarded as a 'bourgeois' art form, and its rise has been coupled with that of the bourgeoisie under the Hanoverians.

The trouble is that not all historians, even Marxist historians, are agreed that the period did witness the rise of a bourgeoisie in the sense of urban business and professional men conscious of forming an independent class. E. P. Thompson explicitly refined the Marxist novel to cater for their alleged failure to act as a class. As we have seen, he sees eighteenth-century English society in terms of two 'classes', the patricians and the plebs, but regards most of those in the middle to have been too dependent upon the landed elite as clients to form a separate bourgeoisie.[1] He has conceded that the business men of London were sufficiently independent of the aristocracy and gentry to constitute a bourgeoisie in the capital, but by implication still denies that those in other towns were recognisable as a distinct class forming a social category which transcended local boundaries to be conscious of having interests in common with men of similar status throughout the nation. Other historians would argue that their counterparts elsewhere were becoming increasingly aware that they formed a separate interest in society, distinguishing themselves from the landowners above them and the mass of the labouring people below.

However, it is unnecessary to become involved in this argument here, since so few writers in this period can be described as provincial. Almost all became associated with London, which was then the cultural capital of the country. London acted as a magnet for writers of all sorts. Playwrights were virtually forced to live there, since opportunities for presenting new plays in the provinces were rare. Although the provincial theatre was firmly established by 1760, with permanent companies in places like Bath and Bristol, Norwich and York, they tended to stage productions first performed in the capital. Without access to the London theatres, therefore, dramatists would not have been able to sustain themselves professionally. Contributors to periodicals on a regular basis also had to be there to get their copy to the printer in time for publication, for while provincial newspapers and even magazines became established at this time, most of their material was copied from the London press. Even poets and novelists, though they were less dependent upon the actual mechanics of production, tended to gravitate to the capital, like Johnson from Staffordshire and Smollett and Thomson from Scotland. As Pat Rogers concludes, 'Few ages have known a more thoroughly metropolitan literary elite.'[2] The only question which need concern us, therefore, is: what relationship did authors have to the city's bourgeoisie?

Pinning down the precise position of individuals in society is notoriously difficult. Does a man's status derive from his family, for instance, or from the group he joins when he becomes independent?

If we take background to be the more important criterion then very few can be identified with the commercial community of the city. Most writers were born in the provinces, even if they migrated to the capital to join the cultural elite. Moreover, they were the sons of country gentlemen and professional men rather than of business men. James Sutherland concluded from an analysis of poets in Johnson's *Lives* that 'Of their parents a considerable number were either noblemen or landed gentlemen, but rather more of them were professional men – lawyers, doctors or clergymen. Eight of the poets (or about one in five) were the sons of parsons.' Pat Rogers discovered from a sample of 100 poets that most received the education of gentlemen. Fifty attended the Universities of Oxford or Cambridge, while a further nine went to Trinity College, Dublin, or Edinburgh University. This led him to conclude that 'Writers of any standing tended to become assimilated into the dominant class.'[3]

Whether they remained so when they embarked on their careers as authors is another question. Should we place writers alongside professional men, since literature is a profession of sorts? That would at least put them in the same social category as the bourgeoisie, if not in the same occupational group. Then again, if we regard writing as a trade, it almost merges them with the commercial classes. In this very broad sense, however, all authorship is the work of a bourgeoisie, and to call literature bourgeois becomes a mere tautology. A further difficulty here, moreover, is that not all authors were professional in the sense of making a full-time living from the profits of their works. Aristocratic writers such as Lords Bolingbroke and Lyttelton had private incomes from land as their primary source of income. Some in addition, like the Earl of Chesterfield, held high office in the state as well as being literary men. Joseph Addison became a Secretary of State, while Matthew Prior was a diplomat. Even Daniel Defoe, who lived more by his pen than did most writers of the time, was employed in government service, albeit at a humbler level. Jonathan Swift and Edward Young were Anglican clergymen. Mark Akenside, John Arbuthnot, Samuel Garth, Bernard Mandeville and Tobias Smollett were medical practitioners. George Farquhar, Richard Steele and John Vanbrugh obtained commissions in the army. George Lillo and Samuel Richardson were tradesmen, as, of course, was Defoe, a man of many lives. Robert Dodsley started out as a footman, and Stephen Duck as a thresher. Remarkably few were directly involved with the business activities of the

London bourgeoisie, an exception being the merchant Richard Glover.

These occupations spanned a wide spectrum and indicate that, beyond the fact that they published their writings, there was no common interest binding Augustan authors to the same class. Indeed, they were acutely conscious of social distinctions among themselves. The more affluent looked down on those who depended on a cheap mass market for their publications to earn them a livelihood. Such 'mercenary scribblers' as their superiors styled them were collectively castigated as Grub Street hacks. Grub Street was the down-market end of the publishing trade, whose products were chapbooks, handbills, ballads and cheap pamphlets. It was mercilessly satirised by Swift in *A Tale of a Tub* and by Pope in the *Dunciad*. Even those with private means, or who earned enough from the up-market trade to maintain themselves, did not share a common ideology. On the contrary, in Anne's reign their political differences were so great that some leading writers formed themselves into exclusive societies, the Tory wits in the Scriblerus and Brothers' Clubs, the Whigs in the Kit-Kat Club. Although the polarisation of the literary world was not quite so institutionalised under the first two Georges, this does not mean that an ideological consensus had been achieved which authors could share.

In this respect the characterisation of the age by historians as one of political stability, or by literary scholars as 'the peace of the Augustans', is deceptive. Although in comparison with the seventeenth century, when it was torn apart by civil war, and with the nineteenth century, when it was divided by reform, Augustan England seems remarkably stable and peaceful, there were nevertheless profound disagreements about the ways in which society was developing. Some reacted to change with unease and even with apprehension. They regretted the passing of a more structured society which they imagined had existed in the recent or remote past. Politically they found refuge in what has been called the politics of nostalgia. Others welcomed change, some cautiously, some eagerly, discerning in it signs of progress rather than of decadence. There were too many shades of opinion to classify every writer as being on either one side or the other.

Yet broadly speaking, those who held the first outlook subscribed to the Country tradition, while those who held the second maintained a Court Whig philosophy. It would be a mistake to distinguish the two groups of writers socially, for the differences within them were greater than those between them. Country authors ranged from aristocrats like Lords Bolingbroke and Lyttelton to Dr Johnson, arriving penniless in London from Lichfield. Court apologists spanned a range from the affluent Addison to the impecunious Stephen Duck. Their pessimism or optimism about the changes they detected going on around them cannot be directly ascribed to their own positions in society.

Although the rival ideologies were not propagated by writers from different sections of society, the two groups did identify themselves with different interests. Those who wrote in the Country tradition idealised the traditional landed elite, representing its members as patriarchs who upheld a moral economy in their communities. Swift's Lord Munodi and Pope's Man of Ross were archetypes of this ideal. They were critical of *nouveaux riches* landowners who allegedly exploited their position ruthlessly as patricians. They also criticised the plutocrats of the business community. Pope's Timon and Balaam were the archetypal representatives of these interests. Court Whig writers reversed these priorities, attacking the interests identified with the Country opposition and defending those allegedly supporting the Whig regime. Thus Addison poked mild fun at Tory landlords in the relatively sympathetic figure of Sir Roger de Coverley, and savaged them with his portrayal of Foxhunter. He also depicted a substantial merchant sympathetically with the character of Sir Andrew Freeport. Defoe praised the world of high finance and its links with the Whig government.

To some extent their works were aimed at different audiences. The Scriblerian wits, Arbuthnot, Gay, Parnell, Pope and Swift, specifically addressed themselves to the 'gentle' reader, by which they meant not 'mild' but 'genteel'. They assumed that they were writing for gentlemen, and accused their opponents of catering for Grub Street. The *Spectator* was directed towards readers 'in Clubs and Assemblies, at Tea tables and in Coffee Houses', i.e. at cosmopolitan rather than country gentlemen.[4] Defoe wrote for a less polished readership, apparently assuming that his works were read primarily by tradesmen.

How far they reached their target readers is a question which cannot be satisfactorily answered in the present state of knowledge about the market. However, what few nuggets of facts and figures there are suggest that, in considering the Augustan audience, we should not be contemplating a single reading public. The notion entertained by Q. D. Leavis that the audience for 'Literature' was homogeneous in the eighteenth century, to be fragmented into readers of 'high-brow' and 'popular' fiction in the nineteenth, is an elitist fantasy.[5] There were at least three groups of readers in the Augustan age: the 'gentle', the middling sort, and the masses.

Pope's *Works* cost £1 7s for the nine-volume set in 1751, while his *Iliad* cost 6 guineas. At these prices only 'gentle' readers could afford to read him, 575 of whom undertook to purchase copies in advance of publication by way of subscription.

The 'gentle readers' to whom the Scriblerians appealed recorded their names in the lists of subscribers which usually accompanied books published by this method. Although quite humble people occasionally feature amongst them, by and large such publications were inevitably sponsored by the more affluent readers. A breakdown of almost any subscription list soon reveals how far this market was dominated by the social and economic elite rather than by the bourgeoisie.[6] Aristocrats, baronets and knights subscribed to books out of all proportion to their numbers in society. The number of subscribers to any one title was relatively small: of 765 books published by subscription between 1700 and 1750, 627 listed fewer than 500 names. Steele's *Lucubrations of Isaac Bickerstaff* (1710) was exceptional, therefore, in attracting 752 subscribers. Yet 71 of these were English peers, 35 were Irish or Scottish peers, 26 were sons of peers, 8 were bishops, and 66 were baronets or knights. To this total of 206 could be added the names of 62 women related to them by marriage. Thus over a third of Steele's subscribers belonged to the aristocracy or titled gentry, and included about 44 per cent of all English peers. Nicholas Rowe obtained a similar proportion of elite subscribers for his *Pharsalia*, published in 1718: 156, including two members of the royal family, out of 391. When Henry Fielding published his *Miscellanies* by subscription in 1743 he obtained 428 subscribers. Of these, 58 were peers of the realm, including no fewer than 12 dukes. Of the 37 women who subscribed, as many as 14 were peeresses. Below these were 12 baronets and 2 knights. Over half the subscribers were distinguished as 'esquires'. A very high proportion of these were lawyers, there being at least 78 identifiable members of the legal profession in the subscription list.

An analysis of subscription lists also reveals that some titles appealed to specific audiences. Predictably, legal tomes appealed to lawyers, local histories to subscribers from particular regions, Scottish works to Scots. Some discrimination can also be detected along political lines. For example, Joseph Trapp, the High Church Tory Professor of Poetry at Oxford, was sponsored not only by fellow-Oxonians but also by other Tories when he published his *Aeneid*, while the Whig historian John Oldmixon appealed to subscribers who shared his politics. Henry Brooke's *Gustavus Vasa*, a Country play so anti-Court that it was banned by the Lord Chamberlain under the Licensing Act of 1737, was published with a subscription list which reads like a roll-call of the opposition.

By and large, however, works which can be positively identified as attracting a particular political constituency were remarkably few. Of about 500 subscription lists which were published between 1710 and 1740, only a small proportion seem to have attracted a disproportionate support from MPs of different persuasions. Moreover, the bias appears to have been induced by the politics of the authors rather than by the subject-matter they discussed. Whig authors like Addison and Steele attracted Whig subscribers, while Tory authors like Matthew Prior appealed to Tories. Court poets like Stephen Duck obtained subscriptions from government Whigs, while Country playwrights like Henry Brooke received them from opposition politicians.

Even works by such partisans could have a more universal appeal if their contents were not obviously polemical. Despite

Alexander Pope's Catholicism and links with Tories, his *Odyssey* and *Works of Shakespeare* were supported by subscribers of all political persuasions, with no significant bias in favour of one group. The same can be said for the *Spectator*, thus justifying the claims of its Whig authors to be nonpartisan. Fielding, too, attracted subscriptions from a wide political spectrum for his *Miscellanies*, even though the Prince of Wales headed the list. The politics of his subscribers ranged from the staunch Hanoverian Whiggery of the Duke of Newcastle to the suspected Jacobitism of the Tory Sir John Hinde Cotton.

The further one moves from the clearly committed author or title to the apparently impartial essay or novel, then probably the wider was the political gamut spanned by readers. Although, as we have seen, much creative literature was charged with an ideological message, its creators were not just preaching to the converted.

They were also able to reach a wider public socially as well as politically. While the market for literary works might still have been dominated by the social elite, there can be no doubt that there was a rapid growth of reading amongst the middling sort in the Augustan period.

This is apparent from the development of the press during the years from 1695 to 1760. The lapsing of the Licensing Act in 1695, and with it the ending of a pre-publication censorship, encouraged the growth of a periodical press. At first this was largely confined to London, where several newspapers were established by 1702, one of them a daily. Together they might have sold about 44,000 copies a week, rising to between 67,000 and 78,000 before the death of Queen Anne. By 1760 the capital produced some ten papers, four of them dailies, which together accounted for at least 200,000 weekly sales. In that year London's population probably numbered around 700,000, so that the ratio of newspapers to potential readers was remarkably high, though, of course, many produced in the capital were also distributed to the provinces. Since there were some 6,620,000 inhabitants of England and Wales in 1761, the proportion of papers to possible readers in the country as a whole is not so impressive. Many, however, had increasing access to their own local papers as well as to the London press. The number of provincial papers rose from none in 1700 to nearly forty in 1760.[7] By then twenty-eight towns had their own local papers, five boasting two apiece while Bristol and Newcastle-upon-Tyne supported three. These radiated out from their places of publication to wide hinterlands. The *Newcastle Journal* circulated far beyond the Tyne, reaching the border at Berwick and the Cumberland coast at Whitehaven. The *Cambridge Chronicle* boasted on its masthead that it was distributed to thirteen counties. These distribution areas became wide enough to overlap, until there was probably complete coverage of the country by metropolitan or provincial periodicals at the accession of George III.[8]

This network communicated far more than the latest news-worthy events. The periodical press carried advertisements for books and pamphlets, along with editorials, essays and letters, as well as news. It helped to create a market for literature which could be exploited by more durable works. The period saw a rapid growth of provincial booksellers, while circulating libraries were established in several towns and even villages by 1760. There was thus built up an infra-structure for a potential mass readership nationwide between 1700 and 1760.

Restrictions of literacy and cost, however, confined this audience in practice mainly to the middle station of life. Contemporaries seem to have been impressed and even alarmed at the general consumption of newspapers. Ned Ward, for instance, observed that

> Ev'ry cobbler quits his Awl
> And twice a day for coffee leaves his stall
> Purely to read, or if he can't, to hear
> What wonders we have done this present year
> Porters at ev'ry corner of the Street
> Read nothing now but *Postman* and *Gazette*.[9]

The coffee which the cobbler allegedly drank twice a day would be served in the coffee-houses which were a major institution in Augustan England. There were 650 of them in London alone by 1714, while many provincial towns could boast them. Their proprietors provided reading matter as well as beverages for their customers. Most patrons perused newspapers, though there were other publications available in some coffee-houses. One in Winchester stocked the monthly magazines, the sessions papers and 'dying speeches', as well as several papers in 1757. The availability of periodicals boosted readership beyond circulation figures. Just how many readers consulted each copy is impossible to calculate. Joseph Addison guessed that every *Spectator* was read by twenty people. This had been criticised as an overestimate, though some contemporaries considered that fifty readers per paper was not impossible.

Whether cobblers did in fact frequent coffee-houses is difficult to determine. There is, however, no dearth of comment on these establishments, for they inspired a great deal of contemporary observation, including two plays which were actually set in them, James Miller's *The Coffee-House* and Henry Fielding's *The Coffee-House Politician.* Many writers commented on the mixing of social classes which they produced. A very early description of one, *The Character of a Coffee-House* (1673), likened it to Noah's ark, since it received 'animals of every sort. . . . Often you may see a silly fop and a worshipful justice, a griping rook and a grave citizen, a worthy lawyer and an errant pickpocket, a reverend nonconformist and a canting mountebank, all blended together to compose an oglio of impertinence.'[10] *Both Sides Pleas'd*, a tract of 1710, imagined a dialogue in one between two people representing High Church and Low Church positions, in the presence of such tradesmen as butchers, carpenters, shoemakers and tailors, and even a weaver and a Thames waterman. Such observations, however, need to be treated cautiously. They tend to come from their more affluent customers, who might have been prone to exaggerate the extent to which coffee-houses were social levellers. Thus somebody who appeared to be a cobbler to a gentleman could well have been a well-established master shoemaker in fact.

How many cobblers were able to read is also hard to gauge, though 58 per cent of Norwich shoemakers were apparently literate in the period 1580-1700. There are some crude literacy tests available, mainly by analysing signatures and marks on the marriage registers which became compulsory after 1753. It is assumed for purposes of measurement that those who could sign their names were able to read, while most of those who could only make a mark were illiterate. Such evidence, fraught with imponderables though it is, indicates, as one would expect, that women were more illiterate than men, and that illiteracy increased as one went down the social scale. It was not, however, as marked as might be assumed. By 1760 about 60 per cent of women were unable to sign marriage registers compared with about 40 per cent of men. The gentry, business and professional men at the apex of society were almost all literate. Most tradesmen and craftsmen could apparently read, while the majority of servants and labourers could not. Even at the lowest levels, however, there was a substantial minority, around 41 per cent, which was literate. In London this could have been a majority, for the geographical distribution of literacy varied enormously from region to region and even from parish to parish within a district. Female domestic servants in rural areas were among the least literate sections of society, which makes the writing of Pamela's highly readable letters a most unlikely feat in reality. London was the most literate centre in the country, while three-quarters of the children in the parish school in Islington were recorded as able to read, with no significant differences between sexes, in the late eighteenth century.[11]

What they read, of course, depended upon what literature was accessible to them. Journeymen earned between 9s and £2 a week in mid-eighteenth-century London. Most skilled workers probably took home about 15s weekly in the capital.[12] Since it was estimated that it cost about 6s for board and lodging, this left a surplus over subsistence which could have been used to acquire novels selling for between 2s 6d and 6s. Some craftsmen therefore could have been among the 5000 readers who bought *Robinson Crusoe* at 5s a copy, or the 6000 who purchased *Joseph Andrews* at 6s. They would, however, have been beyond the means of labourers, who earned little more than subsistence wages. So would most circulating libraries, which demanded subscriptions so high that only gentlemen and substantial professional and business men could afford them. On the other hand, the practice of publishing part books did bring some otherwise inaccessible works within reach of a mass readership. Serial publication, with each part as cheap as 6d and even less, became quite extensive. According to R. M. Wiles, 'More than three hundred new and reprinted works were so issued before 1750, on almost every conceivable subject.'[13] History sold well by this method, Tobias Smollett's serialised *History of England* finding 13,000 purchasers.

There was also a mass of ephemeral literature which circulated even at the lowest levels of the society. Almanacs and chapbooks produced cheaply by the thousand on coarse paper with crude print and cruder woodcuts reached a very wide audience indeed.[14] Few of the literary works with which we have been concerned reached the masses. There were simplified texts of *Robinson Crusoe* and *Moll Flanders* in chapbook editions for semi-literate readers, but Defoe was apparently unique among Augustan authors in having a novel digested in this way.[15] Other novelists, however, might also have found a mass readership, if we are to believe the story of *Pamela* being read to assemblies of villagers, who rang the church bells when the heroine finally married Mr B. Certainly it was well enough known, if not read, for parsons to allude to it in their sermons as though their congregations were familiar with the story, and for dramatists to exploit it on the stage. A play based on the novel, described as 'a comedy' was performed in Goodman Fields theatre in 1742. Young Belmont, a character in Edward Moore's *The Foundling*, upon being invited to consider marriage, replies: 'Faith, I must read *Pamela* twice over first.'[16] Although Fielding thought that few who frequented the upper gallery of theatres would be readers of *Tom Jones*, in 1769 they could see a curious comic opera based on it by Joseph Reed. Reed admitted that he had 'made many material deviations from the novel both in point of fable and character'. He explained the changes thus:

> I have stripp'd its hero of his libertinism to render him, as I imagined, more aimiable and interesting, and have metamorphis'd Parson Supple into a country squire to avoid giving offence to the cloth. The characters of Western and Honour I have divested of their provinciality, lest the

> attention of the performers to the pronounciation of an uncouth and difficult dialect should produce an inattention to the more material business of the drama. I have also endeavoured to purge Western's character of its coarseness and indelicacy, in conformity to the refined taste of the present age; and of its Jacobitism, from an opinion that such political sect no longer exists; as well as from a conviction that nothing of party should appear within the walls of a theatre.[17]

Not much of the original survived such bowdlerisation.

Nevertheless, in one form or another the novel was the most popular genre of the period, reaching the widest audience. It transcended the barriers between the gentle reader and the middling sort, and even made contact with some of the masses.

Conclusion

> As I call my book a novel, not a History, I am not obliged to acquaint the publick whether the story's real or fictitious.
>
> Elizabeth Boyd, *The Happy-Unfortunate; or The Female Page: a novel* (1732)

There are some serious discrepancies between the observations made by contemporary creative writers, and the conclusions reached by modern historians, about the nature of English society in the first half of the eighteenth century. This has led some scholars to suggest that imaginative literature should be completely discarded as a source for the social history of the period. Certainly if we ask the question 'What was life really like in Augustan England?' we would be advised to turn to almost any evidence other than to the literary works of the age: to the private papers of the gentry rather than to Sir Tunbelly Clumsy and Sir Roger de Coverley for the life-styles of country gentlemen; to the records of Queen Anne's Bounty or the ledgers of a trading company rather than to Parson Adams or Sir Andrew Freeport for the professional and business communities; to parish registers or quarter sessions records rather than to Clarissa or Macheath for the family or criminal activity.

Yet if we ask different questions, then literature can be a key which opens many doors into the past. One of the more intriguing problems is: why is there such a variance between the testimony of creative writing and that of quantifiable documentary evidence?

One answer, at least as far as Augustan literature is concerned, is that creators of fiction were not attempting to reproduce reality, as the writer of a documentary might try to do. At best they reflected reality as in a mirror, and the historian must never forget that even an ordinary looking-glass shifts things around from right to left. Moreover, literary reflections are not in plain glass, for the mirror of literature distorts reality. Above all, Augustan authors slanted the reader's vision, adjusting it to their own ideological perception. In order to measure the degree of distortion, and to make adjustments for it, the historian needs to have recourse not only to historical method but also to some techniques of literary criticism.

Of course, historians are trained to evaluate the documents they cite as evidence. Even quantitative materials need careful interpretation, since they were rarely compiled to answer the same questions as modern scholars seek to solve. Moreover, in practice all but the most unimaginative historians have to rely on 'intuitive' sources, since not enough statistics can be generated about past societies to satisfy their curiosity. Reconstructions of previous communities have perforce to be eclectic in their documentation, and to accommodate such qualitative testimony as newspapers and pamphlets, and even personal correspondence and diaries. The routine procedures of historical analysis must include weighing the value of documents by establishing the credentials of their authors and the significance of their audiences. Traditional historical methodology therefore asks questions about the authorship of any document. For example, it tries to ascertain the level of the author's understanding of the matter under discussion; to determine whether or not he is biased; and to discover the nature of his relationship with his reader.

These automatic tests for the reliability of a source can be applied to literary evidence too. Authors should not be accepted as authorities without question. Historians who would hesitate to accept the testimony of a backbench MP on the topic of ministerial discussions should be sceptical of Defoe's dogmatic assertions about almost anything from adultery to xenophobia. Those who would suspect the impartiality of a JP who was also a landlord dealing with a tenant found poaching should have doubts about the objectivity of the *Spectator* on the subject of servants. Those who make adjustments for whether a letter is sent to a relative, a friend, an enemy, a superior or an inferior should take into account the fact that a play was aimed at a particular audience in London.

Indeed, the difference between letters and the kind of literary evidence discussed in this book is not very marked. Epistolary correspondence can even be considered as a literary genre, especially when it was intended for publication anyway, as was frequently the case in this very period. Pope's letters to Swift and his *Epistles* to Bathurst and Burlington might, from one point of view, be considered as much the same kind of testimony.

Yet though slight, the distinction between such materials as autobiographies, diaries, letters and memoirs, which are the stock-in-trade of traditionally trained historians, and imaginative literature, is significant. Such genres as essays, novels, plays and poems which create manifest fictions also pose unique problems of historical interpretation. The relationship between the author and the reader, for instance, is crucial. The author is creating a fictitious world in order to persuade an imagined reader to accept his view of reality.

The anonymous hacks who cobbled together poems on affairs of state exploited a whole variety of fictional situations, including advice to a painter, mock litanies, midnight conclaves with the spirit of faction, the auction of a pack of hounds, dreams, visions and calves'-head feasts. It took a Pope to create an imagined universe presided over by the Goddess Dulness, but these rhetorical devices paved the way. They also preceded the creation of other fictional worlds in the early novel. Before Defoe wrote *Robinson Crusoe* he had conjured into existence a poetic 'Poland', peopled with politicians who passed for peers and MPs actually alive in contemporary England but who were in fact ideological stereotypes.[1]

Dramatists, too, created their own fictional worlds. In tragedy these were usually settings for well-known figures of world history, remote in time and place from Augustan England. There were exceptions to this, such as George Lillo's *The London Merchant*, which involved humbler characters than emperors and their noble retinues, and though placed in Elizabethan England, could be said to represent modern times. Comedies were even more familiar to their contemporary audiences, peopled by country gentry, business and professional men and their servants, and set in a part of the town not far from the theatres, rather than in ancient Rome or some historical or even fabulous location.

Unlike tragedy, therefore, which is manifestly 'unreal', contemporary comedies are the most seductive of literary sources, since they tempt the historian to accept them at face value as 'realistic' drama. Macaulay could not resist the temptation, accusing the comic dramatists of the Restoration of creating 'a world which is a great deal too real':

> Here the garb, the manners, the topics of conversation are those of the real town and of the passing day. The hero is in all superficial accomplishments exactly the fine gentleman whom every youth in the pit would gladly resemble. The heroine is the fine lady whom every youth in the pit would gladly marry. . . . A hundred little touches are employed to make the fictitious world appear like the actual world.[2]

Yet characters in comedies were not taken from real life so much as from a traditional portrait gallery of dramatic archetypes. Even those which claim to be realistic turn out on examination to be engravings from the stock portraits, perhaps hand-coloured by the playwright. John Mottley, for instance, wrote a comedy, *The Widow Bewitched*, in which the prologue boasted:

> No monstrous characters his Muse invents
> But draws what real life too oft presents.

Nevertheless, it includes Stanza, 'a fop of good estate and pretender to poetry', of whom another stock character, Colonel Courtly, says: 'With what pleasure have I observed you, when a whole room full of company have been put out of humour by some serious reflections on religion or morality, change the discourse in a trice to a topknot or a tweezer case.' Stanza goes through a marriage ceremony disguised as a monk, thinking his bride is Arabella when she is really Mimic in masquerade costume, only to discover that the wedding is invalid because the officiating parson was really the Colonel in clerical garb. Even Mottley acknowledged that this totally unreal situation was a dramatic convention, putting into Stanza's mouth the words 'Upon my soul, Colonel, I believe the adventures of this day might be work'd up into a good comedy; but these sham marriages have been a little too frequent upon the stage.'[3]

Although few nowadays would agree with Macaulay that drama reflected reality, it seems to be generally accepted that realism is a predominant characteristic of the early novel. Certainly location in a particular time and place is one of the features of such works as *Moll Flanders*, *Pamela*, *Clarissa*, *Joseph Andrews*, *Tom Jones*, *Amelia*, *Roderick Random* and *Peregrine Pickle* which makes them recognisable as novels in the modern sense. Previous writings which were called novels were for the most part set either in fabulous places like Atlantis, or in rather sketchy parts of France, Italy, Spain or some other European country. Relatively few were located in England, and even these tended to be vague about their actual settings. The modern novel arrived with Moll Flanders threading her way through the alleys of London, and with Tom Jones and Sophia Western chasing across the English countryside from Somerset to the capital.

The transition from a fabulous to a realistic environment gives Augustan novels the impression of being factual as well as fictitious. Early novelists took pains to stress this element in order to make their works more attractive to contemporary readers. As Eliza Tryon observed:

> If the Histories of Foreign amours and scenes laid beyond the seas, where unknown customs bear the greatest figure, have met with the approbation of English readers, 'Tis presumed that Domestick Intrigues, manag'd according to the humours of the town, and the natural temper of the inhabitants of this our island, will be at least equally grateful [*sic*]. But above all, the weight of Truth, and the importance of real matter of fact, ought to overbalance the feign'd adventures of a fabulous knight errantry.[4]

Defoe and Swift passed off the adventures of their fictitious characters as autobiographies or memoirs. Fielding apparently consulted almanacs to establish that the moon really did shine very brightly on that December night in 1745 when

Tom Jones kept his ill-fated assignation with Mrs Waters in the inn at Upton.

This concern to represent fiction as fact should make the historian even more suspicious of novelists as the depictors of 'real life' than of dramatists. Indeed, the early novel has more in common with contemporary plays than with the socially concerned novels of a later age. Henry Fielding developed from a dramatist into a novelist, and his theatrical experience colours much of his later writing, being especially noticeable in *Tom Jones*. Like his plays, the novels have a strong moral element, censuring as well as satirising the age.

Other early novelists were also moralists rather than realists. This is probably more obvious in the work of a minor writer like Eliza Haywood than it is in the works of Defoe, Fielding, Richardson or Smollett. Her novels span the gap between those set in places remote from contemporary England and those in a recognisable setting. *Love in Excess* and *The Fatal Secret* take place in France, *The Rash Resolve* and *The Force of Nature* in Spain, *Idalia* in Venice. The characters are mainly aristocrats, while *Lassalia* revolves around the court of Louis XIV. *The Surprise*, *The British Recluse* and *Fantomina*, on the other hand, are located in England, and while their heroes and heroines have traditionally fabulous names like Euphemia and Bellamant, Cleomira and Lysander, Fantomina and Beauplaisir, they nevertheless move in gentry circles and visit places like London, Bath and Wiltshire. Despite this apparent realism, however, all these novels have highly improbable plots. Fantomina, a lady of quality, disguises herself in turn as a whore, a chambermaid and a rich widow in order to keep Beauplaisir as her lover. Even Mrs Haywood admits that her deceiving him in these disguises is implausible, but tries to explain it away by claiming that she was a consummate actress. So she must have been to pass herself off as the rich widow and the whore in successive bedroom encounters with the presumably dim-sighted Beauplaisir. Insofar as these plots are not mere vehicles for pornography, at which Eliza was an accomplished mistress, they have rather dubious morals. After her sexual adventures in various guises Fantomina at last becomes pregnant and is sent to a French nunnery by her mother, the implication being that ladies of easy virtue will end up badly. The morals of the equally far-fetched *The Surprise* and *The British Recluse* are stated explicitly, the first in the subtitle, *Constancy Rewarded*, the second as 'The effects of love are not tranquillity and ease.'[5]

Although the morality of more celebrated novelists was rather more subtle, their works nevertheless carried similar messages. In *Pamela* it was conveyed in the subtitle, *Virtue Rewarded. Tom Jones* could perhaps have been subtitled 'Prudence Rewarded'. They can be regarded as being the literary equivalent of Hogarth's prints, which also tend to be wrongly regarded as realistic. How often, for instance, is 'Gin Lane' reproduced as though it was the eighteenth-century equivalent of a photograph of a real London street? How rarely is its companion piece, 'Beer Street', also reproduced? Yet they belong inseparably together as a diptych. Hogarth was making a moral point about the social consequences of a culture addicted to gin and one associated with ale. And behind the prints was an ideological message, made explicit in the accompanying verses:

> Beer happy Produce of our Isle
> Can sinewy Strength impart,
> And wearied with Fatigue and Toil,
> Can chear each manly Heart.
>
> Labour and Art upheld by Thee
> Successfully advance,
> We quaff Thy balmy Juice with Glee
> And Water leave to France.
>
> Genius of Health, thy grateful Taste
> Rivals the Cup of Jove,
> And Warms each English generous Breast
> With Liberty and Love.

The obvious moral is that beer is healthy and invigorating, whereas

> Gin, cursed Fiend, with Fury fraught,
> Makes human Race a Prey;
> It enters by a deadly Draught
> And steals our Life away.

The message is that beer, again unlike gin, strengthens not only the robust and cheerful workmen depicted in the print but also the English economy. It is a native 'Produce of our Isle', while spirits are represented as an alien distillation poisoning the workforce. Hogarth drives home the point that beer-drinking is patriotic and gin-drinking unpatriotic by depicting a copy of the king's speech on the table in 'Beer Street' and by including a statue of the Pretender on a stepped pyramid, with the Stuart symbols of the Lion and the Unicorn at the base, in the background of 'Gin Lane'. His message is therefore ultimately ideological, identifying beer with Revolution principles of 'Liberty' and gin with Jacobitism.

Much Augustan literature had a similar moral purpose and ideological message. Of course, the political bias of such leading Augustan authors as the members of the Tory Scriblerus Club and the Whig Kit-Cat Club has long been known. Obviously the Toryism of such men as Arbuthnot and Swift, and the Whiggism of Addison and Steele, need to be taken carefully into consideration when reading the John Bull tracts, the *Examiner* and the *Spectator*. What is not quite so obvious is the degree to which this bias suffuses the other major works of the period, including fictions such as *Gulliver's Travels* and *Robinson Crusoe*. For politics were not just a matter of scoring party points in polemical pamphlets and periodicals: they were the manifestation of ideological attitudes which coloured most aspects of life. Such themes as marriage and the family, which lie at the heart of contemporary plays and novels, got caught up in the conflicting ideologies.

The extent to which the literature of the period was suffused with ideological preconceptions was extraordinary. Even minor anonymous works were saturated with them. Indeed, from the point of view of the historian, the obscure and mediocre authors are often more rewarding than the celebrated and gifted, for they expressed crudely views which were enunciated with greater sophistication and ambiguity in the major works of literature. A remarkably high number of works, even plays, were published anonymously in these years. It used to be held that writers were reluctant to append their signatures to works at this time for fear of prosecution.

In fact the risks, though not negligible, were nothing like as great as they had been under the early Stuarts, when Star Chamber censored publications. Writers at that time risked having their ears cropped and other savage mutilations. Although the punishment of standing in the pillory could still be inflicted upon men convicted of seditious libel, it was no longer accompanied by such barbarities, despite Pope's reference to Defoe appearing there 'earless on high'. Attempts to control literary activity were far less repressive under the Hanoverians than they had been under the Stuarts. The lapsing of the Licensing Act in 1695 dismantled the official censorship and left the libel laws as the only check on publication. Although these gave the government extensive powers of prosecution, the state could only intervene after a work was published, and its intervention tended to be arbitrary and capricious rather than methodical and systematic. Not many authors can have been deterred by fears of the consequences of publication in the eighteenth century.

The resort to anonymity, therefore, was not entirely or even mainly due to attempts to evade detection by the authorities. Concealment of the author's true identity from his readers enabled him to develop a fictitious author or *persona*. Daniel Defoe did this in *The Shortest Way with the Dissenters* by impersonating a fanatical High Church Anglican who was completely intolerant of Dissenters. He was so successful that people took it seriously, thinking that it had been a genuine work by a fiery 'high-flyer' and not a satire by a Dissenter. Swift similarly disguised himself as a Grub Street hack in *A Tale of a Tub* and as a mad projector in *A Modest Proposal.* He also created pseudonymous authors, passing himself off as a Dublin tradesman in the *Drapier's Letters* and as a ship's surgeon in *Gulliver's Travels*. These imagined authors provided a convenient vehicle for satire. They could be used as mouthpieces to express views which the real author wished to attack, thereby condemning themselves out of their own mouths.

Among these *personae* were literary archetypes. These ran the whole gamut of society: modish beaux and fops; booby squires; quack doctors; pettifogging lawyers; grasping city merchants and their cuckolding wives; idle apprentices;

Arcadian shepherds and shepherdesses; and insubordinate servants. Many of these were traditional archetypal characters, traceable back to Elizabethan and even classical drama. To some extent they are timeless devices. Fielding's lawyer in the stage-coach, whom he claimed had lived for four thousand years, is still alive and well, being currently employed in the offices of *Private Eye*'s solicitors Sue, Grabbit and Run. Like the anonymous and pseudonymous authors, however, they could also be used as characters to express contemporary attitudes towards such types. Thus stage squires were exploited by Whig dramatists who regarded country gentlemen as their ideological opponents. Grasping city merchants, on the other hand, were usually creations of Tory writers, like Pope's Balaam, being used to criticise materialistic values attributed to the Whigs.

In response to these satirical attacks authors also developed sympathetic stereotypes to represent values which they admired. Thus Pope portrayed the Man of Ross as a patriarchal figure, while Addison and Steele depicted admirable business men in the characters of Sir Andrew Freeport and Sealand.

The ideal types which appeared in periodical essays or as characters in plays spill over into the pages of the early novel. Fielding's novels especially swarm with them, perhaps because he was an essayist and dramatist before he became a novelist. Squires Allworthy and Western develop the patriarch and the booby, while quack doctors and pettifogging lawyers abound. Fielding's ideology was basically that of a Country Whig, so that like Pope he could admire a patriarch such as Allworthy, but could also find fault with Tory gentry like Western, and even appreciate a member of the business community like Heartfree.

Creative literature is consequently useful as prime source material for historians if they try to establish how it works to persuade the target reader to accept its author's point of view. The techniques mentioned, and many others, were used to manipulate the assumed readers into concurring with the ideological perceptions of Augustan authors. During the reign of Queen Anne Tory writers sustained the social hierarchy and traditional values and attacked those elements in society, particularly the monied interest, which they accused of subverting both. During the reigns of George I and George II they were joined by dissident Whigs who came to acknowledge, or at least to assert, that Walpole was further undermining the fabric of society and the liberties of Englishmen. These opposition arguments fused into a Country ideology in contrast with alleged Court values. The rival ideologies, Tory and Whig, or Court and Country, inform the literature of the Augustan age to an extent which is probably without parallel in any other era of English history.

Notes

Introduction
(pp. 1-13)

1. B. Williams, *The Whig Supremacy* (revised ed., Oxford 1962), 144.
2. W. A. Armstrong, 'The Use of Information about Occupation' in E. A. Wrigley, ed., *Nineteenth-Century Society* (Cambridge 1972), 191, referring to T. S. Ashton.
3. P. Laslett, *The World We Have Lost* (1971), 90-1.
4. T. B. Macaulay, *The History of England*, ed. Sir C. Firth (6 vols, 1913), i, 310-13.
5. Sir C. Firth, *A Commentary on Macaulay's History of England* (1964), 96.
6. *Ibid.*, 97.
7. Lord Macaulay, *Essays* (1893), 735.
8. J. Addison, *The Freeholder*, ed. J. Leheny (Oxford 1979), 130-4.
9. Firth, 133.
10. Macaulay, *History*, i, 384.
11. Firth, 134.
12. *Ibid.*, 132.
13. C. Wilson, *England's Apprenticeship* (1965), 151.
14. J. Collier, *A Short View of the Prophaneness and Immorality of the English Stage* (1698), 215.
15. J. Vanbrugh, *Aesop* (1702; repr. 1734), 265-9.
16. J. Vanbrugh and C. Cibber, *The Provok'd Husband* (1741), 40.
17. J. Hopes, 'Politics and Morality in the Writings of Jeremy Collier', *Literature and History*, viii (1978), 159-74.
18. G. Burnet, *History of My Own Time* (6 vols, Oxford 1833), vi, 207-8, 212. This passage was written around 1708.
19. W. Wotton to Bishop Wake, 21 Mar. 1710 (Christ Church, Oxford, Wake MSS, vol. XVII: Misc. i., letter 243).

Chapter 1
Politics and Literature
(pp. 14-40)

1. G. M. Trevelyan, *English Social History* (1942), vii.
2. *Poems on Affairs of State*, vii, ed. F. H. Ellis (1975), 396.
3. *The Character of a Whig under Several Denominations* (1700),

15-34, 42-5. Interestingly, much of this tract was republished, stripped of its political connotations, in *The True Characters of – viz a Deceitful Pettifogger, vulgarly call'd Attorney, a Know-all Astrological Quack or Feigned Physician; a Female Hypocrite or Devil in Disguise; a Low Churchman or Ecclesiastical Bisarus, a Trimmer or Jack of All Sides* (1708).

4. C. Davenant, *The True Picture of a Modern Whig* (1701), 15-31.
5. *Poems on Affairs of State*, vi, ed. F. H. Ellis (1970), 19-20, 198, 221; vii (1975), 41, 488, 538.
6. J. A. Downie, *Robert Harley and the Press* (Cambridge 1980).
7. J. A. Downie and W. A. Speck, 'A Tract by Robert Harley', *Literature and History*, iii (1976), 100-10.
8. *Poems on Affairs of State*, vii, 90, 93.
9. Downie and Speck, 101; *Prose Works of Jonathan Swift*, ed. H. Davis (14 vols, Oxford 1939-68), vi, 59.
10. *Ibid.*, iii, 3-8.
11. *Ibid.*, vi, 10, 16, 41, 44, 55-6, 59.
12. J. Trenchard and T. Gordon, *Cato's Letters* (4 vols, 1755), i, 117-23: no. 18, 25 Feb. 1720.
13. *The Craftsman*, no. 1, 5 Dec. 1726.
14. See Alan Downie's forthcoming biography of Swift.
15. *Gulliver's Travels*, ed. H. Davis (Oxford 1956), 127-32, 196, 199.
16. J. Gay, *The Beggar's Opera*, ed. J. Hampden (1928), 112, 137.
17. *The Craftsman*, no. 85, 17 Feb. 1728.
18. *The Poems of Alexander Pope*, ed. J. Butt (1963), 420.
19. B. A. Goldgar, *Walpole and the Wits: The Relation of Politics to Literature, 1722-1742* (1976), 76.
20. *The Poems of Alexander Pope*, 349, 372, 425.
21. *Ibid.*, 800.
22. *Ibid.*, 573-4, 578.
23. *The Poetical Works of James Thomson*, ed. W. M. Rossetti [1873], 292, 450.
24. G. Lyttelton, *Letters from a Persian in England to his Friend at Ispahan* (1735), 177.
25. R. Glover, *Leonidas, a poem* (1769), 5.
26. *The Works of . . . Henry St John, Lord Viscount Bolingbroke*, ed. D. Mallet (5 vols, 1754), iii, 75, 77, 78, 85-6.
27. G. Lillo, *Fatal Curiosity* (1737), 6.
28. I. Kramnick, *Bolingbroke and his Circle: The Politics of Nostalgia in the Age of Walpole* (Cambridge, Mass. 1968).
29. Goldgar, 217-21.
30. J. H. Plumb, *Sir Robert Walpole* (2 vols, 1956-60); H. T. Dickinson, *Walpole and the Whig Supremacy* (1973).
31. E. P. Thompson, *Whigs and Hunters* (1975); L. Colley, *In Defiance of Oligarchy: The Tory Party, 1714-1760* (Cambridge 1982).
32. R. Browning, *Political and Constitutional Ideas of the Court Whigs* (1982).
33. Colley; J. C. D. Clark, *The Dynamics of Change: The Crisis of the*

1750s and English Party Systems (Cambridge 1982); E. Cruickshanks, ed., *Ideology and Conspiracy: Aspects of Jacobitism, 1689-1759* (Edinburgh 1982), 6-8.

34. *The Works of Sir Charles Hanbury Williams* (3 vols, 1822), i, 61-70; cf. Colley, 98; Cruickshanks, 7-8.
35. D. Thomson, 'The Conception of Political Party in England in the period 1740 to 1783' (PhD thesis, University of Cambridge, 1938); H. T. Dickinson, *Liberty and Property: Political Ideology in Eighteenth-Century Britain* (1977), 121-92. A partial exception is Browning, 176n, which asserts that 'the Whig/Tory axis remained at least of equal significance'. Certainly a study of Court thought essentially involves an aspect of Whiggism, for there were no Court Tories under the first two Georges. Yet this is precisely what makes their reigns so different from Anne's, and also makes the Court/Country dimension more significant than a Tory/Whig dichotomy.
36. H. T. Dickinson, ed., *Politics and Literature in the Eighteenth Century* (1974), 105.
37. See below, p. 148.

Chapter 2
Social Structure and Literature
(pp. 41-93)

1. For a brilliant survey of the field see R. Porter, *English Society in the Eighteenth Century* (1982).
2. P. Laslett, *The World We Have Lost* (1971), 23-54.
3. E. P. Thompson, 'Patrician Society, Plebeian Culture', *Journal of Social History*, vii (1974), 395.
4. N. Rogers, 'Money, Land and Lineage: The Big Bourgeoisie of Hanoverian London', *Social History*, iv (1979), 437-54.
5. P. Borsay, 'The English Urban Renaissance: The Development of a Provincial Urban Culture, *c.* 1680-*c.* 1760', *ibid.*, ii (1977), 581-603; repr. (1980) by the Open University in *Supplementary Material A322.* Cf. G. Holmes, *Augustan England* (1982).
6. J. Vanbrugh, *Aesop* (1702), 31.
7. Thompson, 395.
8. Borsay, 17.
9. Cf. Laslett; Thompson; G. Mingay, *The Gentry: The Rise and Fall of a Ruling Class* (1976).
10. H. Fielding, *Tom Jones*, ed. F. Bowers (2 vols, Oxford 1974), ii, 742.
11. J. Swift, *Gulliver's Travels*, ed. H. Davis (Oxford 1956), 175-6.
12. *The Poems of Alexander Pope*. ed. J. Butt (1963), 592-4.
13. H. Carey, *Dramatic Works* (1743), 221.
14. *The Spectator*, ed. D. F. Bond (5 vols, Oxford 1965), i, 439-40, 445.
15. W. A. Speck, 'The Harlot's Progress in Eighteenth-Century England', *British Journal of Eighteenth-Century Studies*, iii (1980), 126-39.

16. S. Richardson, *Pamela*, ed. P. Sabor (1980), 43.
17. S. Richardson, *The History of Sir Charles Grandison*, ed. J. Harris (3 vols, 1972), i, 142, 213.
18. *The Spectator*, i, 444, 460, 464, 498.
19. *The Poems of Alexander Pope*, 581-2.
20. *Gulliver's Travels*, 176.
21. H. Erskine-Hill, *The Social Milieu of Alexander Pope* (1975), 15-41.
22. G. Lyttelton, *Letters from a Persian in England to his Friend at Ispahan* (1735), 117-20.
23. *The Spectator*, ii, 20-1, 187; iv, 467-8.
24. J. Dorman, *Sir Roger de Coverley; or The Merry Christmas* (1740), 11.
25. *Guilliver's Travels*, 179.
26. *The Character of a Whig under Several Denominations* (1700), 62-72, 132-4.
27. *The Poems of Alexander Pope*, 594-5; and see Erskine-Hill, 279-317.
28. *The Coquet's Surrender; or The Humourous Punster* (1732), 2.
29. D. Hume, *Essays, Moral, Political and Literary* (Oxford 1963), 579.
30. D. Defoe, *Robinson Crusoe*, ed. J.D. Crowley (1972), 4.
31. D. Defoe, *Moll Flanders*, ed. J. Mitchell (1978), 77-8.
32. *Tom Jones*, i, 185, 515.
33. H. Fielding, *Joseph Andrews*, ed. M. C. Battestin (Oxford 1967), 282.
34. A. Langford, *The Lover His Own Rival* (1736), 10.
35. J. Ralph, *The Cornish Squire* (1734), scene viii.
36. *Bickerstaff's Unburied Dead* (1743), 4.
37. *The Lawyer's Fortune; or Love in a Hollow Tree* (1736), 24.
38. *The Plays of Richard Steele*, ed. S. S. Fenny (Oxford 1971), 36.
39. *Eighteenth-Century Drama: Afterpieces*, ed. R. W. Bevis (Oxford 1970), 79-108.
40. L. Welsted, *The Dissembled Wanton* (1727), 26.
41. For a model of how to interpret dramatic stereotypes see J. Loftis, *Comedy and Society from Congreve to Fielding* (Stanford 1959).
42. J. Gay, *The Distressed Wife* (1743), 13.
43. *The Plays of Richard Steele*, 359.
44. P. Holland, 'The Restoration Theatre and Changes in Urban Society', Open University tape, summarised (1978) in *Supplementary Material A322*, 36.
45. *The Spectator*, i, 10-11; iv, 468.
46. *Ibid.*, i, 296.
47. D. Defoe, *Roxana*, ed. J. Jack (Oxford 1981), 170.
48. *Robinson Crusoe*, 17-18, 48.
49. *Ibid.*, 40.
50. *Ibid.*, 241.
51. D. Defoe, *Farther Adventures of Robinson Crusoe* (3 vols, Oxford 1927), iii, 80.

52. D. Defoe, *Tour through the Whole Island of Great Britain*, ed. P. Rogers (1971), 43.
53. *The Versatile Defoe*, ed. L. A. Curtis (1979), 262.
54. J. Trenchard and T. Gordon, *Cato's Letters* (4 vols, 1755), iii, 206-13: no. 91, 25 Aug. 1722.
55. J. Arbuthnot, *The History of John Bull*, ed. A. W. Bower and R. A. Erickson, (Oxford 1976), 11, 38, 64.
56. *The Spectator*, iv, 466; *The Poems of Alexander Pope*, 585, 627.
57. *Gulliver's Travels*, 19, 20, 56, 252-4.
58. Defoe, *Tour*, 54.
59. B. Mandeville, *The Fable of the Bees*, ed. P. Harth (1970), 236.
60. *Gulliver's Travels*, 128, 198-9, 256-7, 283, 296.
61. *The Works of the Rt Hon. Joseph Addison*, ed. R. Hurd (6 vols, 1854-6), i, 44, 46, 50.
62. *The Prose Works of Jonathan Swift*, ed. H. Davis (14 vols, Oxford 1939-68), iii, 46.
63. *Poems on Affairs of State*, vii, ed. F. H. Ellis (1975), 370.
64. G. Farquhar, *Love and a Bottle* (1699), 1.
65. *Gulliver's Travels*, 131.
66. D. Defoe, *Colonel Jack*, ed. S. H. Monk (1965), 276.
67. *The Complete Works of Henry Fielding*, ed. W. B. Henley (16 vols, 1967), xv, 260-5, 269-79, 283-7.
68. *Tom Jones*, ii, 741.
69. However, interesting changes were rung on these themes in the seventeenth and eighteenth centuries. Maid Marion, for instance, made her début then. (I owe this information to Professor J. C. Holt.)
70. D. Defoe, *The Great Law of Subordination Considered* (1724), preface. See also D. Defoe, *Everybody's Business Is Nobody's Business; or Private Abuses, Publick Grievances: Exemplified in the Pride, Insolence and Exorbitant Wages of our Women Servants, Footmen, etc.* (1725).
71. *The Prose Works of Jonathan Swift*, xiii, 28.
72. *The Spectator*, i, 373.
73. J. J. Hecht, *The Domestic Servant Class in Eighteenth-Century England* (1956), 71-101; D. Marshall, 'The Domestic Servants of the Eighteenth Century', *Economica*, ix (1929), 15-40.
74. R. Dodsley, *The Footman's Friendly Advice* (1731), 6, 27-32.
75. J. Miller, *The Man of Taste; or The Guardians* (1735), 3.
76. W. Popple, *The Double Deceit; or A Cure for Jealousy* (1736), 51.
77. C. Johnson, *The Village Opera* (1729), 5.
78. G. Lillo, *Fatal Curiosity* (1737), act 2, scene ii.
79. J. Miller, *Art and Nature* (1738), 39.
80. *Tom Jones*, ii, 666.
81. *Gulliver's Travels*, 259.
82. *Fable of the Bees*, 279-82.
83. *Cato's Letters*, iv, 236-46; no. 133, 15 Jun. 1723.
84. *The Spectator*, iii, 48.

85. *Colonel Jack*, 1.
86. I. Watts, *An Essay towards the Encouragement of Charity Schools* (1728), 20, 21.
87. *Fable of the Bees*, 121.
88. *Ibid.*, 70.
89. *English Poetry, 1700-1780*, ed. D. W. Lindsay (1974), 28-9.
90. *The Spectator*, ii, 402-3.
91. D. Defoe, *The Shortest Way with the Dissenters and other pamphlets* (Oxford 1927), 166-7.
92. R. Dodsley, *The Blind Beggar of Bethnal Green* (1740), 12-13.
93. D. Defoe, 'Reformation of Manners' in *Poems on Affairs of State*, vi, ed. F. H. Ellis (1970), 446.
94. T. Curtis and W. A. Speck, 'The Societies for the Reformation of Manners: A Case Study in the Theory and Practice of Moral Reform', *Literature and History*, iii (1976), 45-64; E. Duffy, 'Primitive Christianity Revived: Religious Renewal in Augustan England', *Studies in Church History*, xiv (1977), 287-300; T. Hayes, 'The Anglican Hierarchy and the Reformation of Manners, 1688-1738', *Journal of Ecclesiastical History*, xxxiii (1982), 391-411.
95. J. Barker, *A Patchwork Screen for the Ladies; or Love and Virtue Recommended, in a collection of instructive novels* (1723), 116.
96. Watts, *Essay*, 14.
97. *The Poems of Alexander Pope*, 537.
98. Defoe, *The Great Law of Subordination Considered*, 17.
99. *Cato's Letters*, i, 238: no. 31, 27 May 1721. In no. 33, 17 Jun. 1721 (i, 257) they cite Hobbes as 'a great philosopher' who called 'the state of nature a state of war'.
100. *Fable of the Bees*, 83, 220, 351.
101. *The Poems of Alexander Pope*, 538, 544, 547.
102. *The Spectator*, ii, 165-6.
103. M. Collyer, *Felicia to Charlotte* (1744), 20.
104. *The Spectator*, ii, 338.
105. *Fable of the Bees*, 69.
106. *The Poems of Alexander Pope*, 594.

Chapter 3
The Wheel of Fortune
(pp. 94-115)

1. D. Defoe, *Moll Flanders*, ed. J. Mitchell (1978), 188.
2. D. Defoe, *Colonel Jack*, ed. S. H. Monk (1965), 1, 6.
3. *Moll Flanders*, 49, 199.
4. *Colonel Jack*, xvii.
5. D. Defoe, *The Compleat English Tradesman* (2 vols, 1732), i, ix.
6. J. Barker, *A Patchwork Screen for the Ladies* (1723), 63.
7. *Fortune's Tricks in Forty-Six: an allegorical satire* (1747), 10-11, 18.
8. C. Gildon, *All For the Better; or The World Turned Upside Down; being the History of the Headlongs and the Longheads* (1720), 3.

9. *Poetical Works of Jonathan Swift*, ed. H. Davis (Oxford 1967), 202.
10. J. Trenchard and T. Gordon, *Cato's Letters* (4 vols, 1755), i, 131-44: no. 20, 11 Mar. 1721. No. 21, 18 Mar. 1721, published 'A letter from John Ketch Esq., asserting his right to the necks of the overgrown brokers'.
11. H. Fielding, *Amelia* (2 vols, 1930), i, 3-4.
12. H. Fielding, *Joseph Andrews*, ed. M. C. Battestin (Oxford 1967), 202, 220, 224.
13. H. Fielding, *Tom Jones*, ed. F. Bowers (3 vols, Oxford 1974), i, 465, 467, 447. In revising the Man of the Hill's story for the third edition Fielding altered the passage dealing with the desirability of providential intervention against James II, and the justification of resistance: see *Tom Jones*, ed. R. P. C. Mutter (1966), 426.
14. *Amelia*, i, 152, 154, 161; ii, 68-9, 299, 311.
15. S. Richardson, *Pamela*, ed. P. Sabor (1980), 441.
16. S. Richardson, *Clarissa* (8 vols, Oxford 1930), i, 59, 282.
17. *The Dramatic Works of the Celebrated Mrs Centlivre* (3 vols, 1968), iii, 331.
18. H. Ward, *The Happy Lovers* (1737), 14-15.
19. J. Baillie, *The Married Coquet* (1746), 7.
20. 'The Rival Nymphs; or The Merry Swain' in D. Bellamy, ed., *Miscellanies in Prose and Verse* (1750), ii, 46.
21. Ward, *The Happy Lovers*, 17.
22. L. Welsted, *The Dissembled Wanton* (1727), 24, 26.
23. C. Bodens, *The Modish Couple* (1732), 3.
24. Baillie, *The Married Coquet*, 39.
25. J. Miller, *The Humours of Oxford* (1730), 20.
26. J. Miller, *The Man of Taste; or The Guardians* (1735), 8.
27. *The Complete Works of Henry Fielding*, ed. W. B. Henley (16 vols, 1967), x, 91.
28. *Tom Jones*, ii, 801, 836, 888-9.
29. *The Complete Works of Henry Fielding*, x, 60.
30. *The History of Tom Jones the Foundling in his Married State* (1750), 28, 142.
31. C. Coffey, *The Merry Cobbler* (1735), 2. Coffey portrayed another wife-beating cobbler in *The Devil to Pay; or The Wives Metamorphosed* (1731). Jobson orders his wife to 'get in and spin, or else my strap shall wind about thy ribs most confoundedly'. (p. 3)
32. J. Arthur, *The Lucky Discovery; or The Tanner of York* (1737), 3.
33. E. Ward, *Nuptial Dialogues and Debates* (1723), 125.
34. L. Stone, *The Family, Sex and Marriage in England, 1500-1800* (1979), 17, 175, 188, 197.
35. L. Trumbach, *The Rise of the Egalitarian Family: Aristrocratic Kinship and Domestic Relations in Eighteenth-Century England* (1978), 108.

Chapter 4
The City and the Country
(pp. 116-138)

1. Lord Macaulay, *Essays* (1893), 574.
2. D. Defoe, *Moll Flanders*, ed. J. Mitchell (1978), 191.
3. W. Taverner, *The Artful Husband* (1716), 30; *The Artful Wife* (1718), 7, 20.
4. *The Dramatic Works of William Burnaby*, ed. F. E. Budd (1931), 233.
5. J. Mottley, *The Widow Bewitched* (1730), 46-7.
6. *Ibid.*, 22.
7. J. Gay, *The Distressed Wife* (1743), 25.
8. J. Miller, *The Humours of Oxford* (1730), 18-19.
9. *The Masquerade* (1719), 23, 50.
10. *The Poems of Alexander Pope*, ed. J. Butt (1963), 243-4.
11. S. Johnson, *The Rambler*, ed. W.J. Bate and A. B. Strauss (1969), 230-1.
12. *Boswell's Life of Johnson*, ed. G. B. Hill and L. F. Powell (6 vols, Oxford 1934), i, 129, 320.
13. *The Complete English Poems of Samuel Johnson*, ed. J. D. Fleeman (1971), 61-8.
14. *English Poetry, 1700-1780*, ed. D. W. Lindsay (1972), 16, 31.
15. P. Rogers, *Grub Street* (1972), 37-70.
16. P. Aubin, *The Life of Madame de Beaumont* (1721), 17-18.
17. J. Vanbrugh, *Aesop* (1702), 17-18.
18. *Works of the English Poets*, ed. S. Johnson and A. Chalmers (21 vols, 1810), xiii, 107.
19. *Ibid.*, xv, 168.
20. *English Poetry, 1700-1780*, 1.
21. J. Thomson, *The Seasons*, ed. J. Sambrook (Oxford 1981), 5-6, 150, 196, 198, 232-3.
22. S. Duck, *Poems on Several Occasions* (facsimile of 1st ed. (1736), Menston 1973), 14, 24.
23. S. Jenyns, 'An Epistle Written in the Country, 1735' in *Works of the English Poets*, xvii, 595-6.
24. D. Defoe, *Tour through the Whole Island of Great Britain*, ed. P. Rogers (1971), 300, 303, 306, 308-9, 323.
25. I. Kramnick, *Bolingbroke and his Circle* (1968), 189.
26. M. Byrd, *London Transformed: Images of the City in the Eighteenth Century* (1978), 36.
27. A. Henderson, *London and the National Government, 1721-1742* (1945), 33-45.
28. *Ibid.*, 44, 54.
29. Defoe, *Journal of the Plague Year*, ed. L. Landa (1969), 7.
30. *Ibid.*, 15. Defoe could not resist a Whiggish jibe at Charles II's court when observing that it was unaffected by the plague 'tho' they did not want being told that their crying Vices might, without breach of Charity, be said to have gone far, in bringing that terrible Judgment upon the whole Nation'.

31. *Ibid.*, 60.
32. *Ibid.*, 93.
33. *Ibid.*, 198.
34. B. Mandeville, *Enquiry into the Causes of the Frequent Executions at Tyburn* (Los Angeles 1964), 20, 48.
35. B. Mandeville, *The Fable of the Bees*, ed. P. Harth (1970), 57-8, 68, 76, 144.
36. Byrd, 84.
37. *The Complete Works of Henry Fielding*, ed. W. B. Henley (16 vols, 1967), x, 35.
38. H. Fielding, *Tom Jones*, ed. F. Bowers (2 vols, Oxford 1974), ii, 689.
39. H. Fielding, *Jonathan Wild*, ed. J. H. Plumb (New York 1961), 74, 96.
40. J. Sekora, *Luxury: the Concept in Western Thought, Eden to Smollett* (1977), 63-109.
41. R. Floud and D. McCloskey, *Economic History of Britain since 1700* (1981), 64.
42. *Ibid.*, 21; E. A. Wrigley and R. Schofield, *Population History of England, 1541-1871* (1981), 207.
43. P. Borsay, 'The English Urban Renaissance: The Development of a Provincial Urban Culture, *c.* 1680-*c.* 1760', *Social History*, ii (1977), 581-603.
44. *A Tract of the National Interest* (1757), 7-8.
45. *Works of the English Poets*, xvii, 17-22.

Chapter 5
Henry Fielding and the Historian
(pp. 139-166)

1. A. R. Humphreys, 'Fielding and Smollett' in *The Pelican Guide to English Literature*, iv: *From Dryden to Johnson*, ed. B. Ford (1957), 315.
2. B. A. Goldgar, *Walpole and the Wits* (1976), 98. For a recent discussion of Fielding's politics see B. McCrea, *Henry Fielding and the Politics of Mid-Eighteenth-Century England* (Athens, Georgia 1981).
3. Historical Manuscripts Commission, *Egmont Diary* (1923), ii, 390.
4. H. Fielding, *The Grub Street Opera*, ed. E. V. Roberts (1968), 11-12, 68.
5. H. Fielding, *Historical Register for the year 1736*, ed. W W. Appleton (1967), 47.
6. *Ibid.*, 30, 33-4.
7. M. M. Goldsmith, 'Faction Detected: Ideological Consequences of Robert Walpole's Decline and Fall', *History*, lxiv (1979), 19.
8. P. Rogers, *Henry Fielding: A Biography* (1979), 112-13.
9. H. Fielding, *Miscellanies*, ed. H. K. Miller (Oxford 1972), 4.

10. H. Fielding, *Jonathan Wild*, ed. J. H. Plumb (New York 1961), 215, 218.
11. *Ibid.*, 35, 39, 166-8.
12. H. Fielding, *Joseph Andrews*, ed. M. C. Battestin (Oxford 1967), 112, 140, 281.
13. H. Fielding, *The True Patriot*, ed. M. A. Locke (1965), nos 2, 14, 17.
14. H. Fielding, *The Jacobite's Journal and related writings*, ed. W. B. Coley (Oxford 1974), 20.
15. H. Fielding, *Amelia* (2 vols, 1930), ii, 225-32.
16. See above, p. 44.
17. *Joseph Andrews*, 157-8.
18. *Amelia*, ii, 310.
19. H. Fielding, *Tom Jones,* ed. F. Bowers (2 vols, Oxford 1974), i, 42-3, 58, 357.
20. *Ibid.*, ii, 612-13.
21. *The Poems of Alexander Pope*, ed. J. Butt (1963), 697.
22. *Tom Jones*, ii, 613.
23. *Ibid.*, i, 272-3, 276, 440.
24. *Joseph Andrews*, 201, 217-18.
25. *Tom Jones*, ii, 771-2.
26. *Jonathan Wild*, 69.
27. *Joseph Andrews*, 63.
28. *Tom Jones*, i, 380-1, 412.
29. *Ibid.*, 423.
30. *Joseph Andrews*, 67.
31. *Ibid.*, 286.
32. *Tom Jones*, i, 431-2.
33. *Joseph Andrews*, 103.
34. *Tom Jones*, ii, 936-7.
35. *Amelia*, i, 47; ii, 294, 310.
36. *Tom Jones*, ı, 371.
37. M. C. Battestin, *The Moral Basis of Fielding's Art: A Study of 'Joseph Andrews'* (1959), 143.
38. *Joseph Andrews*, 267.
39. H. Fielding, *An Apology for the Life of Mrs Shamela Andrews*, ed. D. Brooks (1970), 353.
40. *Amelia*, ii, 157.
41. *Tom Jones*, i, 408.
42. *Amelia*, ii, 157, 159.
43. *Joseph Andrews*, 344.
44. *Ibid.*, 162.
45. R. Browning, *Political and Constitutional Ideas of the Court Whigs* (1982), 67-88.
46. *Tom Jones*, ii, 620.
47. *Amelia*, ii, 50.
48. *Joseph Andrews*, 53.
49. H. J. Shroff, *The Eighteenth-Century Novel: The Idea of the Gentleman* (1978), 26.

50. *Jonathan Wild*, 45-6.
51. *The Complete Works of Henry Fielding*, ed. W. B. Henley (16 vols, 1967), xiii, 141, 149.
52. *Tom Jones*, i, 126.
53. Fielding, *Miscellanies*, 153.
54. *Tom Jones*, i, 270.
55. *Amelia*, i, 114; ii, 131.
56. *Joseph Andrews*, 230-1.
57. *Tom Jones*, i, 8.
58. *Amelia*, i, 125.

Chapter 6
Tobias Smollett and the Historian
(pp. 167-185)

1. D. Greene, 'Smollett the Historian: A Reappraisal' in G. S. Rousseau and P. G. Bouce, ed., *Tobias Smollett: Bicentennial Essays presented to Lewis M. Knapp* (1971), 25-56.
2. T. Smollett, *The Complete History of England* (11 vols, 1758-60), x, 54-5.
3. *Ibid.*, 259.
4. *Ibid.*, 325.
5. J. G. A. Pocock, 'Machiavelli, Harrington and English Political Ideologies in the Eighteenth Century', *William and Mary Quarterly*, xxii (1965), 549-83; repr. in *Politics, Language and Time* (1972).
6. J. G. A. Pocock, *The Ancient Constitution and the Feudal Law* (Cambridge 1957).
7. I. Kramnick, *Bolingbroke and his Circle* (1968), 111-36. An exception was Samuel Squire, who came to see constitutional continuity dating from the reign of Edward I: see R. Browning, *Political and Constitutional Ideas of the Court Whigs* (1982), 117-50.
8. Smollett, *op. cit.*, vii, 472.
9. *Ibid.*, viii, 291.
10. *Ibid.*, viii, 291-2.
11. T. Smollett, *The Continuation of the Complete History of England* (4 vols, 1760-1), i, 56.
12. J. Sekora, *Luxury: the Concept in Western Thought, Eden to Smollett* (1977).
13. T. Smollett, *Roderick Random*, ed. H. W. Hodges (1927), 245, 253.
14. *Ibid.*, 79, 98.
15. *Ibid.*, 78, 100.
16. *Ibid.*, 250, 259.
17. *Ibid.*, 87, 214.
18. *Ibid.*, 230.
19. *Ibid.*, 426.
20. T. Smollett, *The Adventures of Peregrine Pickle*, ed. J. L. Clifford (1969), 78, 354.

21. *Ibid.*, 188-9.
22. *Ibid.*, 197-8.
23. C. Robbins, *The Eighteenth-Century Commonwealthman* (1959).
24. *Peregrine Pickle*, 229, 231-2.
25. *Ibid.*, 232.
26. *Ibid.*, 148, 163, 364-5, 575.
27. *Ibid.*, 609.
28. *Ibid.*, 615.
29. *Ibid.*, 637, 667.
30. *Ibid.*, 672.
31. *Ibid.*, 770.
32. *Ibid.*, 772.

Chapter 7
Augustan Writers and their Readers
(pp. 186-198)

1. See above, p. 42.
2. P. Rogers, ed., *The Context of English Literature: the Eighteenth Century* (1978), 21.
3. *Ibid.*, 17.
4. *The Spectator*, ed. D. F. Bond (5 vols, Oxford 1965), i, 44.
5. Q. D. Leavis, *Fiction and the Reading Public* (1965), 132.
6. W. A. Speck, 'Politicians, Peers and Publication by Subscription, 1700-1750', in I. Rivers, ed., *Books and their Readers in Eighteenth-Century England* (Leicester 1982), 47-68.
7. G. A. Cranfield, *The Development of the Provincial Newspaper, 1700-1760* (Oxford 1962); R. M. Wiles, *Freshest Advices* (1965).
8. J. Brewer, *Party Ideology and Popular Politics at the Accession of George III* (Cambridge 1976), 142-6.
9. E. Ward, *Nuptial Dialogues and Debates* (1723), 205.
10. 'The Character of a Coffee-House' in *Harleian Miscellany* (1808), vi, 467.
11. D. Cressy, *Literacy and the Social Order: Reading and Writing in Tudor and Stuart England* (Cambridge 1981); L. Stone, 'Literacy and Education in England, 1640-1900', *Past and Present,* xlix (1969); V. E. Neuberg, *Popular Education in Eighteenth-Century England* (1971), 173.
12. J. G. Rule, *The Experience of Labour in Eighteenth-Century England* (1981).
13. R. M. Wiles, *Serial Publication in England before 1750* (Cambridge 1957), ix.
14. B. S. Capp, *Astrology and the Popular Press: English Almanacs, 1500-1800* (1979).
15. P. Rogers, 'Classics and Chapbooks' in Rivers, ed., *Books and their Readers in Eighteenth-Century England*, 27-45.
16. E. Moore, *The Foundling* (1748), 4.
17. J. Reed, *Tom Jones, a comic opera* (1769), preface.

Conclusion
(pp. 199-209)

1. D. Defoe, 'The Dyet of Poland' in *Poems on Affairs of State*, vii, ed. F. H. Ellis (1975), 72-132.
2. T. B. Macaulay, *Critical and Historical Essays* (2 vols, 1907), ii, 417-18.
3. J. Mottley, *The Widow Bewitched* (1730), 6, 7, 64.
4. E. Tryon, *The Lover's Secretary; or The Adventures of Lindamira*, revised and corrected by T. Brown (3rd ed., 1734), preface.
5. E. Haywood, *The British Recluse* (1742), 82.

Index

Titles of works are listed under authors where known.